BUSINESS IN ASIA

BUSINESS IN ASIA

Edited by
Russell Smyth and Marika Vicziany

Monash University Press
Clayton

Monash University Press
Building 11
Monash University
Victoria 3800, Australia

www.monash.edu.au/mai

All Monash University Press publications are subject to double blind peer review

© Monash Asia Institute 2008

National Library of Australia cataloguing-in-publication data:

Business in Asia.

Bibliography.
SBN 9781876924539 (pbk.).

1. Business - Asia. 2. Business enterprises - Asia - Case studies. I. Smyth, Russell L. (Russell Leigh), 1969- . II. Vicziany, Marika.

338.7095

Cover design by Minnie Doron.
Printed by BPA Print Group, Melbourne, Australia - www.bpabooks.com

contents

	Glossary	vii
	Contributors	ix
Chapter one	Asian dominance: imperialism, entrepreneurship and the new growth era *Russell Smyth and Marika Vicziany*	1
Chapter two	Japan: globalisation and multiculturalism *Ross Mouer*	29
Chapter three	South Korea: the reign of the unreinable chaebol? *Lesley McKaig*	53
Chapter four	China: privatisation and enterprise restructuring in a socialist market economy *Russell Smyth*	71
Chapter five	India: energy and the role of the state and private sectors in a rising giant *Marika Vicziany*	87
Chapter six	Vietnam: the search for a socialist market economy *Keith Trace*	109
Chapter seven	Thailand: financial institutions and regional trade *David Treisman*	129
Chapter eight	Indonesia: an improving business climate *Robert Rice*	147
Chapter nine	Malaysia: the contradictions of a remarkable economic transformation *Marika Vicziany*	165

Chapter ten	Singapore: economic success and resilient authoritarianism	
	Lesley McKaig	185
	Bibliography	205

Glossary

AFTA	ASEAN Free Trade Area
AMC	asset management company
ASEAN	Association of Southeast Asian Nations
BIBF	Bangkok International Banking Facilities
CPI	consumer price index
CTVE	collective township and village enterprise
FIDF	Financial Institutions Development Fund
GAIL	Gas Authority India Limited
GDP	gross domestic product
GLCs	Government Linked Companies
IMF	International Monetary Fund
MITI	Ministry of International Trade and Industry (Japan)
MNC	multinational corporation
NEP	New Economic Policy
NPO	non-profit organisation
OECD	Organisation for Economic Co-operation and Development
ONGC	Oil and Natural Gas Corporation (previously Oil and Natural Gas Commission)
OPEC	Organization of the Petroleum Exporting Countries
OVL	ONGC Videsh Limited
PAP	People's Action Party

PIL	Pacific International Lines
RM	Malaysian ringgit
RMB	Chinese renminbi
Rp	Indonesian rupiah
Rs	Indian rupees
S$	Singaporean dollar
SEC	Securities Exchange Commission
SMEs	small and medium-sized enterprises
SOE	state-owned enterprise
US$	United States dollar
VND	Vietnamese dong
WTO	World Trade Organization

contributors

Leslie McKaig is a former lecturer in the Department of Economics, Monash University, where she taught for more than ten years. Her research interests focus on the economic development of East Asia.

Ross Mouer is Professor of Japanese Language and Studies in the School of Languages, Culture and Linguistics, Monash University. He is currently Director of the Centre for Japanese Studies in the Monash Asia Institute. His research interests embrace the broad areas of Japanese sociology; the organisation of work and industrial relations in Japan; images of Japanese society and meta-theories of Japanese society.

Robert Rice is an honorary associate in the Department of Economics, Monash University, and served as a consultant to USAID on the reconstruction of Aceh following the 2004 Boxing Day Tsunami. His research on Indonesia spans some 30 years and includes studies of employment creation, resources, and development planning.

Russell Smyth is Professor and Deputy Head of the Department of Economics and Director of the Asian Business and Economics Research Unit in the Faculty of Business and Economics, Monash University. His research interests include Asian economies, Chinese economic reform, law and economics and applied time series econometrics.

Keith Trace is a former associate professor with the Department of Economics, Monash University and currently serves as a consultant to various Australian and international agencies on ASEAN economic development.

David Treisman is a PhD candidate in the Monash Asia Institute, Monash University. He holds an MA from Witwatersrand University (South Africa) with a dissertation on the Asian Financial Crisis in Thailand, and is currently completing a doctoral thesis on the political economy of ASEAN integration.

Marika Vicziany is Professor of Asian Political Economy and Director of the Monash Asia Institute, Monash University. Her research focuses on questions of mass poverty, minorities, long term economic development and regional security in India, Pakistan, western China and Malaysia.

chapter one

Asian dominance: imperialism, entrepreneurship and the new growth era

Russell Smyth and Marika Vicziany

The Asian financial crisis of the late 1990s, according to Andre Gunder Frank (1929–2005), was not a meltdown at all, but a start-up. Actually, it was a re-start. At a time when the majority of the world's leading commentators were wringing their hands and declaring that the 'Asian economic miracle' was really a mirage based on shaky financial foundations, Frank insisted that the economic fundamentals of production in Asia were sound; and if the financial architecture was weak, it was weak partly because it suited the West to keep it so. The argument about the start-up was based on the observation that the Asian financial crisis had global impact. It was the first Asian crisis in two centuries to have such an effect, indicating for Frank that despite the triumphalism of the West, the crisis proved that Asia had not only again becoming an integral part of the global economy, but had done so in a manner that increasingly suggested that Asia was taking centre stage. Beyond this, Frank suggested even more heretically that the Asian financial crisis heralded the rebalancing of global economic power in a manner that reasserted the earlier and much longer dominance of Asia in the pre-1800 world. According to Frank, Western capitalism, Western technology and even the industrial revolution needed to be conceived as a blip in the long run of world history: Europe had dominated the world economy for fewer than 200 years—from about 1800 (at the earliest) to 1997—and now Asia was back (Frank 2003; see also Eslake 2006).[1]

These opening remarks locate the present volume: our timeframe is the past 200 years of European domination, the impact of that domination and how that domination has receded thanks to the rise of modern Asian entrepreneurship. However, we have not undertaken a comprehensive history or chronological approach to the subject of Asia's decline and then re-emergence in this period. Rather, the individual chapters presented in this collection focus on the economic growth of the key Asian economies in the five decades since the end of the Second World War. We are preoccupied with how the Asian economies have re-grown and the economic, political and social factors behind that resurgence.

Why focus on the post-Second World War era? The end of the Second World War coincided roughly with the end of European imperialism in Asia. The process of decolonisation was long and complex, but gradually the whole of Asia re-emerged with independent political actors divided by modern national boundaries that reflected contemporary nation states born from the combined forces of colonial design and local ethnic, religious and political aspirations. Perhaps one of the most potent symbols of this long, drawn-out process occurred at midnight on 18 December 1999 when the Portuguese colony of Macau was returned to China after 400 years of foreign rule. The handover of Macau came some two and a half years after the hand-back of Hong Kong on 30 June 1997. Europe had given an even older colony back to Asia 36 years earlier—Goa was returned to Indian control in 1961 after 451 years of Portuguese rule and after a short 'invasion' by Indian troops (Vicziany 1969).

In the first part of this chapter we provide a snapshot of the socioeconomic characteristics of the countries included in the collection and explain the rationale for choosing these particular economies. In the second part we develop the background for the subsequent chapters by providing an historical account of how contemporary business elites emerged in the modern era. Specifically, we explore the legacy of imperialism for the independent nation states that emerged in Asia after the Second World War. Our focus is on the role of state entrepreneurship and the rise of the private entrepreneurs of Asia, their relationships with imperial authority, and how these entrepreneurs provided the mechanism for the Asian transition into a global, industrial world of continuous technological change. The third part of the chapter gives an overview of the growth trajectory of the selected countries since the Second World War and provides an introduction to remaining chapters.

Overview of the selected countries

The volume contains chapters on Japan, South Korea, China, India, Vietnam, Thailand, Indonesia, Malaysia and Singapore. The extraordinary economic performance of East Asia is arguably the most important economic phenomenon of the second half of the 20th century. Writing prior to the Asian financial crisis, Hill (1997:131) stated, 'No country in world history has grown so quickly, for so long' as Japan, South Korea, China and the majority of the countries of the Association of Southeast Asian Nations (ASEAN). Compared to countries such as Japan and South Korea, India is a relative latecomer in the growth stakes but has made giant strides since economic liberalisation in the early 1990s.

Japan and South Korea were the first countries in Asia to industrialise: they both grew rapidly, had similar industrial structures (characterised by the *keiretsu* in Japan and the *chaebol* in South Korea) and relied on state-led development programs. Japan and South Korea are now members of the Organisation for Economic Co-operation and Development (OECD) and, along with Singapore, are the major high-income economies in the region. China and India are included in the collection for their status as the emerging giants of world business. Both countries represent sizeable markets with rising middle-class incomes, and both countries are developing sizeable export sectors. China is often referred to as the world's factory. Large numbers of migrant workers flooding into cities along China's coastal seaboard have allowed China to emerge as a leader in manufacturing (see Nielsen, Smyth & Vicziany 2007). Meanwhile, India is developing as a world leader in exports of information technology, electronics and other high-technology services. India's emergent role as an exporter of information technology is being facilitated by an extensive Indian Diaspora in the United States that now has a central role at the top of the management ladder in American companies, non-government organisations and United States government departments and agencies (Vicziany 2001).

The other five countries in this volume were selected because they are the economic powerhouses of ASEAN. Hill (1997:131) dubs Malaysia, Indonesia, Singapore and Thailand as the 'high-growth "ASEAN Four"'. We add Vietnam to this 'Gang of Four' because, although its rapid growth is of more recent origins, throughout the 1990s it was one of the fastest-growing economies in the world. Vietnam is an interesting case; similar to China, it has been successful with policies that have not attracted the acclaim of the mainstream (see Dollar 2004 on Vietnam; Smyth's chapter on China in this volume). However, Vietnam's *Doi Moi* (renovation) economic reforms in the late 1980s and early 1990s were applauded by the World Bank (2002). As Hill (1997) notes, until the late 1980s the literature on the East Asian development model focused primarily on Japan and the four newly industrialised economies of Hong Kong, Singapore, South Korea and Thailand. The experiences of Southeast Asia (excluding Singapore) were largely ignored. However, from the early 1990s a major change began to occur in the literature on the East Asian model. The World Bank's (1993) controversial report, *The East Asian miracle,* examined economic development in the high-growth ASEAN countries, in addition to Japan and the newly industrialised economies. Young (1994) and Krugman (1994) turned the spotlight on Southeast Asia, in particular Singapore, by arguing that economic growth in East Asia was primarily input-driven, with little or no productivity gains. The Asian financial crisis (1997–99) had its origins in Thailand, and its effects and the responses to the crisis centred on Indonesia, Malaysia, the Philippines and Thailand, in addition to Japan and South Korea. The responses of the world lending and labour agencies to the Asian financial crisis gave a lot of attention to the prospects for recovery in the key Southeast Asian countries (see ILO 2000; IMF 2001; World Bank 2001a).

Table 1 presents an overview of key indicators for the selected countries in 1990, 2000, 2004 and 2005. There are large disparities in population size across the countries—China and India, which are the most populous countries on earth, are at one extreme and the small city-state of Singapore is at the other. In countries such as China, Japan and South Korea, population growth is near zero, while in Malaysia and Singapore population growth is relatively high. Indonesia, Thailand and Vietnam have experienced declining population growth. With the exception of Japan and South Korea, where the period of high growth occurred prior to the 1990s, in the 15 years since 1990 each country has had a high average gross domestic product (GDP) growth rate. The economies in the sample affected by the Asian financial crisis, such as Indonesia and Thailand, have rebounded strongly, while growth in China, Malaysia and Singapore was largely uninterrupted by the crisis. In terms of GDP per capita, while China and India are on course to become two of the three largest economies in the world over the course of the next decade, their population size means that in per capita terms they are still relatively poor countries. GDP per capita in India and Vietnam is less than US$ 600 per annum, and in China and Indonesia it is lower than US$1,500 per annum. Thailand and Malaysia have *slightly* higher GDP per capita, while Japan, Singapore and South Korea have *much* higher GDP per capita. Singapore and, to a lesser extent, Malaysia and Vietnam have a high ratio of foreign direct investment to GDP, while Japan, which has been openly hostile to inward foreign direct investment, has a very low ratio of inward foreign direct investment to GDP. In terms of basic human capital, the primary school enrolment ratio is at least 85% in each of the countries, and in China, Japan and Singapore the primary school enrolment ratio is 100%. Literacy rates are around 90% or higher in each of the countries except India, where the literacy rate in 2004 was 61%, up from 49.3% in 1990. As for broader socioeconomic indicators, the Human Development Index (which is a comparative measure of poverty, literacy, education, life expectancy and other factors) varies considerably across the region—from 0.5–0.6 in India through to in excess of 0.9 in Japan.

These variations do not detract from the impressive past growth of all the countries in this collection; nor will they hold back the projected growth rates of the future. Even India, where some of these indicators are much less favourable than for the other Asian countries, appears to be set on a path of persistent economic expansion during the next 50 years. Such growth will make a great difference to the living standards of ordinary Indians, although it will at the same time continue to leave many millions behind in conditions of mass poverty. Fundamental to the growth scenarios throughout the region is the role of the Asian entrepreneur, as both investor and innovator. As we argue in the next section, modern entrepreneurship was re-invented in Asia in the midst of the colonial regimes that dominated the region from about 1850 to 1960.

Background to modern growth: the legacy of imperial rule

The colonial legacy

European imperialism in Asia had an impact on all the nations and peoples in this region, even though Japan, Thailand and China were never directly under colonial rule. Table 2 summarises the sequence by which particular Asian nations gained their independence. Japan, Thailand and China do not appear in this table because they remained nominally 'independent', which does not mean that they escaped the overwhelming presence of European imperial powers in the Asia–Pacific region.

Japan's modernisation in the 19th century was driven primarily by the determination of the Japanese elite to avoid falling under foreign domination. They feared the Europeans, and they feared the Russians in particular. In 1904 Japan defeated the mighty navy of the Russian Tsar, a victory that vindicated its long-term strategy of striking out on an independent path to modernisation. The rise of European dominance in Asia in the 19th century also had the paradoxical effect of making Japan itself into an imperial power. The determination to remain free from colonial domination and become a strong nation in modern technological terms saw the Meiji Restoration develop into Japan's industrialisation program. The major obstacle to this was that Japan was a resource-scarce country—but the resource-rich provinces of China and Korea stood at Japan's doorstep. In 1910 Japan annexed Korea, a blatant act of imperialism driven by the example of European expansion. This was followed by the rising economic power of Japan in Asia; by 1931 Japan's imperial dominion extended to Manchuria. China's loss of Manchuria had been a long time coming. The Qing dynasty had been in steady decline for about a century, with European powers nibbling away at China's treaty ports on the eastern seaboard, while Russia, a landed imperial power, nibbled away at China's western frontier. The Ili valley in today's north-western Xinjiang Uygur Autonomous Region became part of the Russian Empire during the 1870s.

Imperial rule in Asia was traumatic for all host countries, regardless of the level of wanton destruction and authoritarian control and whether the imperial powers were European or non-European. India suffered because, despite the high mortality rate amongst the European communities in the new colonial cities on the subcontinent, the technological and cultural impact of foreign rule unsettled the existing order. The Muslims who ruled India prior to the arrival of the British, namely the Mughals, went into deep cultural shock. It has been suggested that they rejected modern, Western education largely because it was associated with the new masters who had displaced them. The relative socioeconomic backwardness of India's contemporary Muslim community can be partly attributed to the long resistance to modernisation, which was closely associated in the minds of Indian Muslims with Westernisation. In parts of India not ruled by the Mughal dynasty, the British came to arrangements to protect Hindu rajas and princes; throughout the subcontinent the local indigenous elites outside the large cities remained intact, as did the old, non-Muslim feudal landlords. In rural India the British presence was 'light' and mainly visible in the form of the district collector, who kept his eyes on the revenue capacities of villages and on law and order. In other words, the British ruled India indirectly through local power elites and by recognising the place of indigenous laws, customs and authorities—provided that these did not contradict the interests of the metropolitan elites living in London and other British cities.

In Malaysia the British adopted the same principles of indirect rule as applied to India but with the difference that the migration of Indian and Chinese labour into colonial Malay began to change the ethnic composition of the land. Indian labour was recruited for the British plantations and mines, and Chinese labour came not only to work but also to serve as trading compradors. The result was that independent Malaya inherited a social character that had been greatly transformed by British rule and a society in which the Malay inhabitants felt disadvantage. This legacy ultimately fed into the *bumiputera* policies of the independent government of Malaya during the 1970s; the disadvantages suffered by the Malays were not merely economic but also cultural, and stemmed from new colonial myths about the 'lazy native' (Alatas 1977).

Colonial Korean society was possibly the most deeply traumatised by foreign rule. Cummings has noted that in 1950 one Korean out of three had no association with the area in which he or she had been born (Cummings 1984). The physical mobility of Koreans both inside Korea and in East Asia occurred in response to a drastic reorganisation of Korean society and polity. In contrast to indirect rule in British India and Malaya, imperial Japan thoroughly shook up the Korean system and installed Japanese landlords in Korean villages,

Japanese managers in both old and new factories, and Japanese tax collectors throughout the economy. The Dutch in Indonesia and the French in Vietnam were also highly interventionist, preferring direct rule because it enabled the imperial authorities to mould the structure of the Asian economies to the needs of the European treasuries. The Dutch *Kultur* system in Indonesia was a direct attempt to link the production of plantations and other cash crops to the national economy of Holland. The Japanese in Korea were similarly interventionist (McNamara 1996:182).

Imperialism and the rise of Asia's private entrepreneurs

Despite the differences in the degree of foreign penetration into Asia, there are some broad similarities in the impact that European dominance had. This legacy had important long-term consequences for the economic development of Asia in the post-Second World War era. Imperialism had two faces: on the one side, the naked economic ambition of all the imperial powers drove them to various degrees of economic and social exploitation; on the other side—in ways that the imperial authorities never intended and could never have imagined—their disruptive and destructive impact on Asia also contained the seeds for Asian revival.

In particular, imperialism saw the emergence of new elites in Asia, especially entrepreneurs who came to play a critical role in economic modernisation and growth. These new elites appeared not only in the new colonial cities that sprang up in response to the economic and political needs of foreign powers, but also in the smaller towns and ports of the hinterlands. It was not the intention of the imperial authorities to create these business elites—rather, their intentions focused on the creation of new bureaucratic elites who would help them to govern and control the 'unruly natives'. Yet the new business classes emerged in any case, partly because European commercial exploitation in Asia depended critically on borrowing capital from indigenous merchants and moneylenders. Contrary to what Vladimir Illych Lenin believed, imperialism did not see the massive transfer of capital surpluses from Europe to Asia. Rather, European capital was sucked into the European colonies where Europeans lived, namely Canada, South Africa, Australia and New Zealand. The economies of these settler colonies were radically different from the traditional economies subjugated by European and Japanese imperial might. Hence, the economic development of Asia in the 19th and 20th centuries depended on local capital and on local entrepreneurial and managerial talent—even though all of this was recruited and organised by foreign interests. In some cases (such as the Chinese in Singapore,

Malaysia and Indonesia) the new entrepreneurial trading groups were themselves relative newcomers to the regions.

As a result of this financial dependency by imperial rulers, local sources of capital, production and entrepreneurship developed. Inevitably, these new capitalists extended their business interests well beyond what served the needs of their imperial masters. A particularly dramatic example of this is provided by the economic evolution of the Parsi community during the British Raj. At first the Parsis acted as translators for the early British. Through this they discovered the world of international commerce, and by the 1840s large Parsi trading firms were beginning to emerge in India and to establish business branches in the Far East. The rise of the house of Tata is an example of this. Having accumulated vast sources of capital by selling Indian opium in China, the Tatas diversified into exporting cotton to Britain and from this they began to establish cotton textile factories in India. By the end of the 19th century the Tatas were ready to expand into iron and steel production and, despite British indifference and even opposition, they began producing modern steel in Jamshedpur in 1911. Today the Tata business house is one of the largest in India and internationally renowned for its chain of Taj hotels and the discrete brilliance of Tata Consultancy Services Ltd, one of the world's leading information technology companies. The transition made by the Tatas from servicing the needs of imperial rulers to becoming modern agents of industrialisation became a common story throughout Asia. In India, in particular, the new entrepreneurial class was a large and diverse one and included Marwari, Hindu and Jain business houses (Mukherjee & Mukherjee 1983; Goswami 1991).

Even in Korea, despite the economic stranglehold of Japanese rule, many new modern Korean firms emerged. These became role models of how to build and structure a modern company in a competitive industrial or agricultural setting. One of the most interesting cases was that of Kim Yon-su, the founder of a major Korean spinning mill (known by the name of Samyang). The capacity of Kim Yon-su to establish and then retain control of his company was based on personal family wealth, the productivity of his company, and the founding director's ability to adapt his corporate strategies to the demands of the Japanese authorities in Korea. Those demands compelled Kim Yon-su to take up the business of land reclamation, a priority enterprise for the Japanese, who were busy converting Korea into a major supplier of food and forest products to Japan (McNamara 1988:172). Kim Yon-su continued to adjust his growth strategies in line with Japanese priorities, with the result that when Japan annexed Manchuria in 1931, his agricultural and textile enterprises were extended to mainland China (McNamara 1988:173).

Kim's relationship with the Japanese government in Korea was not a smooth one—the Japanese sought to restrict his movements and would have preferred to promote Japanese entrepreneurs rather than Korean ones. At the same time, the Japanese were pragmatic and recognised the effective management style and growth record of Kim. Kim in turn used his position of entrepreneurial control to transfer Japanese technology to his company by training his own technical staff and employing only Korean workers in his enterprises (McNamara 1988:176). He also developed powerful Japanese clients, including the Japanese Imperial Army, which became a 'captive customer' (Eckert 1991:123).

Japanese colonialism saw a rapid growth in modern Korean companies and entrepreneurs—in 1904 there were only six factories controlled by Koreans: by 1927 the number had mushroomed to about 2,500 (Lim 1999:616–17). During the 1930s, in the interest of providing Japan with more sophisticated industrial goods, Japanese controls over Korean industry were greatly reduced, with the result that a considerable heavy industry grew rapidly (Lim 1999:619). Economic pressure from Japan helped to generate a culture of business efficiency, which formed an important post-colonial legacy. The collaboration between the state and *chaebol* on national economic goals today resonates with relationships developed in colonial times. Moreover, as with Asian entrepreneurs throughout the region, the direct experience that the emerging business elites had of living and travelling abroad generated new ideas and ideals about modernisation. The achievements of Kim Yon-su, for example, are difficult to comprehend without considering that he lived in Japan between 1911 and 1921, breathing in the air of Japanese modernisation and even modelling his own image on Japanese Meiji heroes (Eckert 1991:35–6).

It was not only the epicentres of metropolitan power that created new entrepreneurs in Korea—small trading and merchant networks grew up in rural areas, small towns and ports once they had worked out ways of accommodating themselves to the unique demands and pressures of imperial rule. These entrepreneurs provided 'a critical human link between early trade and later *chaebol*' (McNamara 1996:2). According to Eckert, about 60% of the entrepreneurs who set up the top 60 South Korean *chaebol* in the post-Second World War era 'had some kind of colonial business experience' (Eckert 1991:254). These new entrepreneurs destroyed the power of Korea's conservative literati who had opposed modernisation (McNamara 1996:65) and understood that the success of modern Japan depended on 'a highly centralized, and extremely capable state apparatus' (Lim 1999:603). The model for a powerful, modern Korean state had been created thanks to Japanese rule. It is, therefore, not unrealistic to suggest that the rapid economic growth of the South Korean economy after the 1960s was partly possible because of the state–private sector nexus that the Koreans inherited from the Japanese.

India, by contrast, emerged from colonial rule with a Westminster parliamentary democratic system, which was not designed to serve the needs of industrialisation. Rather, the newly independent Indian state had to graft onto the parliamentary system the essentials of Soviet-style socialist planning. Over time that socialist planning model assumed increasing importance and reached its pinnacle with the vigorous nationalisation program instituted by Prime Minister Indira Gandhi during the 1970s and 1980s. Despite state subsidies to the private sector and special privileges to large companies that provided funds for election campaigns, the relationship between governments and entrepreneurs was much more adversarial and lacked the co-operative framework typical of Korean, Japanese and, most recently, Chinese industrialisation.

The impact of imperial rule on island Southeast Asia was vastly different to the industrial base that had been established in Korea and India before independence. The fragmented nature of island Southeast Asia made it far more difficult to create integrated economic and political systems. Indonesia, in particular, continues to suffer from the vast regional diversities generated by its 18,000 islands, despite the fact that about 60% of Indonesia's people live on the two islands of Java and Madura. Indonesia and Malaysia also lacked the heritage of vast landed pre-modern bureaucracies, which, in the case of India and China, had moved over the centuries towards creating more integrated socioeconomic systems. In this fragmented environment, the British in Malaya and the Dutch in Indonesia created further division by attracting migrant labour and capital from India, mainland Southeast Asia and China. The upward mobility of the Chinese, in particular, in these new colonial settings was considerable.[2] The result is that today both Malaysia and Indonesia have an influential Chinese middle class—something that has not been especially valued by the post-colonial regimes. In both countries official policies during the past 30 years have sought to promote 'the sons of the soil' in order to encourage the rise of non-Chinese and non-Indian middle-class elements.

The other legacy of colonial rule in Malaysia and Indonesia was that the middle classes created by colonialism were mainly small to medium businesses that did not evolve into the large business houses that emerged in India, Korea and China. Indeed, Furnivall goes much further than this in his classic study of Indonesia: 'the natives had made no appreciable advance in industry, commerce or shipping, and there has been no emergence of an Indonesian middle class' (Furnivall 1939:398). Outside petty trade and the cottage industries, the modern economy that emerged in Indonesia was in the hands of state-owned enterprises

(Macintyre 1994:245). The same was true of Malaysia. Since independence it has been difficult to diversify the entrepreneurial bases of these two societies—in the case of Malaysia the *bumiputera* policies have promoted state-linked companies rather than a vigorous culture of innovation and business, and in Indonesia the business clout of the Chinese (representing some 5% of the population) has not been weakened owing to the willingness of Indonesian businessmen to on-sale their licenses and privileges to the Chinese (Macintyre 1994:247).

In Singapore the Chinese community found the political haven that had eluded them in Malaysia and Indonesia. Ironically, despite accounting for some 77% of the Singaporean population,[3] the Chinese in Singapore have not proven to be any more entrepreneurial than their Malaysian and Indonesian counterparts. While they dominate petty trade, urban services and cottage industries, big business in Singapore has been in the hands of the multinationals. The involvement of foreign business was the focus of an impatient Lee Kuan Yew, Singapore's first prime minister, who wanted to catapult Singapore to the status of a developed country. In the 1960s he concluded that this ambitious strategy could not wait for the Chinese entrepreneurs to transform themselves into big businesses undertaking large, risky investments. Although the broad patterns of entrepreneurship outlined above applied to island Southeast Asia, this did not prelude some exceptions—some large Chinese business houses did emerge in the region. Despite this, overwhelmingly the largest and most influential companies outside the agricultural sector in Southeast Asia have been the multinationals, whose histories extend back into the colonial era.

The most unlucky country in Asia was Vietnam, where colonial rule metamorphosed into colonial war and eventually civil war. At a time when the rest of Asia was experiencing the fresh winds of decolonisation in the period 1945–1975, Vietnam was thrown into direct conflict with the world's most powerful economy, the United States, because Western perceptions of colonialism became thoroughly distorted by American preoccupations with the Cold War. Vietnam did not rid itself of foreign rule until 1975: at first, in order to shore up French power in the reconstruction of Europe, the United States supported the resumption of power by the French once the Japanese were expelled from Indochina; then, when the Vietnamese nationalists appeared to favour the communist system over the capitalist one, the United States became directly engaged in the Vietnam War. As discussed in Keith Trace's chapter, the consequences of the Vietnam War were disastrous for Vietnam at an economic and humanitarian level.

Only three Asian nations escaped direct imperial control in the 19th and 20th centuries: Japan, Thailand and China. Japan was protected by its lack of land

and resources and by the Meiji Restoration, Japan's early response to European pressure. Thailand was shielded because it became a buffer state between British possessions to the west and French possessions to the east. The Thai kings were, like the Japanese, well aware of the Western threat and began a series of major administrative and other reforms under King Mongkut (1851–68) and King Chulalongkorn (1868–1910). This progressive Thai reform process has continued into the present era. China also survived being placed under direct colonial control, although, unlike Japan and Thailand, China lost many 'treaty ports', which were given over to numerous European powers via the Treaty of Nanjing (1842) and the Treaty of Tientsin (1858). China also lost land to Russia, Portugal, Britain and, most notably, to Japan—Taiwan was ceded to Japan on China's defeat in the Sino–Japanese war of 1895. China's battered condition then opened the country up to further foreign control, whereby the key European powers and the United States divided China into 'spheres of influence'.

European interests in China remained largely focused on trade concessions and privileged access to China's domestic markets, rather than the exercise of imperial control of the kind that defined European rule in India, Malaysia, Indonesia and Vietnam. The result of having such large conglomerations of foreign traders and bankers in the cities of China was that eventually this gave rise to new kinds of indigenous Chinese entrepreneurship, fuelled by foreign ideas of business finance and management. Innovative ideas came from Chinese students studying within Western-oriented institutes in China or abroad, especially in the United States. As Morgan notes, many of these students formed the core of professional life in China during the 1920s and 1930s, with many of them becoming industry leaders (Morgan 2004:7). Mu Ouchu, who became one of Shanghai's best known industrialists, was so deeply attracted to Taylorism[4] that he translated Taylor's work on 'scientific management' in 1916 (Morgan 2004:8). These ideas, and many others, had an enduring impact on the emerging industrial elites, especially an influential group of entrepreneurs who emerged in the Jiangsu–Zhejiang region (Morgan 2004:10). The massive growth of the private sector in the Shanghai industrial zone today continues this tradition of entrepreneurship that was evident in the first three decades of the 20th century. Many scholars have insisted on the even longer history of entrepreneurship in this region, based on the view that the lower Yangtze River area had been a region of prosperity for centuries and in the modern period had all the preconditions for industrialisation (Morgan 2004:12, n35; Frank 2003). The success of the Maoist revolution of the late 1940s and the subsequent destruction of bourgeois culture and private entrepreneurship marked an end to the private sector that had emerged in response to colonial intrusion. It is therefore reasonable to argue that the re-emergence of private entrepreneurship since the reforms of

Deng Xiaoping in 1981 mark a return to patterns of the past, rather than just the importation of foreign market models.

Imperialism and state entrepreneurship

Private entrepreneurship has been the single most dynamic factor in the emergence of the Asian economies in the post-Second World War era. Yet much of that achievement would not have been possible without state entrepreneurship, which provided not only the nurturing environment that private, indigenous entrepreneurs needed but also a force that was willing to step in and undertake the production and organisation that private capital was reluctant to undertake. Paradoxically, state entrepreneurship did not feature in most Asian countries during the colonial era. Despite the history of intervention by the colonial state (see above), that intervention was driven by the self-interested, financial compulsion of the imperial authorities. Rarely did that compulsion involve local industrialisation. Indian railways, for example, were built after the Indian mutiny of 1857 largely in order to establish a modern communications and transport system able to provide the rapid transport of troops to quell any future rebellions. Very quickly India's railway arteries facilitated a rapid growth in domestic and international commerce, and this helped Britain to use India in its international balance of payments system (Saul 1960:58). Indian export surpluses helped to offset Britain's costs of importing commodities from the United States, Canada and Australia. When the Tata business house began to establish a fledgling Indian iron and steel industry, it encountered nothing but opposition from the British Indian government (Harris 1958; Bagchi 1972). Similar stories of the indifference and opposition of imperial powers to Asian industrialisation can be told for the rest of Asia. Japan's industrialisation program for Korea provides a remarkable exception, yet the motivations were identical. The interests and needs of the colonial state remained supreme and pro- or anti-industrialisation policies in colonies reflected that directly.

The result of this history of state indifference before the independence movements of Asia was that decolonisation inevitably brought to power indigenous regimes committed not merely to industrialisation but also to giving the state a special role to ensure that the industrialisation process happened. This also meant that many Asian regimes were attracted to socialist planning systems and Lenin's dictum that the state needed to have a firm grip on the 'commanding heights of the economy' (Lenin 1922). The exact nature of the relationship between state and private entrepreneurship varied from country to country, depending in particular on the degree to which the new national states adhered to socialist ideas and the precise contours of what they inherited from colonial rule.

In the case of India, democratic parliaments and private entrepreneurs shared the role of agents of development with the mechanisms of state planning and the 'licence permit Raj'. The basic principles of state planning were borrowed from the Soviet Union and mixed with a system of controlled private capitalist production through the distribution of licences to private entrepreneurs. Imports of components, for example, were channelled through state agencies. The result was a mixed economy, which remains the defining feature of India today, as Vicziany has argued in her analysis of the leading private and public sector companies that dominate oil and gas production in India (see chapter five). In China's case, the revolution of 1950 saw the emergence of the most socialistically oriented economy in world history. The state's role as an entrepreneur went even further in China than in the Soviet Union—as exemplified by the 'Great Leap Forward', which was a unique attempt by the Communist Party of China to industrialise the countryside using primitive technology. In the case of these two emerging Asian giants, state-owned companies continue to play a critical role in the economy even if the overriding laws and regulations of India and China are now favourable to the development of *private* entrepreneurship. To ignore the role of state entrepreneurship would result in an incomplete and, indeed, incomprehensible analysis of the business environments of India and China.

State entrepreneurship has also been important in Vietnam and Malaysia, where, as elsewhere, governments have often provided the initial impetus for industrialisation. Moreover, throughout the region the linkages between state and private entrepreneurship persist to this day. Not all these aspects of entrepreneurship can be addressed in a single study of the kind presented in this book; but it is worth noting in passing that individual entrepreneurs have frequently moved from state to private sector employment in order to go beyond the constraints they faced in the state sector. Moreover, many of the institutional structures for private sector development in Asia continue to depend on state entrepreneurship—for example, the leading national banks throughout much of the region remain firmly within state control (Zhang 2006).

Business in the Asian economies since 1945

In the previous section of this chapter we argued that the era of European dominance from about 1850 to 1960 was defined by a remarkable economic transition in Asia: the very period of Asian economic subordination to Europe and America saw the Asian economies experience a modernisation process, which gave rise to new entrepreneurial classes. These entrepreneurs have fuelled the resurgence of Asia during the past two decades. Decolonisation marked a major discontinuity in that modernisation process—the entrepreneurial renaissance, which began under colonial tutelage, continued but was now under the umbrella of new nationalist Asian governments, which were committed to the delivery of indigenous economic growth and a better standard of living for their own people (rather than for the coffers of colonial powers).

This section provides a snapshot of the development policies and growth paths of the selected countries since the Second World War and shows how the chapters in this collection cohere into a persistent story of rapid modernisation and industrialisation. In the next chapter Ross Mouer examines the factors shaping Japan's economic performance since 1955 and the resultant social outcomes. Between 1900 and the start of the Second World War, Japan's economy grew at about 4% per annum which was higher than most other countries in that period. However, from 1955 up until the mid-1970s, Japan grew at close to 10% per annum which was unprecedented. The income-doubling plan, which existed from 1955 to 1965 with the aim of doubling GDP in ten years, was an important stimulus and set off growth rates of 10% per annum growth, which continued well into the mid-1970s. Between 1946 and 1976 the economy grew 55-fold (Johnson 1982). By the mid-1970s Japan was producing 10% of world manufacturing output, but had just 3% of the world's population, 0.3% of the world's total surface and few natural resources.

The reasons for Japan's economic success are controversial. There was extensive use of commercial policies. The Ministry of International Trade and Industry (MITI) adopted a number of selective policies to promote exports. MITI targeted potential export winners and used a range of export incentives, including subsidies, tax credits, directed credit, exemptions from import duties on certain goods and licensing of foreign technology. These incentives were offered subject to strict market criteria. If the firms did not meet targets, the incentives were revoked, consistent with the Darwinian principle of 'survival of the fittest'. MITI used 'administrative guidance' to influence the number of firms in particular industries and to influence the business strategies that firms adopted. As Johnson (1982: 8) notes:

> The government did not normally give direct orders to businesses, but those firms who listened to the signals coming from the government and then responded were favoured with easy access to capital, tax breaks and approval of their plans to import foreign technologies.

MITI also pursued import substitution—for instance, Johnson (1982) points out that at different times Japan used tariffs, import quotas and import restrictions based on foreign currency allocations. The main difference between Japan and countries like India is that import substitution was coupled with export promotion. MITI facilitated a close 'collaborative relationship' between business and government (for example, MITI has provided a vehicle for the *keiretsu* to lobby the Japanese government). When senior bureaucrats retired from agencies such as MITI they took up senior positions in private businesses, which cemented the close relationship.

There appears, initially, to be a strong positive correlation between the use of commercial policies and Japan's economic success over this period. At least, as scholars such as Johnson (1982) have argued, in the absence of evidence to the contrary there is an a priori case that Japan's use of commercial policies was responsible for Japan's economic success. There have, however, been critics of this perspective. One argument is that Japan's economic success in the high-growth period was due to the high level of personal savings, stable macro-economic policies and favourable world conditions. The critics of interventionism argue that targeting was not always successful. At times MITI missed certain industries such as electronics, while other industries, such as the car industry, developed in spite of opposition from MITI (Ito 1997). It might also be argued that Japan's success was due to a series of events that, with hindsight, turned out to be fortuitous for promoting economic growth. These fortuitous events are one-offs, which cannot be replicated in other countries. Bombing by the United States during the war destroyed a lot of out-dated technology, which was replaced with up-to-date technology financed by the Marshall Plan. In the period 1945–55 the United States put in place administrators that were Western-educated and receptive to new ideas about how to facilitate economic growth. Economic reforms in the occupation period also freed the *zaibatsu* from familial domination, which had been restrictive. Japan received defence protection at a low cost (because Japan was of strategic importance to the United States during the Cold War), allowing it to invest in growth-enhancing policies. And the United States provided a ready market for Japanese exports in the 'golden age of world trade' (1945–75), which no longer exists because of saturation and slower growth.

By the 1980s Japan was an economic superpower and, it was thought, on the verge of overtaking the United States as the world's largest economy. As Krugman (1999:60–3) points out, top-selling books on Japan in the early 1980s focused on how the United States should become more like Japan. In the early 1990s, though, Japan's growth rate started to slow—Mouer refers to the 1990s as Japan's lost decade. The Asian financial crisis exposed weaknesses in the main bank relationship with the *keiretsu* and the close relationship between government and big business, which had long been considered strengths of the Japanese approach. From the 1990s the tenor of book titles about Japan, such as Michael Porter's *Can Japan compete?* instructs Japan to become more like the United States. The lost decade has caused Japan to re-evaluate where it is heading. As Mouer notes, there is increasing discussion in Japan of the phenomenon of *nihonbyo* (the Japanese disease) and what is the best approach to kick-start the Japanese economy again.

As is clear from Lesley McKaig's chapter on South Korea, there are many similarities between the state-led approach to development in Japan and South Korea in the 1950s, 1960s and 1970s. As noted earlier, the essence of the Japanese modernisation model was subconsciously transferred to Korea during the period of imperialism. In both countries, a strong state manipulated prices to promote national growth objectives. McKaig notes that in South Korea the same debate exists as in Japan between those who argue that South Korea's success from the 1950s to the 1980s was due to a strong development state and those who advocate that the success was market conforming and, in particular, that it reflected the ability of the *chaebol* to respond to market signals and outward-looking export-led trade strategies. McKaig argues that both market-led and state-led models contributed to South Korea's rise from the 1960s and that both were found wanting in the fallout from the Asian financial crisis. There are other similarities between Japan and South Korea in the form of one-off fortuitous events that smoothed Korea's path to success. In South Korea's case, aid from the United States and the inflow of Japanese capital following the normalisation of the Korea–Japan relationship were important stimuluses for growth (Cho 2001). McKaig emphasises that the Asian financial crisis represented a major structural break for South Korea. The rate of growth in GDP fell from 5% in 1997 to –6.6% in 1998. As with Japan, the crisis exposed fundamental flaws in the South Korean development model. Recognition of these flaws has led to a shift in approach to development. In the decade since the beginning of the crisis, South Korea has moved more from the state-led to the market-led model and much emphasis has been placed on reforming the corporate practices of the *chaebol*.

Following the chapters on Japan and South Korea, Russell Smyth and Marika Vicziany examine the growth experiences of China and India respectively. While Japan and South Korea were pursuing selective policies to promote exports from the 1960s, China and India chose similar economic development strategies of near-autarky, industrialisation and the dominance of the state in the economy. The result was near-economic disaster. China emerged from the Cultural Revolution (1966–76) in virtual economic collapse. Following the Second World War, most pundits considered that India would be a development success compared with East Asia because in contrast to Japan, India remained largely unscathed by the war. And unlike countries such as Indonesia, where there was a vacuum in the civil service when the Dutch left, in India, Indian nationals occupied relatively senior positions in the civil service when the British went. However, India's growth record from the 1950s to the 1980s was disappointing relative to the high-performing East Asian economies. China introduced piecemeal market reforms in the late 1970s, while India commenced hesitant economic reforms in the 1980s and systematic liberalisation from 1991 onwards. Since opening up, both countries have experienced rapid economic growth, with China growing at around 10% per annum and India at 6% per annum. China and India are now widely regarded as the emerging economic superpowers of the 21st century (Srinivasan 2004; Das 2006). Estimates by Consensus Economics suggest that by 2015 China will overtake the United States as the world's largest economy and India will move past Japan to occupy third place (cited in Eslake 2006). As Eslake (2006:18) suggests, the rise of China and India in the world economy is arguably the most significant economic event since the collapse of the Bretton Woods agreement at the start of the 1970s. It is at least as important as Japan's sustained economic growth from the 1950s through to the beginning of the 1990s.

Vietnam makes an interesting comparison with China and, as a member of ASEAN, represents a link between the chapter on China and the later chapters on Southeast Asia. As discussed in Keith Trace's chapter, following the reunification of Vietnam in 1976, the new Socialist Republic of Vietnam imposed Soviet-style planning on the South. The planning system in Vietnam generally performed poorly, similar to that of China prior to the introduction of market reforms. While China introduced economic reforms from the late 1970s, the policy of *Doi Moi* in Vietnam was formally introduced almost a decade later in December 1986. The focus in both instances has been on creating a market economy with socialist orientation. In the late 1980s and early 1990s a number of economic reforms were introduced in Vietnam, including liberalisation of trade; devaluation of the Vietnamese currency, the Dong; abolition of subsidies to state-owned enterprises; and relaxation of price controls. As Trace puts it, by 1992 the Vietnamese economy had made a substantial transition towards a market economy. There was a brief period in the mid-1990s when economic reforms were halted because of concern amongst conservatives in the Communist Party that the reforms were proceeding too fast, but otherwise the reforms proceeded relatively smoothly through the 1990s and the first half of the 2000s. Through implementation of the *Doi Moi* economic reforms, Vietnam has experienced remarkable growth in its GDP, savings rate and foreign direct investment, seating Vietnam comfortably amongst the high-growth ASEAN countries. Economic expansion was accompanied by a sizeable increase in oil revenues and transformation of what was an inefficient agricultural sector into a world-class rice exporter (Alpert & Sanders 2005). Vietnam was largely unscathed by the Asian financial crisis, managing to largely avoid the balance of payments, banking and fiscal crises that affected some other countries in Southeast Asia. Reflecting on Vietnam's experience in the Asian financial crisis, the World Bank (2002) has suggested that macro-economic management is one of the main strengths of the Vietnamese economy.

Following the chapter on Vietnam, the last four chapters of the book examine the high-growth ASEAN 'Gang of Four'. As Hill (1997) emphasises, Indonesia, Malaysia and Thailand stand apart from Singapore and the other newly industrialised economies (Hong Kong, South Korea and Taiwan). Compared with the newly industrialised economies, Indonesia, Malaysia and Thailand are latecomers to development. The three larger countries differ in that they are geographically larger, their natural resource bases are stronger, they are ethnically more diverse and their political economy structures differ. There are, however, also important similarities between Indonesia, Malaysia, Thailand and Singapore that help to explain their high rates of economic growth. Hill (1997:133) suggests that macro-economic orthodoxy, openness and equity constitute the 'irreducible core' of explanations for economic growth. As discussed in the respective country chapters in this volume and by Hill (1997) in considerable detail, all four countries perform well in these three core areas.

In addition to discussing the reasons for economic growth prior to the Asian financial crisis, the chapters on the ASEAN high-growth economies examine the effects of the Asian financial crisis and how each country has responded to the crisis; the chapters also look at the prospects of each country in the 21st century for continued and sustained high rates of growth. David Treisman provides an overview of the Thai business environment through an analysis of Thailand's financial liberalisation and its subsequent impact on the Thai economy. Robert Rice reviews the factors that have affected Indonesian economic development, with a focus on the role of the state in business, factors affecting the development of private enterprise, and positive and negative factors affecting the business climate. Marika Vicziany examines what she describes as Malaysia's 'remarkable economic transformation', but also suggests that in the first decade of the 21st century serious questions exist about the future of Malaysia's long-term development strategy. Malaysian competitiveness is weakening and the country's innovation strategies appear to have stagnated. Vicziany argues that these uncertainties are taking their toll by inducing social disharmony within families, between generations and between diverse economic regions. In the volume's final chapter Lesley McKaig reviews the debates surrounding Singapore's economic success, focusing on the role of the state and the relative contribution of Singapore's entrepreneurial classes; namely, the local private business sector, the multinational corporations and government-controlled enterprises.

Conclusion

The Asian economies are back. In 2003 a Goldman Sachs report estimated that by 2041 the Chinese economy would be larger than that of the United States and that by 2032 India would exceed Japan in terms of total annual GDP measured in US dollars (Wilson & Purushothaman 2003:3). Fuelling that growth is the rise of dynamic, local private industries. And China and India are not the only emerging giants—Indonesia is said to be next on the list. Most important of all, growth is generic to the region as a whole. Asia was first propelled by the intervention of the indigenous state using a wide range of protectionist instruments; increasingly, over time, the dynamism of local entrepreneurship took over and economic liberalisation emerged as the key policy instrument to unfetter local initiative. Today the world of business in Asia is a rapidly changing scenario in which home-grown companies compete against multinationals for market share and market access. These multinationals, themselves, reflect the changing order of our times—we now have Indian multinationals exporting palm oil from Malaysia, Chinese multinationals investing in animal feeds in the Philippines and Vietnam, and Korean multinationals running factories in Ireland, Poland and Mexico. The multinational is no longer the exclusive terrain of American or European entrepreneurs. Moreover, giant multinationals now operate alongside mini-multinationals. Bigness is not everything. One estimate notes that in 1990 there were 30,000 multinationals operating across the globe and now there are 60,000; and the most rapid expansion is amongst the 'Lilliputs' (Ewing 2006). The story of the rise of the Asian multinationals goes beyond the objectives of this book. Here we have mapped out a wide terrain that identifies the key features of the Asian economies in the post-Second World War era as European colonialism retreated and opened up unprecedented opportunities for Asian entrepreneurs.

Table 1: *Economic and social indicators*

	JAPAN			
	1990	2000	2004	2005
Population size (millions)	123.5	126.8	127.3	127.5
Population growth (%)	0	0.1	0.1	n.a.
GDP/per capita US$ (2000 base year)	33,252	37,409	39,195	n.a.
GDP growth rate (%)	5	3	2.3	2.8
Industrial growth rate	n.a.	n.a.	5.3	1.7
FDI stocks (as % to GDP)				
Inward	n.a.	1.1	2.1	n.a.
Outward	6.6	5.8	7.9	n.a.
Literacy rate (%)	n.a.	n.a.	99	n.a.
Primary enrolment ratio (%)	100	100	n.a.	n.a.
Secondary enrolment ratio (%)	97	101	n.a.	n.a.
Exports of goods and services (% of GDP)	10	10.8	11.8 (2003)	13.6
Imports of goods and services (% of GDP)	11	9.4	10.2 (2003)	−10.8
Unemployment rate (%)	n.a.	n.a.	n.a.	4.4
Inflation (% change YOY)	n.a.	n.a.	n.a.	n.a.
HDI trends	0.89	0.932	0.941	n.a.
	SOUTH KOREA			
	1990	2000	2004	2005
Population size (millions)	n.a.	47.3	48.2	48.5
Population growth (%)	1	0	1	n.a.
GDP/per capita US$ (2000 base year)	n.a.	n.a.	17,971	n.a.
GDP growth rate (%)	n.a.	n.a.	3.7	4.0
Industrial growth rate	n.a.	n.a.	10.2	5.0
FDI stocks (as % to GDP)				
Inward	n.a.	n.a.	n.a.	n.a.
Outward	n.a.	n.a.	n.a.	n.a.
Literacy rate (%)	n.a.	90.9	97.9	n.a.
Primary enrolment ratio (%)	100	103	n.a.	n.a.
Secondary enrolment ratio (%)	86	88	n.a.	n.a.
Exports of goods and services (% of GDP)	28	38	n.a.	51.6
Imports of goods and services (% of GDP)	29	36	n.a.	48.1
Unemployment rate (%)	n.a.	n.a.	3.7	3.7
Inflation (% change YOY)	n.a.	n.a.	n.a.	n.a.
HDI trends	0.818	0.884	0.901	n.a.

CHINA				
	1990	2000	2004	2005
Population size (millions)	1,135.20	1,262.20	1,296.50	1,307.56
Population growth (%)	1	1	0.58	0.589
GDP/per capita US$ (2000 base year)	364	856	1,486	n.a.
GDP growth rate (%)	4.7	8	10	9.9
Industrial growth rate	7.8	n.a.	17.1	1.7
FDI stocks (as % to GDP)				
Inward	5.8	17.9	14.9	n.a.
Outward	1.3	2.6	2.4	n.a.
Literacy rate (%)	78.3	93.28	90.9	n.a.
Primary enrolment ratio (%)	97	104.2	n.a.	n.a.
Secondary enrolment ratio (%)	n.a.	n.a.	n.a.	n.a.
Exports of goods and services (% of GDP)	18	25.9	40.2	13.6
Imports of goods and services (% of GDP)	14	23.2	29.2	−10.8
Unemployment rate (%)	n.a.	8.2	9.9	4.4
Inflation (% change YOY)	3.4	0.3	3.9	n.a.
HDI trends	0.627	n.a.	0.755	n.a.

INDIA				
	1990	2000	2004	2005
Population size (millions)	n.a.	1,001.00	1,073.00	1,091.00
Population growth (%)	n.a.	1.7	1.4	n.a.
GDP/per capita US$ (2000 base year)	322	391.65	518.17	593.00
GDP growth rate (%)	n.a.	6.06	8.51	6.91
Industrial growth rate	n.a.	6.61	7.02	8.35
FDI stocks (as % to GDP)				
Inward	0.5	3.7	5.2	n.a.
Outward	n.a.	n.a.	1.0	n.a.
Literacy rate (%)	49.3	n.a.	61.0	n.a.
Primary enrolment ratio (%)	n.a.	87	n.a.	n.a.
Secondary enrolment ratio (%)	n.a.	n.a.	n.a.	n.a.
Exports of goods and services (% of GDP)	7	13.9	15.3	19.1
Imports of goods and services (% of GDP)	9	14.6	17.2	16.3
Unemployment rate (%)	n.a.	40.37	9.80	9.90
Inflation (% change YOY)	0.513	4.0	4.3	n.a.
HDI trends	n.a.	0.577	0.602	n.a.

VIETNAM				
	1990	2000	2004	2005
Population size (millions)	66.20	78.52	82.16	83.80
Population growth (%)	2	1	1	n.a.
GDP/per capita US$ (2000 base year)	227	397	550	n.a.
GDP growth rate (%)	5	7	8.4	7.7
Industrial growth rate	n.a.	n.a.	16	15.6
FDI stocks (as % to GDP)				
Inward	25.5	65.7	66.3	n.a.
Outward	n.a.	n.a.	n.a.	n.a.
Literacy rate (%)	90.4	n.a.	90.3	n.a.
Primary enrolment ratio (%)	90	94	95.5 (2003)	n.a.
Secondary enrolment ratio (%)	n.a.	65	n.a.	n.a.
Exports of goods and services (% of GDP)	36	55.0	59.7 (2003)	69.6
Imports of goods and services (% of GDP)	45	57.5	67.6 (2003)	76.5
Unemployment rate (%)	n.a.	4.4	2.2	n.a.
Inflation (% change YOY)	n.a.	−1.7	7.8	n.a.
HDI trends	0.617	0.695	0.704	n.a.

THAILAND				
	1990	2000	2004	2005
Population size (millions)	55.59	60.72	62.38	65.50
Population growth (%)	2	1	0.6	n.a.
GDP/per capita US$ (2000 base year)	1,427	2,021	2,399	n.a.
GDP growth rate (%)	11	5	6.2	4.5
Industrial growth rate	n.a.	n.a.	8.2	n.a.
FDI stocks (as % to GDP)				
Inward	9.7	24.4	29.7	n.a.
Outward	n.a.	1.8	2.1	n.a.
Literacy rate (%)	n.a.	92.4	92.6	n.a.
Primary enrolment ratio (%)	n.a.	76	85	n.a.
Secondary enrolment ratio (%)	n.a.	n.a.	n.a.	n.a.
Exports of goods and services (% of GDP)	34	66.8	65.6 (2003)	70.5
Imports of goods and services (% of GDP)	42	58.1	58.9 (2003)	−65.8
Unemployment rate (%)	n.a.	3.6	2.1	2.1
Inflation (% change YOY)	n.a.	1.5	2.8	n.a.
HDI trends	0.714	n.a.	0.778	n.a.

INDONESIA

	1990	2000	2004	2005
Population size (millions)	178.2	227.7	238.6	242.0
Population growth (%)	2	1.3	1.3	n.a.
GDP/per capita US$ (2000 base year)	612	800	1,151	n.a.
GDP growth rate (%)	9	5	5.1	n.a.
Industrial growth rate	n.a.	n.a.	6.9	5.1
FDI stocks (as % to GDP)				
Inward	7.7	16.5	4.4	n.a.
Outward	n.a.	4.6	n.a.	n.a.
Literacy rate (%)	n.a.	n.a.	87.9	n.a.
Primary enrolment ratio (%)	92	89	n.a.	n.a.
Secondary enrolment ratio (%)	n.a.	n.a.	n.a.	n.a.
Exports of goods and services (% of GDP)	25	42.9	31.3	30.9
Imports of goods and services (% of GDP)	24	33.5	26.5	26.9
Unemployment rate (%)	n.a.	6.1	10.9	11.8
Inflation (% change YOY)	0.625	3.7	6.1	n.a.
HDI trends	0.178	0.680	0.697	n.a.

MALAYSIA

	1990	2000	2004	2005
Population size (millions)	18.20	23.27	25.20	25.90
Population growth (%)	3	2.4	1.7	n.a.
GDP/per capita US$ (2000 base year)	2,498	3,881	4,221	n.a.
GDP growth rate (%)	9	9	7.1	5.3
Industrial growth rate	n.a.	12.1	11.3	4.0
FDI* stocks (as % to GDP)				
Inward	23.4	58.6	39.3	n.a.
Outward	6.1	23.6	11.7	n.a.
Literacy rate (%)	80.7	92.0	88.7	n.a.
Primary enrolment ratio (%)	84	94	93	n.a.
Secondary enrolment ratio (%)	n.a.	n.a.	n.a.	n.a.
Exports of goods and services (% of GDP)	75	124.4	121.3	121.8
Imports of goods and services (% of GDP)	72	104.5	99.7	−100.4
Unemployment rate (%)	n.a.	3.1	3.6	n.a.
Inflation (% change YOY[†])	n.a.	1.5	1.5	n.a.
HDI[‡] trends	0.721	0.790	0.769 (2003)	n.a.

SINGAPORE				
	1990	2000	2004	2005
Population size (millions)	3.04	4.01	4.20	4.30
Population growth (%)	4	2	2	n.a.
GDP/per capita US$ (2000 base year)	14,401	22,767	25,170	n.a.
GDP growth rate (%)	9	9	8.7	6.4
Industrial growth rate	n.a.	n.a.	4.8	n.a.
FDI stocks (as % to GDP)				
Inward	83.1	123.1	150.2	n.a.
Outward	21.3	62.1	94.5	94.5
Literacy rate (%)	n.a.	88.8	92.5	92.5
Primary enrolment ratio (%)	96	n.a.	n.a.	n.a.
Secondary enrolment ratio (%)	n.a.	n.a.	n.a.	n.a.
Exports of goods and services (% of GDP)	n.a.	n.a.	n.a.	243
Imports of goods and services (% of GDP)	n.a.	n.a.	n.a.	213.1
Unemployment rate (%)	n.a.	4.4	5.3	n.a.
Inflation (% change YOY)	n.a.	1.4	1.6	n.a.
HDI trends	n.a.	n.a.	3.4	3.3

*FDI— foreign direct investment

†YOY—year on year

‡HDI—Human Development Index

n.a.—not available

Source: Compiled from World Bank, World Development Indicators (New York: Oxford University Press) and World Bank, World Development Indicators, accessible at http://publications.worldbank.org/WDI/

Table 2: The sequencing of decolonisation

Year	New nation	Old colonial power	Year	New nation	Old colonial power
1945	Korea	Japan	1954	Vietnam	France
1945	Taiwan	Japan	1959	Malay Federation (including the future state of Singapore)	Britain
1945	Vietnam (nominal independence)	Japan	1961	Goa, Daman, Diu absorbed into India	Portugal
1945	Indonesia (nominal independence)	Netherlands	1975	Vietnam (independence and unification)	France, Britain and United States
1946	Philippines	United States	1975	East Timor absorbed into Indonesia	Portugal
1947	India and Pakistan	Britain	1975	Papua New Guinea	Australia
1948	Burma and Sri Lanka	Britain	1997	Hong Kong absorbed into China	Britain
1949	Laos	France	1999	Macau absorbed into China	Portugal
1949	Indonesia	Netherlands	2002	East Timor	Indonesia
1953	Cambodia	France			

Notes

1 For Frank, China now and in the past was the epicentre of the global economy but he was prepared to concede that he did not know enough about the history of India to be 100% sure that China was more important than India in the long run: personal communication with Marika Vicziany 2000–04.
2 The Indian entrepreneurs in Southeast Asia have also been influential—in the past and today. For example, Jakarta has a large Sindhi business community, which is linked to the international Sindhi business diaspora as intimately as the Chinese community.
3 The Malays represent 15% and the Indians 7%.
4 Taylorism is attributed to the work of Frederick Taylor, who in 1911 published *The scientific principles of management*, which was an approach to modern factory production in which the extreme specialisation of tasks and workers' roles was seen as the basis of accelerated output and efficiency. Although regarded as a management approach of benefit to capital and corporations, Taylor himself believed that both employers and employees would benefit by the more scientific arrangement of labour inputs into the manufacturing process.

chapter two

Japan: globalisation and multiculturalism

Ross Mouer

From model to crossroads

Japan is often singled out for being the first Asian economy to heavily industrialise. Following on from the ten-year income-doubling plan introduced in December 1958 (actually the plan became four plans introduced in quick succession as the economy continued to grow beyond expectations), between 1960 and 1975 the economy grew annually by over 10% in nominal terms (see Table 1). By 1970 Japan had come onto the radar of Western observers who drew attention to Japan's economic record as a miracle and as a threat.

Table 1: Real and nominal economic growth rates, the rise in nominal wage rates, unemployment rates and the consumer price index (CPI) 1955–2000

Year	A Average annual growth rate in real GNP*	B Average annual growth rate in nominal GNP	C The ratio of real to nominal growth rates (B/A)	Average annual growth in wages	Average unemployment rate	CPI
1956–60	n.a.	8.50	n.a.	5.68	2.04	n.a.
1961–65	n.a.	10.0	n.a.	10.46	1.26	n.a.
1966–70	n.a.	11.30	n.a.	14.14	1.20	n.a.
1971–75	4.54	15.22	3.35	20.74	1.44	11.56
1976–80	4.40	6.18	1.40	9.82	2.06	6.62
1981–85	3.28	6.04	1.84	5.92	2.50	2.78
1986–90	4.92	6.30	1.28	5.80	2.50	1.36
1991–95	1.40	2.42	1.72	3.42	2.60	1.36
1996–2000	1.46	0.62	0.42	0.14	4.06	0.30

*GNP—gross national product

Sources: Rodo Daijin Kanbo Tokei Joho Bu 1982:12–14. (2) Kosei Rodo Daijin Kanbo Tokei Joho 2002:16, 20.

A common perception in the 1970s was that Japan's industry had suddenly emerged from the ashes of bombed rice paddies. As the economy continued to expand and began to generate sizeable balance of payments surpluses in the 1980s, many people came to regard Japan as a model combining traditional and modern elements. It was seen as a postmodern economy with certain features of the socialist economic ethos that are associated with many pre-industrial societies and the vibrant markets associated with urban societies. Japan was regarded as an industrial economy that maintained a respect for traditional human relationships while pushing ahead with the rationalisation of work practices and the accumulation of savings to support a high level of investment in economic infrastructure and in the replacement of the capital equipment underpinning Japan's very competitive manufacturing industries. The 'Look East' policies adopted by a number of other Asian governments and the general interest of the advanced economies in Japan as a model tended to focus attention on a limited number of practices and institutions that were at the time alleged to be uniquely Japanese and non-Western: enterprise bargaining, quality control circles, just-in-time production systems, and certain aspects of corporate culture and human resource management. This focus was inclined to place an emphasis on the importance of decisions at the micro-economic level. The infatuation with Japanese-style management and the traditional values associated with it often cut across the view that Japan's success was a recent phenomenon.

A look at Japan's longer-term trajectory, however, reveals that Japan's economy was not based on an overnight miracle. Rather, it had resulted from a century of industrialisation and modernisation (albeit in a Japanese mode) following the Meiji Restoration in 1868. Behind that was the existence of (1) sophisticated technology in steel, ceramics, textiles and lacquer ware in developed cottage industries, (2) certain financial and commercial institutions, and (3) high male literacy rates, which could be traced back even further into the Tokugawa period (1615–1868). Considering that history and then looking at the growth in other Asian economies over the past 30 years, the Japanese accomplishment now appears to be less extraordinary than it was believed to have been in the 1970s. Nevertheless, Japan's role as the first Asian society to develop an advanced industrial economy has led many to ask whether it supplied a model for Asian development à la Westernisation, which was more generally applicable around the world, or simply an early example of a particularly Asian approach to late development. Before considering the future of the Japanese economy, several facets of the Japanese experience require close scrutiny.

The major components of the 'Japanese model' for growth as it was commonly understood from the 1960s and through the 1980s included manpower policy, industrial policy, special micro-economic practices at the firm level, and shifts in the outlook and composition of the population. However, during the 1990s the Japanese experienced a number of changes that would shape Japan's economic future and render less relevant many of the discussions about the uniqueness of the Japanese experience. These changes included the impact of high economic growth over the preceding three decades on the Japanese population (especially in terms of the outlook of a younger generation growing up with higher levels of affluence, the aging of the population and the spread of practices associated with civil society). They also included the impact of international and domestic financial shocks and the clamour for greater transparency. Certain labour shortages connected to the reluctance of younger Japanese to engage in dirty, demanding and/or dangerous work spurred the influx of foreign workers to do such jobs. Inward migration, in turn, has generated the multiculturalisation of the labour force. The recessionary conditions associated with the impact of economic globalisation during the 1990s also gave rise to the demand by employers that the labour market be deregulated (in part through further casualisation of employment) at a time when the unionisation rate fell from 25% to 20% (continuing a decline that started in the mid-1970s when the rate was about 35%).

Factors shaping Japan's economic performance: 1955–90

When Japan first drew international attention, emphasis was placed on cultural factors. High savings, the work ethic and the absence of strong class affiliations, for example, were commonly cited to explain Japan's success. Over time, however, as Nakamura (1995) and others have observed, a number of structural factors came to receive more attention. Here three areas might be cited where critical policy choices were made to structure Japan's economic affairs in ways specifically designed to promote growth. Many of the choices in the 1950s and 1960s were made with the aim of promoting and channelling the accumulation of economic surplus into areas where returns would be the greatest. Despite American efforts to democratise Japan by decentralising much economic activity, Japan remained a rather centralised state, and behind this choice was the assumption that the nation state was the major or ultimate unit of social consequence: in 1955 conservative forces united behind the Liberal Democratic Party,[1] and for the next 35 years a cohesive triumvirate of big business, conservative politicians and elite bureaucrats worked closely together with a tacit agreement concerning that assumption. The structures that were institutionalised under that leadership came to be known collectively as the '1955 system'.

Industrial policy

The role of the government in directing Japan's economy has been debated for some time. Debate has also focused on the extent to which the government has played a proactive role, as opposed to a reactive role. Although Nakayama (1975) cautioned against overemphasising the role of the government, most observers would accept that in the post-war years the government has taken a proactive stance in implementing a program of economic growth through industrialisation. Between 1955 and 1999 the government's Economic Consultative Committee (Keizai Shingikai) issued 14 medium-range economic plans. Some observers such as Johnson (1982) have focused on the role of the bureaucracy in picking a few key industries to support through a complex system of administrative guidance, which allowed for market-conforming mechanisms overseen by the state; most observers, however, have attributed Japan's economic growth to a broader range of factors that include the government's policies to promote education, inflationary spending on large public infrastructure projects, the acquisition of large savings through its postal savings system, minimal expenditures on social services and social security, and efforts to undermine and contain left-wing unionism and other populist movements (such as various consumer or anti-pollution movements) that might detract from economic growth.

Still others (especially in the 1960s and 1970s when Japan's economic performance was seen as 'miraculous') have stressed the importance of cultural factors or national character. They have pointed to a penchant for high savings, an innate work ethic, a willingness to serve the nation, an ability to convert that communal orientation into a strong loyalty to the firm, and a certain egalitarian ethos, which is evidenced in the emergence of an extensive middle class without strong or antagonistic class consciousness along occupational lines (as is commonly found in many Western societies).

A third position has focused on structures, some put in place as policy outcomes but many simply evolving out of the chaos following the war and the somewhat ad hoc way in which Japanese society evolved and responded to external stimuluses in the post-war years. These structures included the 1955 system, the relationship between a number of educational institutions and the labour market, various industrial relations and personnel management practices, affiliation with the OECD, the institutionalised flow of rural labour and overseas workers into Japan's urban manufacturing centres, Japan's membership in the United Nations and its return to the international community as a 'non-political' actor. The initial move of Japanese capital overseas occurred through small and medium-sized entrepreneurial firms in light manufacturing, which began to invest in Southeast Asia in the 1970s. The growth of Japanese exports was also supported by the fixed United States dollar–Japanese yen parity (at

360 yen to the dollar) through the 1950s and 1960s, by the opening of the American market to Japan, and by American protection of Japan during the Cold War years. In the northern autumn of 1989 the United States government began its Structural Impediment Initiatives talks with its Japanese counterpart. Attempting to dismantle many of the non-tariff barriers that limited outside access to the Japanese market, American negotiators were frustrated by 'the enigma of Japanese power', a term used by Van Wolfren (1989) as the title for his book. Van Wolfren argued that the decision-making apparatus in Japan was opaque and without a clear locus to which political responsibility could be tied. However, circumstances changed dramatically in the early 1990s with the bursting of Japan's economic bubble, the end of the Cold War, the end of the Liberal Democratic Party's political dominance, and 'globalisation'.

At the same time, considerable attention had been given to the diseconomies or dysfunctions associated with Japan's growth. Pointing to high levels of pollution, excessively small residential spaces, urban crowding and inadequate public recreation facilities (the privatisation of leisure), long hours of work and *karoshi* (death from overwork),[2] critics of the Japanese experience argued that much of Japan's economic growth had been a mirage, with many Japanese themselves coming to decry the paradox of being so rich and yet feeling so poor. Although McCormack captured this sense in the title of his *Emptiness of Japanese Affluence* (1995), arguing that the economy revolved around behind-the-scenes transactions that deceived many ordinary Japanese, several of his concerns had surfaced earlier in the late 1960s and in the early 1970s, before receding in the late 1970s and in the 1980s and the bubble years, only to resurface again in the 1990s. The urgency to answer questions about the origins of Japanese growth waned considerably as Japan entered the 1990s and an extended period with recession-like conditions.

Micro-economic practices

At the beginning of the 1980s, it was Japanese-style management that attracted international attention. Two reports by the OECD in the 1970s had attributed a good deal of Japanese success to its system of industrial relations. Specific mention was made of lifetime employment, seniority wages and enterprise unions. Behind those practices stood Japan's trade union laws, its legislation for settling industrial disputes and the Labour Standards Law. Nevertheless, while this policy framework, largely put in place during the occupation years (1945–52), allowed such practices, it did not provide for any of them. The second OECD (1977) report thus put such practices down to unique Japanese cultural traits, a view readily accepted by many informed writers at the time, but one that came to be increasingly marginalised during the following decades.

With the interest in Japanese-style management peaking in the late 1980s, repeated study tours to Japan by Western managers and the experience with burgeoning Japanese direct investment at home led many people to conclude that the superior productivity of Japan's factories sprang from other less-advertised practices: just-in-time production systems (which shifted costs to lower-rung subcontractors), various quality control measures (including quality control circles, which were not as spontaneous as originally described),[3] highly segmented labour markets internally and externally, an extremely complex wage system with deferred payment of a sizeable portion of worker remuneration, and several strategies to undermine the long-term viability of left-wing enterprise unions. These were all matters that were shaped by micro-economic structures, and depended more on political balances at work than on culture per se.

Although some scholars such as Koike (1988; 1995) pointed to ways in which internal labour markets functioned to impart to regular (male) employees deep and broad skills, and multiskilling, these features were sometimes contrasted with demarcated skilling in other societies. It is generally accepted that regular employees in large firms who have access to such training represent a rather small proportion of the *male* labour force in Japan. At the same time, Koike has carefully argued that even though long-term employment and strictly seniority-based wages may have been confined to only a portion of the labour force, the benefits of such practice were open to a critical number of skilled blue-collar workers, as well as university graduates in professional, technical and managerial work. Putting aside arguments about how widely such practices were implemented, observers saw the importance of such practices normatively as 'best practice'—an ideal outcome to which lower-level employees might aspire *if they worked hard enough*. In this sense the institutionalisation of such practices for a small elite in Japan's largest firms (representing perhaps 10–20% of Japan's employees) is linked to the motivation of many (the other 80–90%) to study and to work hard. Some time ago Koshiro (1982) wrote about the scarcity of good jobs in Japan; the practices of long-term employment and seniority-based wages served to delineate an elite labour force in Japan's large firms and were the envy of other workers both inside and outside Japan.

The lifestyle of the *sarariman* (salaried employees) became a standard to which numerous graduates aspired.[4] They owned their own homes, enjoyed all the latest consumer gadgets and put their children into Japan's better schools. The mainly male salaried employees in Japan's elite labour force and their approach to family life contributed to the institutionalisation of paths for upward mobility, thereby giving the younger generation in Japan hope that by studying hard and excelling academically they, too, might join the ranks of the securely employed.

Very early in the post-war period, the Japanese came to understand the economics of education. During the 1960s the belief spread that Japan was a truly egalitarian middle-class society in which young Japanese had an equal opportunity to achieve both inter- and intra-generational mobility by performing well in the Japanese system of education. One result of such aspirations was a highly educated labour force, with over a third of the designated generation completing some form of tertiary education by the mid- to late 1970s. The motivation to succeed spilled over into work for many Japanese who believed that anything was achievable for regular employees who worked hard. Such employees became the backbone of the Japanese economy and were renowned for their long hours of work as *moretsu shain* (gung-ho company employees). The more capable of those doubtless became the driving force behind Japan's expansion in the 1960s, 1970s and 1980s.

Social outcomes

The major outcome of Japan's rapid growth from the mid-1950s onwards was the birth of a strong middle-class consciousness by the late 1970s. Based on surveys taken by the Prime Minister's Office, it was reported by much of the media and accepted by many academics that 90% of Japanese had come to identify themselves and their lifestyle with a large amorphous middle class. This consciousness was bolstered by surveys (including the Stratification and Social Mobility Survey taken every ten years by the Japan Sociological Association) (Kyujugonen SSM Chosa Kenkyukai 2000) showing that high rates of inter-generational occupational mobility had occurred. There was some evidence to support the idea of a large, growing and prosperous Japanese middle class: national markets had emerged, large segments of the population had moved into standardised urban accommodation, common consumer goods (rice cookers, vacuum cleaners, electric fans, black-and-white and then colour television sets, refrigerators, cars) were widely diffused, and leisure-time activities (such as golf and, later, computer games and a youth-oriented popular culture) were expanding and vigorously marketed. This new national consciousness was reinforced by moves to spread a standardised Japanese language through the schools as part of efforts to centralise control over a national curriculum.

Other changes could also be mentioned. Furuzawa (2005), for example, writes about food technology and how advances in packaging and transport systems allowed for the spread of standard processed foods onto dinner tables around Japan. Further, from the Prime Minister's Office came statistics from the Family Income and Expenditure Survey indicating that income differentials among households had diminished over time, yielding Gini coefficients considerably below the coefficients calculated for other similarly developed economies.

During the 1970s and 1980s Japanese intellectuals continued debates about the extent to which government statistics and journalistic accounts in a somewhat docile media fictionalised images of Japanese society. They pointed to the negative issues raised above: worsening pollution, cramped housing, excessively regimented work processes, unfair labour practices and the repression of unions, and other realities that served to undermine the standard of living and to restrict the emergence of a civil society. In particular they pointed to ways in which a vigorous and, in part, radical labour movement had been weakened by a series of government initiatives and management offences.

At the same time life expectancy rose from under 60 in 1950 to over 80 by the 1990s. Caring for the aged increasingly became a problem for many households. Although the labour force participation rate for married women remained at around 50% for much of the post-war period, women sought regular employment and other roles outside the home. Smaller families and household appliances lowered the pressures associated with looking after the home, although an increasingly competitive education system and aged care meant that some women continued to function mainly at home; the labour force participation rate for wives continued to vary inversely with the income of their husbands well into the 1980s, as families struggled to achieve target incomes while maintaining a balance at home. As homes filled with consumer durables, Japanese began to spend on the softer items: sex, movies, computer games and sport. With the lifting of foreign exchange restrictions at the end of the 1960s, the *sarariman* began to be accompanied by their families when on overseas assignments, and the number of Japanese tourists going abroad increased rapidly in the 1980s. These trends were further bolstered by the huge foreign exchange earnings from Japan's competitive exports in manufactured goods, but Japan came under fire for unfair trade practices and for limited contributions to support the world system while buying up cultural assets abroad. With the 'bubble economy' at its zenith in the late 1980s, Japanese increasingly went abroad with renewed confidence as businessmen, tourists and residents.

The 'lost' decade

The recessions in the 1990s may have undermined some of that burgeoning confidence, but could not reverse the longer-term trends mentioned above. Japanese society had become internationalised in ways that were difficult to reverse. The economy had been integrating with the world for some time, and the newly found patterns of consumption and living were becoming habits. Looking mainly at the further drop in economic growth rates during the 1990s, people came to refer to this time as 'the lost decade'. However, many of the new habits of consumption were intimately connected to far-reaching social change and to altered ways of thinking about work. In terms of the evolution of Japanese society, the decade was certainly not 'lost'.

Japan's long-term growth trajectory culminated with huge balance of payments surpluses during the 1980s, tremendous amounts of private and corporate investment overseas (including the establishment of retirement villages in Spain and elsewhere and talk of building a 'multi-function polis' in Australia), and the growth of sizeable Japanese communities overseas. People began to talk of a forthcoming Japanese century and Pax Nipponica, which would follow upon the American century. Some noted the close relations between these two great capitalist nations and speculated about further integration and the creation of a new geopolitical sphere, which might have been called 'Japamerica'. However, underlying tensions in the trade relationship, which had been articulated in the Structural Impediment Initiative talks in the late 1980s, pointed not only to structural barriers tilting the trade field in Japan's favour, but also to some fundamental weaknesses that accompanied a certain type of social dumping. It is thus more than an interesting coincidence that the end of the Cold War was accompanied by a sudden acceleration in the pace of globalisation and the exertion of externally generated competitive pressures on the Japanese economy. At the same time, the new economic affluence generated at home was having its own impact on the willingness of Japanese to participate in the labour market and on the state of Japan's civil society.

In 1985 nearly 90% of Japan's trade surplus was due to the export of goods, with only a little over 10% coming as a return on its portfolio of foreign investments. By 2001, however, roughly half of the surplus came from investment, about equal to the income derived from the export of goods. Huge balance of payments surpluses meant that firms could invest in overseas operations. Output from factories built overseas came to displace Japanese exports abroad and to compete in Japan with goods produced in Japan. In the 1990s China increasingly replaced Japan as the factory of the world and began producing increasingly sophisticated goods. At the same time the further opening up of the Japanese market put greater pressure on many Japanese firms. In addition to the growing competition in domestic markets from goods produced overseas, the decisions of Japanese firms to invest abroad meant that there were fewer funds to invest in their operations in Japan.

During the 1990s Japan also experienced its own version of the Asian financial crisis, sometimes referred to euphemistically as the 'Big Bang'. A number of major firms such as Yamaichi Securities (in November 1997) went bankrupt, and the number of bankruptcies increased significantly. The costs involved in retiring bad loans were covered by government subsidies (and thereby, ultimately, the average citizen), by various forms of cost cutting at the firm level, and by the loss of many private investments made for retirement. Despite popular scepticism with government policy to liberalise trade, it was nearly impossible for the Japanese state to move backwards and reinstitute the structural barriers to protect local interests in an international climate in which states were moving to embrace the World Trade Organization (WTO) framework. From the mid-1990s those developments created pressures that came to be released through the higher unemployment rates (as shown in Table 1 in this chapter).

At the same time consumers saw benefits in the new regime. By then explanations emphasising the cultural determinants of a uniquely Japanese set of consumer preferences gave way to recognition that there was a more universal demand for products—some needing to be of high quality and commanding higher prices, and others not so and selling at cheaper prices.

The Kobe earthquake in January 1995 served to highlight further the shortcomings of the 1955 system. Although many Japanese took pride in the fact that Japan was a highly networked information society, Japan found it difficult to co-ordinate rescue attempts and was slow to grasp the full extent of the damage. The earthquake also revealed shortcomings in building standards in the construction industry, which accompanied underhand bidding practices and an excessively decentralised or tiered approach in which responsibility (not only for construction but also for relief and subsequent welfare services) was difficult to pinpoint. There was also increasing income inequality, a trend noted by observers. These were the major developments in the national economy at the macro level.

Globalisation and restructuring

In the late 1990s moves were made to restructure the economy. A succession of banks merged, culminating, for example, in the Mizuho Bank being formed in April 2002 by a merger of the Fuji Bank, the Dai-ichi Kangyo Bank and the Industrial Bank of Japan. The Mitsubishi Bank and the Bank of Tokyo had merged earlier in 1996. In April 2001 the Sumitomo Bank merged with the Sakura Bank (itself formed from an earlier merger of Mitsui and Taiyo Kobe Banks). Mergers and restructuring also occurred in the securities and life-insurance industries between 1999 and 2004. These need to be understood in the context of the mergers that had occurred among competing firms in North America and Europe a decade earlier. The pressure points were identical. With global restructuring in the automobile industry reverberating in Japan (with the Ford involvement in Volvo in 2000 and the merger of Chrysler and Daimler in

1998), it was logical that the French Renault company stepped in to bolster the fortunes of Nissan in May 1999, bringing with it a non-Japanese chief executive to guide the Japanese company in Japan's strongest industry. Matsuda followed suit, later coming to invite another foreign executive to oversee its affairs. Such restructuring has also occurred in other high-profile industries such as retailing and telecommunications. In tertiary education, national universities have been privatised and the competition to acquire enrolments from a declining cohort of high-school graduates in Japan has resulted in some institutions merging and others seeking to recruit fee-paying overseas students, in some cases introducing an English-language curriculum to attract them. Administrative reform has also been on the agenda of the government for some time, with a reduction in the number of ministries, agencies and various advisory boards, a continued push to further amalgamate local governments, and ongoing bureaucratic rationalisation aimed at reducing the number of public servants. Under pressure from a significant demographic shift as the population ages, steps have also been taken to consolidate a vast array of pension and healthcare schemes.

Despite these changes, many are still sceptical as to whether the changes will re-establish Japan's economic prominence in the future. Writers such as Sato (2003) argue that the reforms are too slow, and are not resulting in the level of transparency necessary to harness society's full potential. The first in a series of articles on *nihonbyo* (the Japanese disease) in Japan's leading economic newspaper in January 2003 highlighted four major sources of the problem:

(1) how corporate society is organised and run in Japan;

(2) the attachment of Japan's innately conservative leaders to the ways that appeared to have brought Japan so much economic growth over the preceding four decades;

(3) an apparent imperviousness to the full extent of the crisis besetting Japan (especially in terms of globalisation), to changes in Japanese society (including its move towards multiculturalism) and to falls in levels of universal literacy;

(4) a loss of confidence in risk taking following the sudden collapse of the bubble economy in the early 1990s.

Sato (2000) and Tachibanaki (1998) have argued that the new inequalities in income, wealth and education undermined the faith of many Japanese in the system. Sato (2000; 2003) thinks that many Japanese are losing their motivation to study and work hard, believing that the chances for upward mobility are now quite restricted. Rather than class warfare, however, this seems simply to breed alienation from the system, which produced so much of Japan's wealth in the post-war era. A number of Japanese have now come to question the wisdom of reforms based simply on notions of the bottom-line economic rationalism associated with the unbridled free-market capitalism. They see such capitalism as American-led globalisation and as an approach to be avoided.

Deregulation

Moves to rationalise the economy have revealed themselves in various attempts to deregulate the economy. The labour market has been a major target. Structural reform per se did not fundamentally alter labour market segmentation in Japan. Education histories, gender and age continued to shape entry into Japan's labour markets. Mobility in the labour market has traditionally been downward, or often occupationally lateral, as workers moved out of the privileged large-scale sector into smaller firms and from permanent employment to various kinds of casual employment. These facets of Japan's combined labour market are highlighted when contrasted with the situation in countries that have a less segmented approach to the way labour markets are organised, such as Australia (see Figure 1).

Figure 1: The structuring of the labour market, entry into its segments and the paths for downward mobility

A. Labour market flows in Japan

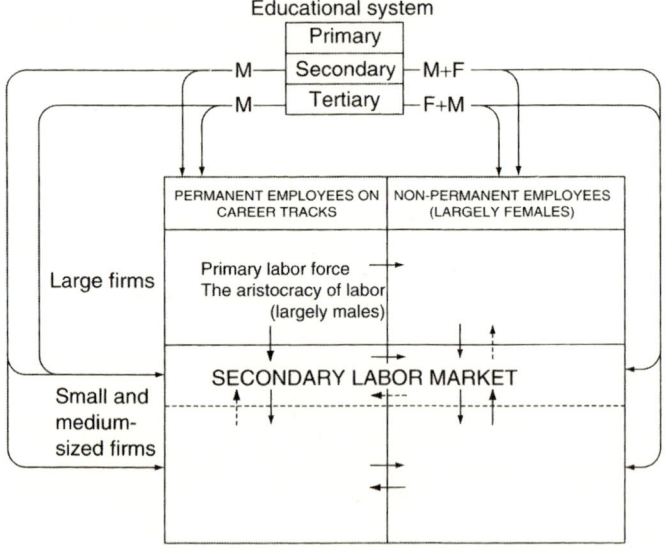

Source: Mouer 1989: 118, as reproduced in Mouer and Kawanishi 2005: 89.

B. Labour market flows in Australia

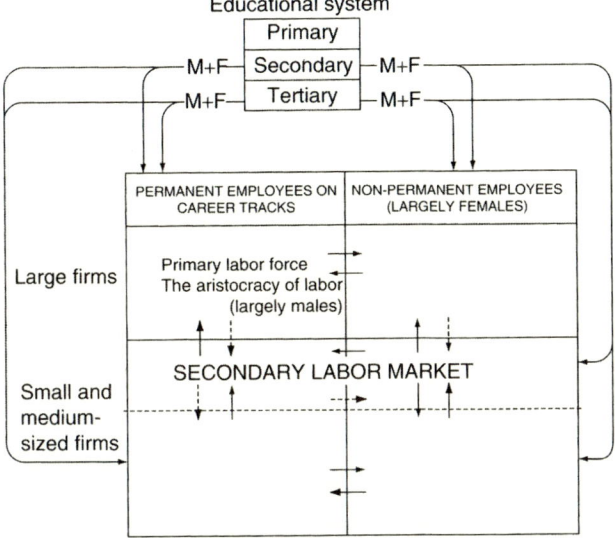

Source: Mouer (1989:118), as reproduced in Mouer and Kawanishi (2005:89).

The proportion of Japan's employees in casual employment has been increasing for some time. In 2001 nearly a third of males and 13.8% of females were aged over 65 and were still working (compared with only 4.5% and 1.6% in Germany or 16.9% and 8.9% in the United States), and their proportion of the total labour force increased from 12% in 1990 to 17.3% in 2000 (Mouer & Kawanishi 2005:102). The percentage of females working casually rose from 41.7% in 1992 to 46% in 1997 (the figures were 18.6% and 19.1% for males): Table 2 shows even greater increases between 1996 and 2000.

Table 2: Percentage distribution of non-regular employees in the non-agricultural private sector by firm size: 1996 and 2000

	Percentage of all employees who are non-regular employees	
Firm size (by number of employees)	February 1996	August 2000
1-29	30.0	34.7
39-99	23.8	34.8
100-499	19.5	24.8
500+	14.6	19.1

Source: Mouer and Kawanishi 2005:117–119.

In the 1990s Nikkeiren (the Japan Federation of Employers' Associations) pushed the Japanese government to deregulate the labour market even though some employers argued that practices contributing to the maintenance of social stability and order at work should be retained. Nikkeiren and the government sought to regain Japan's industrial competitiveness. Two reforms were critical to management's aptitude to command labour. One reform was to enhance management's ability to have employees work at its convenience; the other concerned the ease with which work could be outsourced. Organised labour resisted deregulation, and the legislation was not passed until September 1998. Nikkeiren fought and lost on each count. Because these types of changes are being introduced in Australia and many other economies, it is instructive to examine these trends in Japan in more detail. It is at the micro-economic level and in work organisation and labour markets that we can often detect how society and the economy come together to create society-specific responses to universally felt pressures in order to become and to remain globally competitive. Over the past decade this nexus between the economy and society has evolved for the individual employee with regard to structural change in each of the four ways described below.

First, the proposed legislation allowed for work to be delegated to employees against a nominal time standard. Essentially a return to piecework, it allowed employees to complete designated tasks faster or slower than the standard time (without reference to the actual time required). Although the law had previously allowed for this to occur in very limited areas, management pushed successfully for employers to be able to allocate work in this manner to all white-collar employees.

Second, the legislation changed the Labour Standards Law of 1947, which had allowed labour and management to negotiate at the firm level about limits on the amount of overtime employees could be required to work, with no set upper limit on overtime. Labour and management in many firms had agreed, however, that an employer could require an employee to work up to 15 hours of overtime per week, 45 hours per month and 360 hours per year. Management pushed to remove all constraints. Labour wanted the legal limit on annual overtime set at 360 hours for male employees, dropping to 150 hours in April 1999. The final outcome was the 360-hour limit for men, with the 150-hour limit for women being extended to April 2002.

Third, management pushed for the right to extend the variable work week so that overtime would be calculated in terms of overtime for a standard work year. By giving time off in lieu of overtime worked during busy periods, management had in the past been able to have employees work up to ten hours a day and 52 hours a week for up to three months without paying overtime rates. After three months the limits were set at nine hours and 48 hours respectively. Management wanted employees to work the ten hours a day and 52 hours a week for more extended periods, without being liable for overtime. Unions wanted the 40-hour standard work week respected every week. The revisions to the Labour Standards Law fully incorporated management's demands.

Fourth, previously the maximum length of time for a labour contract was one year. Regular employees worked on the basis of an informal agreement with management, which recognised their firms' policies of a fixed retirement age. The debate on labour contracts mainly concerned two groups of workers. One consisted of casual employees hired as part-timers, *arubaito*, *shokutaku*, *rinjiko* or other temporary help.[5] Management argued that such employers would be able to organise their own everyday affairs at home with more certainty if they were on longer contracts of up to five years. This meant that management could better 'lock in' its casual labour force and have its own measure of certainty, and that the distinction between the labour markets for regular and non-regular employees would be reinforced. Behind this there was, perhaps, the idea that a second group consisting of regular employees in highly technical or professional jobs might also be hired on such contracts in the future. The new law lifted the limit for contracts from one year to three, and it is clear that management will in the future be much more selective in deciding who to hire as regular long-term employees.

The other legislation of particular relevance here is the Law for Dispatching Workers. First passed in 1986, the law provided for certified companies to supply labour to cover (temporary) shortages in 13, and then 16, highly specialised occupational categories. In 1994 Nikkeiren called for categories to be opened up, and the number was raised to 26 in 1996. After further lobbying by Nikkeiren, the supply of such labour was in principle opened up for all occupations in December 1999, and a system of *shokai yotei haken seido* (longer-term job placements through temporary assignments) was established in 2000.

While organised labour has been able to slow this kind of deregulation in some areas, management's push to deregulate has made headway overall, and further changes are likely to follow. Nevertheless, despite the weakening of the labour movement in Japan, the supply of labour has significantly altered and has had its own impact on the way work is organised in Japan. Graduates became a much more diverse lot over the 1990s; fewer now seek the secure but highly pressurised work life associated with regular employment in Japan's prestigious large firms. Also, their drop-out rate after initial employment is higher. Terms such as *furiitaa* (freelance worker)[6] and *parasaito shinguru* (parasite singles)[7] have come to describe sizeable numbers of young people bent on a lifestyle alternative to that of the *sarariman*. Once shunned by Japan's more able graduates, foreign firms are now attracting a steady stream of applicants wanting to be challenged in ways that will allow them to demonstrate a wide range of skills, including information technology communication skills and English-language proficiencies. They welcome and search out opportunities to work abroad.

The equal opportunity legislation of 1986, as revised in 1999, has reinforced gender-related standards from overseas, while also underlining the need for employers in the 'new globalised economy' to proactively embrace women in the labour force if they are to have a competitive staffing profile. As Chan-Tiberghien (2004) argues, global standards are being adopted in Japan with regard to many gender-related practices. Moreover, in the current competitive environment, firms are coming to realise that they can no longer afford to discriminate against women or people with distinguishing features conceptualised in terms of old prejudices. Although many foreign workers have been hired to work in areas characterised by the 'three D's',[8] many companies have opened their doors to more skilled foreigners in order to keep their workforces competitive. There are thus signs that Japan's segmented labour market is loosening up, with many more opportunities for intra-generational mobility through inter-market mobility. This connects directly to the multiculturalisation of Japan and to the emergence of civil society in Japan today.

Civil society and voluntarism

After 1945 leftist intellectuals were outspoken in their support for the state to provide new civil minimums and to guarantee human rights associated with civil society. Although the idea of civil society existed in pre-Meiji Japan, conservatives dismissed such thinking as foreign individualist ideology, which had no place in a collectivistic Japan. In the early 1990s *shibiru sosaitei* (civil society) came to be associated with an interest in the potential for voluntarism in societal affairs, an orientation acceptable to conservatives concerned about the costs of social welfare.

Over the past decade the term 'NPO' (non-profit organisation) has come to be widely used in Japan to differentiate groups with an ongoing interest in 'serving society' from those with clear economic interests or long-term specialised political agendas (KKC 2000:8). Sugishita (2001:5–8) argues that NPOs were stimulated by public discussion of the NPO bill, which passed the Japanese Diet in March 1998 following the enactment of similar legislation in the United States.

A 2001 white paper (Somu Sho) suggested that some 47.08 million Japanese (approximately 37% of the adult population aged 15–79) were internet users, and that the majority logged on every day. The internet enables many Japanese citizens to expand their living spaces beyond the borders of the Japanese state. The enhanced ability of ordinary Japanese to enter and to access space outside the confines of local and national communities has obviously had ramifications on how Japanese think about their life-cycle options within Japan.

Further rationalisation meant that Japan was able to absorb the price increases caused by the sharp rise in the cost of imported oil during the 1990s. The result was that Japan maintained and even enhanced its international economic competitiveness well into the 1980s. Yabuno (1995) describes the period after the oil shocks of the 1970s as a time during which peripheralised local communities experienced depopulation, rapid aging, feminisation, unemployment and various other changes. He argues that several local communities responded by establishing their own international relations, thereby circumventing the national government in activities traditionally seen to be within its exclusive domain. This grassroots diplomacy has allowed Japanese to expand the horizons of their world. At the same time, Japan's 'foreign' population has also grown and diversified. In this regard, Morris-Suzuki (2000) has argued that many of these universally experienced issues require a comparative perspective as the Japan-specific dimensions become relatively less important. This, too, is an occurrence that invites more person-to-person exchanges at the grassroots level.

Including naturalised Koreans and Chinese, Japan's 'foreign' population has traditionally been below 1–2% of the total population. However, the number of foreigners living in Japan began to increase markedly from the late 1980s, owing in part to labour shortages. Based on his reading of disparate studies on Japan's new migrant population, Komai (2001) hints that Japan's newcomers are reaching a critical mass, which can fundamentally change Japanese society. Barriers previously circumscribing the world of the foreigner in Japan are being lowered as contact with 'foreigners' expands in a wide range of areas. Until the 1990s the National Sports Competition had been closed to foreigners. In the 1990s the senior high, junior high, university and open divisions were successively opened to non-Japanese. Baseball used to limit teams to three non-Japanese players, but that ban was lifted in 1996. Foreign wrestlers have dominated the top sumo division since the January 2003 Grand Tournament. Many of the restrictions controlling the appointment of foreigners to senior academic positions at national universities have been relaxed over the past two decades. An oddity on Japanese television in the 1970s, foreigners now commonly appear. The presidents of several large Japanese firms are foreign-born, the best known being Carlos Ghosn (President of Nissan), and in 2002 a naturalised citizen from Finland was elected to the Diet.

These changes are reflected in notions of Japanese identity. Mouer and Sugimoto (1995a; 1995b) and Fukuoka (1996) observed in the mid-1990s that citizenship, blood, language and ethnicity no longer went together in defining Japaneseness. The country's new wealth attracted a growing number of non-Japanese to work in Japan. At first they came mainly as singles and entered as temporary residents. By the 1990s, however, families started to arrive and longer-term settlement began. While this influx was first felt in factories, several rural areas sought to overcome shortages of household labour by 'importing' brides from overseas. Burgess (2003) reported that about one out of every 20 Japanese entering matrimony today marries a non-Japanese, up from one in every 200 only 30 years ago. He also noted that in about 80% of those marriages the foreign partner is female, a reversal of the situation in the early 1970s. Most significantly, perhaps, he found that foreign-born wives in Japan are not simply assimilating into Japanese society in an official sense. Rather, he found them to be actively participating in civil society and shaping the way officially recognised social institutions were evolving around them.

Until the 1970s Japan's foreign exchange restrictions meant that few Japanese could freely enter or access the domain beyond the Japanese state. Since then the number of Japanese travelling abroad has increased exponentially. In 1970 about 1.7 million Japanese exited Japan and about 270,000 nationals lived overseas. Just four years later those figures had jumped to 3.1 million and 380,000. By 2000 they stood at about 18 million and 800,000.

A Japanese diaspora has been slow to form. The growth of overseas Japanese communities has been linked to Japanese direct foreign investment. A survey of 4,800 major Japanese companies in the early 1990s (Tsuchiya 1995:7–13) revealed that many were adopting an integrated approach to production and attached value to the localisation of their operations, underlining the likelihood that Japanese would be communicating and interacting much more closely with their counterparts overseas. Tsuchiya (1995:vi) also pointed to the growing appreciation among Japanese managers overseas that they must 'get their hands dirty' in the everyday affairs of their employees and in the local communities from which those employees come.

The accelerated absorption of English is reflected in the increased use of foreign words in the discourse of many public debates in Japan. Japanese are actively adopting English words (often with a uniquely Japanese nuance) so quickly that it is difficult to trace their origins. Some expressions generated in Japan are now being accepted as local variants of English, along with Singlish

(Singaporean English) and other forms of English. A small number of Japanese firms have introduced English as a second language in running their businesses, and it seems to serve as an important adjunct for many educated Japanese. Vigorous public debate was stirred when an advisory group of the Prime Minister suggested in 2000 that consideration be given to the desirability of having English as Japan's second official national language (see Funabashi 2000). While not receiving wide support, given the climate at a time when English was being criticised for being the conveyor of cultural imperialism (as described in Oishi 1997), the debate underlined the importance of English for Japan's international interface and the extent to which English was impacting on the Japanese language. In July 2002 the Japanese government introduced to schools a new six-point strategy to raise the English skills of Japanese children.

Considering the extent to which other cultural forms are being infused to create a kind of 'MacJapan culture', there is room to speculate about the extent to which bi-cultural literacy is now required to reap the full benefits of living in Japanese society and to shape the directions that society takes in the global era. Although English has been used to infuse the Japanese language with additional vocabulary (rather as Latin and Greek derivatives did for English elites some centuries ago), the usage of English nevertheless tends to set Japan's more privileged citizens apart from its ordinary citizens.

Change, global best practice and restratification in the future of the Japanese economy

While borderlessness may be accompanied by a relative decline in the role of the state in regulating the interface of its citizens with international society, many of the symbols and the discourse for nationalistic consolidation remain. The role of the Japanese government is by no means negligible, and its policies are shaping the way Japanese interact with the world. At the same time, one should take care not to overemphasise the role of the national government in directing society's affairs. Democratically elected governments often choose to respond to populist demands in a democratic fashion by implementing policies that ultimately serve to retard globalisation and the development of civil society. While Japan's post-war conservative governments have structured Japan's foreign policy around a carefully considered line known as 'economic diplomacy', in the 1990s it began to feel pressure to involve Japan with the world across a broader range of areas and to lessen its influence over the way its citizens could interact with the world outside Japan.

The debates on convergence and divergence and on the role of Asian values in shaping the course of economic development in the 1970s focused attention on

Japan as the most advanced economy in Asia. There was speculation about the lessons to be gleaned from Japan's experience, especially as a model providing a different route to development than that which emerged from the Western experience. Following upon Vogel's *Japan as number one* (1979), Johnson's (1982) treatment of Japan as a development state using market-conforming mechanisms and the countless writings of Ronald Dore and others on Japanese-style management (as described in Mouer & Kawanishi 2005:ch1) suggested that Japan offered alternative approaches to social organisation and governance for the advanced economies. On the assumption that cultural difference was an important factor explaining Japanese economic success and a belief that the Japanese approach developed out of ethos loosely labeled 'Asian values', Malaysia, Singapore and other Asian societies sought inspiration from the 'Look East' policies advocated by Lee Kuan Yew in Singapore. Following on from this a number of writers began to comment on various types of capitalism (see Hampden-Turner & Trompenaars 1994). However, Japanese social structures and values are now seen as being less unusual than was thought to be the case in the 1970s and 1980s when *nihonjinron* was at its height as an ideology of cultural difference and national superiority.[9]

Change in Japan over the past decade has been far reaching and complex, not only in the economy but in society at large. Some change has clearly been shaped by inflows of people and ideas from abroad. At the same time change has not been inevitable—at least in the short term. While the government and business circles grope for a way forward in terms of restructuring, individual Japanese have also taken the initiative to make themselves more competitive in terms of international labour markets. At the same time they have become more aware of opportunity costs and have learned to demand more in return for their labour. This has resulted in a Japanese populace that is more attuned to global best practice. While many of these individually driven initiatives may be considered as responses both to Japan's rising levels of affluence and to global forces, it is difficult to separate in a causative sense universally rationalistic processes that are already occurring from those owing mainly to globalisation. It is likely that the functional imperatives universally associated with further capitalist development will result in changes that incorporate forms derived from Japan's cultural heritage. As Japanese society becomes more multicultural and more multilingual, two-way flows of information and ideas will expand and further contribute to Japan's interface with an increasingly globalised world. Japan's impact on that world will likely increase. This can already be seen in the export of Japanese popular culture, although *manga*, *karaoke* and *anime* become less Japanese as they become part of other cultures. These processes are likely to result in Japan becoming less Japanese as it borrows and lends in an increasingly globalised environment. On the other side of that coin, what it means to be Japanese is becoming more blurred. Thus, increasingly when we talk about 'the Japanese model', we are talking about structures that may have derived from Japan (although many unique features were actually imported into Japan, such as quality control circles from the United States) but are now found in Japan and overseas. For this reason, we might, as Ouchi (1981) did, simply refer to Japanese-style management as 'Theory Z management'.

Growing inequality within Japan will continue to temper Japan's globalisation. To negotiate that interface and to maximise the benefits they receive from doing so, Japan's bilingual elite will become increasingly conversant in English, participating fully in the emerging global society being formed by a rising international elite. A major question remains, however, concerning the capacity of other Japanese to become bilingual and to use that bilingualism to invigorate the NPOs and other grassroots bodies that may create a new awareness among the monolingual population of ways in which their interests diverge from those of the bilingual elite. Whether on a global scale (among nation states) or on a domestic scale within Japan, it is unlikely that the issues raised by economic inequalities will recede in the near future. Many of the issues raised in this chapter, including the steps taken to deregulate labour markets, pinpoint a small number of mechanisms affecting the inequalities Japanese will be experiencing in the years ahead. One need not be a Marxist to speculate about how those inequalities will give rise to uncertainties that will invite responses that cannot now be predicted. However, the above discussion suggests that Japanese society and economy are intricately intertwined in the global system and it is unlikely that those responses will occur in isolation.

Notes

1. The Liberal Democratic Party was in government from 1955 for nearly 50 years, with a small break in the mid-1990s during which a coalition of opposition parties was in government.
2. Rather than referring to a death count in a narrow sense, this term came to symbolise the heavy workloads and the ill health (often as stress-related symptoms) that resulted from the intensified workloads in the 1970s, 1980s and early 1990s.
3. Quality control circles were introduced to Japan through training courses organised by the United States-led occupation in post-war Japan. The techniques of quality control were implemented in nearly all Japanese companies in the manufacturing sector during the 1950s and 1960s through a nationally established body. Initially conceived as a way in which workers could voluntarily contribute to the enhancement of their own productivity, the extent to which such groups were led by management and the extent to which they were 'voluntarily' developed from below has varied from firm to firm and over time.
4. *Sarariman* refers broadly to those with the status of full-time employment and a guaranteed monthly income (salary). These were mainly men and mainly in administrative positions, although many production workers with salaries and employment guarantees considered themselves to be in the *sarariman* category. The *sarariman* are distinguished from those employed on an hourly wage, whose monthly income may fluctuate depending upon the time actually worked. The ideal *sarariman* had a long-term employment guarantee, though he or she might have moved one or more times from one employer to another. As part of the salary system, they received bonuses twice a year, which totalled perhaps three to seven months of their annual salaries. Many wore a suit and, most likely, a tie.
5. *Arubaito*: casually employed workers who usually are not on a contract; refers mainly to students who have such work, often on a seasonal basis (as in delivering gifts for department stores during the rushed gift-giving seasons). *Shokutaku*: refers to a special employment status, often for long-term employees who have retired but are retained for some years in rolled-over, one-year contracted positions of less authority (such as security personnel, night watchmen, low-level assistants). *Rinjiko*: a temporary worker hired as an individual (not through a labour hire company).
6. Those who accept *arubaito* as a lifestyle and trade the insecurity that goes with such employment for the freedom to reject requests for overtime and the absence of consideration for the needs of employers (for instance, giving advance notice of quitting). Characterised by low levels of stress at work for young people, but also by an increasing sense of economic insecurity (considerations for later in life if having a family and for other cash flow needs, such as a pension).
7. The term refers to young Japanese in their 30s who have decided to remain single beyond the normal age of marriage and who continue to live with their parents. The term has negative connotations, suggesting that such singles sponge off their parents, receiving free room and board while saving and spending their own incomes as they please. The term refers both to *furiitaa* types and to those in solid employment with good incomes. The term perhaps reflects a sensitivity in Japan in the late 1990s

that many retired employees who worked hard in the 1960s and 1970s to make the Japanese economy what it is today have to struggle on inadequate pensions, and that with the aging of the population the younger generation will need to work hard to provide for the older members of society. Accordingly, the lifestyle of the *furiitaa* and the *parasaito shinguru* is seen by many conservatives as being less than socially responsible.

8   Refers in English to work that is characterised as dangerous, dirty and demanding (or difficult). The 'three K's' is the Japanese equivalent—*kiken* (dangerous), *kitanai* (dirty) and *kitsui* (demanding or difficult).

9   *Nihonjinron* refers to a large literature that takes a culturally essentialist view and espouses the uniqueness of Japanese society, Japanese culture and the way Japanese people think. In terms of work organisation, those in the *nihonjinron* mode would argue/assume that lifetime employment, seniority wages and enterprise unions were uniquely Japanese institutions, which came from Japan's unique cultural values. In some ways this line of thinking represents, and is a precursor to, the Asian Values approach to understanding Asia.

chapter three

South Korea: the reign of the unreinable chaebol?

Lesley McKaig

The issue of state versus markets has long preoccupied social scientists, especially in the debate over the rapid rise of Asian economies after the Second World War. In the second half of 1997 the debate was reignited by the Asian economic crisis. South Korea has often featured in this discussion.

This chapter uses the case of South Korea's rapid economic development since the 1960s to not only illuminate the respective roles played by the state and the market, but also to assess their contributions towards the structural problems that became apparent after 1997.

Although the 1997 Asian financial crisis in South Korea was part of a broader cyclical economic crisis associated with a downturn in the market, it revealed some of the essential contradictions (which go to the core of South Korea's model of economic development) that were inherent in its growth process since the early 1960s. To that extent, both models—state-led and market-led—contributed to the rise of South Korea's economy from the 1960s and, more importantly, both could be found wanting, as is clear from the need for economic restructuring in the period following the Asian financial crisis.

Under the market-led model, economic growth occurred in South Korea because the South Korean business sector, dominated by the *chaebol* (large-scale corporations), successfully responded to the market signals, in the form of prices, factor costs and market opportunities (such as growth in world trade and its liberalisation over time). Outward-looking strategies that favoured export-led growth and a neutral, or non-discriminatory, government policy towards the *chaebol* were part of the market-led explanation of South Korea's economic development. Any problems in this process of development were usually attributed to a failure of government policy, notably in its zealous economic intervention (see World Bank 1987; Hughes 1993b; Song 1990).

The state-led camp asserted that economic development was caused by enlightened state policy and was not subjected to frequent government failure, as the neoclassical economists always emphasised. Economic prosperity was achieved by a developmental state that was both strong and capable and had a vision for national economic growth. This capability was achieved by utilising institutions such as the bureaucracy, military police and the central intelligence agency. Meanwhile the state's strength was derived from its autonomy from pressure interest groups, which might have undermined national prosperity. This theory maintained that South Korea's economic development was driven by the state artfully manipulating market prices to achieve its national plan of growth (see Deyo 1987; Amsden 1989; Haggard 1990; Wade 1990; Johnson 1982).

It is clear that these contending theories were each seeking vindication in claiming the same prize—South Korea's spectacular economic development (see Table 1 for rates of economic growth). Admittedly such high growth rates sprang from a very low base—by 1953, the end of the Korean War, the nation had been devastated economically and socially. Growth was fuelled by export-led industrialisation and facilitated by the swift yet relentless upgrading of the industrial structure. From the early 1960s to the early 1970s, South Korea utilised its comparative advantage of abundant, low-cost labour for labour-intensive, simple manufacturing in sectors such as textiles, clothing and footwear. Annual percentage changes in exports for each of the first three five-year planning periods between 1962 and 1976 were 43.7%, 35.2% and 47.1% respectively.

Table 1: Performance of the first six five-year plans, 1962–66 to 1987–91

	1962–66	1967–71	1972–76	1977–81	1982–86	1987–91
Economic growth rate (%)	7.8	9.5	9.1	5.7	9.8	10.0
Investment (as % of GNP)*	17.0	26.1	27.1	30.7	30.0	34.5^0
Domestic saving (as % of GNP)	8.8	16.1	20.8	23.5	27.2	36.3^0
Foreign saving (as % of GNP)	8.2	10.2	6.7	5.9	2.6	-2.3^0
Current account (millions of US$)	-103.4^1	-847.5^2	-313.6^3	$-4,464.0^4$	$+4,600.0^5$	$-8,700^6$
Exports[a] (average annual % change)	43.7	35.2	47.1	21.6	10.8	16.3
Imports[a] (average annual % change)	19.1	26.2	31.0	24.1	4.3	21.0

* GNP—gross national product
[0] As a % of gross national disposable income
[a] Figures are based on balance of payments statistics
[1] In 1966 [2] In 1971 [3] In 1976 [4] In 1981 [5] In 1986 [6] In 1991
Source: Bank of Korea, National Accounts, 1990, as reprinted in Cho Soon (1994:29,35,40,46,49,51).

Structural change occurred during the 1970s, with the development of higher value-added industrial production, as heavy industries such as chemicals, iron and steel, and shipbuilding were established and promoted for both export and import replacement purposes. An upward trend in South Korea's wage levels (which had begun in the 1970s largely due, initially, to labour shortages), together with greater international competition from foreign firms with access to cheaper production costs elsewhere (notably cheaper labour in Southeast Asia), meant that South Korean industries from this time had to rely on a more skilled and technologically intensive basis if the nation was to sustain its growth rate. By the 1990s South Korea had achieved developed status. This was formally recognised in 1996 when it joined the ranks of developed nations as a member of the OECD.

But the 1997 Asian financial crisis caught South Korea by surprise; it brought the economy to its knees and the nation's people feared their treasured prosperity was in jeopardy and were shamed by the International Monetary Fund (IMF) record bailout of US$57 billion. The rate of growth of real GDP fell from 5% in 1997 to –6.6% the following year (EIU 2002a:7). Events in 1997 exposed fundamental flaws, which had long existed. Structural problems inherent in South Korea's particular method of industrialisation could no longer be camouflaged. What followed has been an overhaul of many entrenched practices and policies as South Korea has struggled with economic reform. The government is deregulating, foreign investors are slowly being accepted and even accommodated, the financial sector is developing, and the *chaebol* are being challenged to reform corporate structures and behaviour. While some elements of reform are more successful than others, there has nevertheless been a marked shift from the previous pattern of economic growth to one that accords the market mechanism more control.

Balance of power between the state and corporate sector

From early on the South Korean state asserted the primacy of economic growth over social and political development. President Syngman Rhee, supported by the United States, emerged from exile in the United States in 1948 to rule the newly formed Republic of Korea until 1960. Rhee, while not successful in developing the economy, nevertheless proved to be savage and swift in repressing any social opposition. This quashing of protest, undertaken in accord with the desire of the United States to remove leftist forces, was at times more violent than was supported by the United States (Hamilton 1983:46). Thus was established the basis of an often antagonistic state–society relationship, one which, at least until the mid-1980s, was dominated by the government. This era laid down an early pattern in which the major components of society, such as domestic consumers, labour, the agricultural sector, and small and medium-sized enterprises, gave way to the greater forces of economic growth, and this trend was to deepen in subsequent years. Paradoxically, however, it also established the roots of future social protest and political opposition—the very roots of democracy.

It was not until Park Chung Hee became President in 1961, however, that the strong and autonomous state acquired a developmental capacity. Park instigated an 'amazing transformation' of the economy (Kwon, Cordell & Kim 1985:262) from a primary sector-based economy to an industrial economy, from an inward-looking to an outward-looking economy, and from a tentative and corrupt business–state alliance to a stronger alliance. The *chaebol* came to dominate the economy and national economic progress was made. This strong state–business relationship worked to good effect and produced mutual benefit for each party: South Korea industrialised and the *chaebol* expanded their empires.

Many analyses of South Korea's economic history since the Korean War have focused on the balance of power between the state and the market and on the respective roles played by South Korea's various state regimes and the capitalists of the *chaebol*. In fact, our vocabulary has even been expanded to accommodate the various interpretations of this close relationship. Moon (1994) wrote of state-centric and business-centric fluctuations. Evans's (1989) 'embeddedness' reflected the interwoven state–business nexus that pervades all levels. Johnson (1982), in writing about Japan, used the concept of the 'capitalist development state', which can also be applied to South Korea. Wade (1990) created 'governed markets'. Samuels (1987), in asserting the business sector's independence from the state, described the relationship as one of 'reciprocal consent'. Weiss (1994:92, 86), tired of the simplistic state–market dichotomy, wrote of a capable but co-operative state, and described it as 'governed independence'.

The bond between the state and business sectors in South Korea fluctuated over time, which lent credibility to each of the contending positions, market-led or state-centred, at different stages in South Korea's growth. Initially the state, under Park, had a dominant, even disciplinarian, role (Amsden 1989:14; Moon 1994:146). As long as the mutual dependence of the state–business relationship was maintained, economic development was generated. But such a relationship could not survive indefinitely. The co-ordination of the corporate sector's goal, to expand market share, with the state's aim to expand the nation's share of the world surplus (Weiss 1994:95) was a special feature of this growth and was responsible for the rapid rate of economic growth for many years. But such a coalition was both tenuous and tense. Many accounts have explored the nature of the relationship. Its success has frequently been attributed to the role of South Korea's bureaucracy in preventing the government–business co-operation from collapsing into pressure group pluralism (Weiss 1994:97), in separating the functions of the politicians and bureaucracy so that special interest groups did not deter the path of economic development (Johnson 1982), and its underpinning of the long-run infrastructural power of the state, leading to co-operation with business.

The basis of this process was undermined only when the state–business relationship began to weaken—that is, once the *chaebol* gained financial independence from the state by accessing outside funds in the 1980s. But the emerging *chaebol* independence did not mean increased efficiency or improved business methods. Instead the *chaebol* used their economic size and power to further enlarge their empires, to cling more firmly to the family ownership structure, to maintain the complex cross-shareholding pattern that allowed ailing companies within the *chaebol* group to be cross-subsidised, to increase debt-to-equity ratios by continuing to eschew equity-based finance, and to diversify into even more industries and so exasperate government attempts (which had begun in 1974) to force some economic specialisation of their activities. It seemed that the weakening of the capitalist developmental state, in conjunction with a more assertive private business sector, still failed to generate the economic benefits meant to accompany economic deregulation. Moves in this direction, however halting, were reducing the degree of economic competition within South Korea, not enhancing it. The small and medium-sized enterprise sector still failed to thrive, choked off from the state opportunities readily granted to the big firms. Was this a case of the market (the *chaebol*) failing?

A further outcome of this state–business alliance was the underdeveloped nature of South Korea's financial sector. And here the state failed. This arose because the allocation of capital funds to local producers was invariably on the basis of political whim. At times this generated national economic growth, such as with the favouring of export production in the 1960s. In the 1970s this subsidised method of capital allocation also facilitated Park's policy for capital-intensive industrialisation, the HCI program. Assessment of this economic program has been controversial; however, some people (statists in particular) claimed that the state was successful in transforming the structural base of South Korea's economy away from labour-intensive production (Amsden 1989:144, 152). Today's internationally successful motor vehicle and shipping industries are testament to that. Others claimed that by artificially changing the prices of the factors of production (capital in particular), a cyclical downturn was exacerbated and was made worse by a poor international economy that was still reeling from the second Organization of the Petroleum Exporting Countries (OPEC) oil crisis in the late 1970s (Cho 1994:180; Kuznets 1994:128; Chang 1993:135). Often, the *chaebol* used state loans to fund non-productive investments and thereby created non-performing loans. Driven by the need to be big rather than economically efficient, they used their economic size and power to command loans to further diversify their production rather that boost profits or efficiency.

State control mellowed over time to state influence, but by the 1980s the state regimes were still reluctant to release their final grip on the financial sector (which had been the source of their control over the economy) and hence their source of state power over the private sector. The consequences were significant. South Korea's insufficiently developed financial sector was not capable of withstanding international capital liberalisation once this was required of the nation. Problems such as these underpinned South Korea's 'economic miracle' yet, once exposed, in December 1997, they had to be addressed quickly for they now threatened the future economy.

Unbalanced growth

These were just some of the structural problems caused by the unbalanced nature of South Korea's economic development. While the success of the developmental state in South Korea had been contingent on the public–private alliance, its survival depended on the continuation of unbalanced (high-speed) growth, and it also perpetuated that unbalanced growth. In the long run this model, and the resultant 'economic miracle', had produced a mixture of good and bad. Unbalanced growth generated spectacular statistics but it also produced fundamental, latent problems—not only social and political problems, but economic problems, which were exposed in the second half of 1997. What, then, was the nature of South Korea's unbalanced economic development? What was out of balance?

South Korea's economic growth hinged on export-led industrialisation at the expense of the development of the domestic market. Export producers were matched against international competitors and realised economies of scale in a world where trade was growing exponentially. During the 1960s and 1970s it was the state that often chose the investment activities of the *chaebol*, and the *chaebol* in turn continued to grow larger to accommodate new export markets. The *chaebol* diversified production activities to reflect their grandiose ambitions. The pursuit of size rather than profit, coupled with subsidised capital for investment, in the quid pro quo arrangement with the state rendered the South Korean *chaebol* almighty powers. These huge conglomerates had no obligation to reveal their business activities or to placate shareholders with short-run profits. They had a penchant to beat rival *chaebol* at whatever cost, and since selling equity out of the family was shunned, they borrowed capital excessively—typically four to five times the asset value (Haggard 2000:151; Chowdhury & Islam 1995:141). Their alliance with the state over the decades, especially in terms of access to capital, enabled the *chaebol* to evade the rigours of the market. In fact until the 1980s the state functioned as the risk-taker on much investment activity. The *chaebol* were seen to be invincible, champions of the nation's economic growth, ubiquitous within society.

As a result, the structure of South Korea's industry was highly concentrated, so that small and medium-sized enterprises were left undeveloped. While the *chaebol* used smaller companies for supplier goods, they either owned them directly or held great power over them. Thus the potential for innovation, flexibility and specialisation coming from smaller-scale businesses was thwarted. Too much emphasis had always been placed on the success of the conglomerates. With their size they were able to generate rapid growth on the scale required by the state and in accordance with South Korea's particular level of economic development. Yet their growth masked economic inefficiency, misallocation of resources and high levels of debt; indeed, they were considered 'too big to fail' (Amsden 1989). This, together with the government's role in causing such industrial concentration in the first place, illustrates a failing of both the state and the market.

The absence of a balanced industrial structure also had implications for technological development, since South Korea did not have access to the potential creativity and dynamism often found in smaller-scale corporations. The most appropriate comparison is with Taiwan, which, while lamenting its lack of large-scale private firms, has been able to utilise its small-scale enterprises to generate new technology, if not from within, then by using 'guerilla tactics' to obtain advanced foreign technology (McKay & Missen 1994:22). In contrast, South Korea had to upgrade its production processes by using foreign technology, which typically came through government channels (for example, in the form of industrial licensing). According to Amsden (1989:4), South Korean firms were adept at learning, less so at inventing and innovating. This has been a problem for a nation poised, for more than a decade, on the edge of higher technological production and more sophisticated production levels. Since the 1980s private investment has been poured into research and development to execute this transformation as the access to advanced levels of technology from Japan and the United States dries up (Cho 1994:175–6). The *chaebol* have been faced with either generating their own successes in research and development or embarking on joint ventures in order to access foreign technology. The formation of joint ventures for this purpose has increased since December 1997.

Unbalanced growth also affected South Korea's savings and consumption patterns. While the high savings rate of the South Koreans facilitated the massive industrial investments, it was at the expense of local consumption and proved costly in the long run. Repression of local demand during the high-growth decades of the 1960s and 1970s could not be contained by the 1980s, when the latent desire for materialism was let loose in a massive consumer boom. This expansion of middle-class demand was accompanied by a rise in imported luxury goods, unproductive investment activity and flagrant waste. This change reflected the dawning to the South Koreans, under democratisation, that for the first time in their history they might substantially influence their future social, political or even economic environment.

Another structural problem produced by South Korea's high-growth policy affected its component parts for production. Despite Park's heavy industrialisation drive in 1973 to develop capital goods as inputs, South Korea has always remained dependent on imported intermediate goods, most particularly from Japan. The *chaebol*, as export producers, tended to concentrate on production of final goods, not intermediate goods, and this imbalance, ironically, had implications for South Korea's balance of trade, leaving South Korea vulnerable to Japanese producers and other international sources of capital goods.

So, too, the economic and political development of South Korea was out of balance. South Korea's high-speed 'growth at all costs' policy was necessarily at the expense of, and detrimental to, social and political development. Admittedly the standards of living within South Korea have improved since the 1960s, and a relatively low level of income inequality has typified South Korean economic development (Chowdhury & Islam 1995:217). But it can be argued, nevertheless, that some components of society (labourers, savers and consumers) reaped a less than proportionate benefit (Chang 1992:50). Economic growth was predicated upon the authoritarian government's exploitation of South Korean savers, consumers and workers. In fact, for most of the growth years until 1987 the growth of labour productivity tended to outstrip the rise in real incomes (Cho 1994:84; Amsden 1989:201).

The development of social infrastructure (health, education, social services) was always considered secondary to economic development. It was not until the 1980s that social development policy even featured in the government's political rhetoric, and even then it was hastily set aside when economic matters became more urgent, as happened with President Chun Doo Hwan's policy of stabilisation, liberalisation and social equity in the 1980s.

So, the changing role of the state in South Korea was triggered by economic and political factors. In economic terms, the more successful the capitalist developmental state, the greater the economic development and the greater the inevitability of eroding that state power. In other words, the very success of the capitalist developmental state had created the means of its own demise as it facilitated the emergence of a more powerful private business sector, which in turn eroded the state's influence over the *chaebol* (Chang 1992:41–53; Moon 1994:160–1). Partly the changing state role was in response to external pressures to deregulate. Ironically, the South Korean state, keen to demonstrate an international responsibility and join the ranks of international institutions such as the OECD and the WTO, chose to comply. Economic circumstances within South Korea, such as the increasing ability of the *chaebol* to obtain outside finance from a variety of sources including reinvested profits, also diminished the impact of state intervention.

A significant political catalyst in changing the role of the state was South Korea's democratisation in 1987. This reduced the ability of the state to intervene in the economy and in society, at least to the extent that it had done in the past. The basis of state autonomy, the subjugation of social interest groups, appeared to be disintegrating during the preceding years under the Chun Doo Hwan regime (1979–87). With his highly unpopular policies and general neglect of social development, Chun was no longer considered politically legitimate as his regime increasingly resorted to social repression. Public opinion would no longer support such an unbalanced national development. Thus from the 1980s the conjunction of economic growth, nascent political liberalisation, and the loss of mutual dependency between state and business made the maintenance of the strong autonomous interventionist state difficult.

But why, then, did the process of economic liberalisation take so long and why had it still not been achieved by the end of 1997? Fortuitous economic circumstances in the 1980s disguised economic problems and delayed the immediate pressure on the state to restructure the economy and thereby deregulate. Indeed, one could well marvel that South Korea managed to avoid economic disaster for so long because, despite spectacular economic growth over the decades, structural problems within South Korea's economy were already apparent in the early 1980s, if not earlier. These issues were ignored and they did go away, temporarily at least, as they were subsumed by fortuitous factors, mostly external. The 1985 appreciation of the Japanese yen not only gave the relatively more competitively priced South Korean exports a reprieve, but flooded the international capital markets with cheap yen-based loans. South Korea's luck lay also in the resurgence in the international economy, with its 'three lows' (lower interest rates, low United States dollar and low oil prices), and more importantly with the successful staging of the 1988 Olympic Games in Seoul, which celebrated the culmination of three years of unprecedented rapid growth in South Korea. According to Chung (1990:47), during the years 1986–88 the economy grew at 12% per annum. These factors all boosted South Korea's macro-economic indicators and hid the more fundamental economic problems.

It is important to note that the various state regimes since the 1980s (Chun Doo Hwan 1979–87, Roh Tae Woo 1987–92 and Kim Young Sam 1992–97) all expressed varying degrees of commitment to economic liberalisation, and even made some progress with economic reform policy, yet it was halting and inconsistent. Part of the problem lay with the private sector's response. The private corporate sector failed to meet the challenge of the state's first tentative steps towards deregulation under Chun Doo Hwan. Business methods continued to lack economic discipline as the private sector responded to incentives other than those offered by the market. The *chaebol* still driven by rivalry, chose to be grandiose not efficient, and emphasised diversified production at the expense of specialisation. Encouraged by cheap international loans (especially in a world 'awash with yen' after 1985), the *chaebol* increased the pace of their debt-financed expansion. Even though the government failed to restrain the escalating external debt, it had reduced its dominance over the micro-economic sector. Yet a more efficient and productive private business sector had failed to emerge. The *chaebol* were not taking the opportunities being made available to them.

The labour movement, long resentful of its exclusion from the elite state–business alliance, released a torrent of demands to redress the inequity after 1987. These were detrimental to the economy. Indeed, by the time Kim Young Sam entered office, he was facing a society deemed by some to be 'sick'. This South Korean 'sickness' meant a decline in industriousness and ingenuity, the erosion of values and a rise in narrow self-interest, the loss of confidence and a sense of defeatism (Oh 1993). South Korea's economy and its society were less than stable for some time and this volatility rendered the nation highly vulnerable to the external triggers of late 1997.

Another change was occurring in the 1980s. The internationalisation of capital and currency markets, which increased the freedom and speed of capital movement, rendered South Korea's underdeveloped financial sector vulnerable. Mobile capital not only responds instantly to market changes but also anticipates and perhaps even initiates them. December 1997 forced a public exposure of South Korea's massive scale of debt, especially foreign debt incurred by the *chaebol*. This was often deployed into non-productive investments such as speculative land development and was no longer funded by the high export earnings of the past. An alarming amount of non-performing loans was the result.

Nevertheless, South Korea's recovery from the Asian financial crisis was outstanding. Economic growth had recovered by 1999 (see Table 2), the Korean won had stabilised and the foreign reserves had recovered from their precariously low levels. The full extent of the IMF bailout was not subsequently required and South Korea had repaid the debt by mid-2001 (Colebatch 2001:6). Economic reform, however, has not kept pace with recovery. The *chaebol* have continually thwarted corporate reform by proving to be innovative in circumventing the intentions of these policies (EIU 2002b:9).

Table 2: Major economic indicators, 1996–2006

	1996	1997	1998	1999	2000	2001	2002	2003	2004	2005[1]	2006[2]
Real GDP growth rate %[3]		5.0	−6.7	10.9	9.3	3.0	6.3	2.7[4]	4.6	4.0	5.5
Current account (US$ billions)	−23.0	−8.2	40.4	24.5	12.2	8.2	6.0	12.0	28.2	16.6	16.4
FDI* (US$ billions)	3.2	7.0	8.9	15.5	15.2	11.3	9.1	4.7			

[1] Recent data subject to revision
[2] IMF/Economist Intelligence Unit forecast
[3] At 1995 prices, unless stated otherwise. Source: Economist Intelligence Unit country data.
* FDI— foreign direct investment
Sources (unless stated otherwise): Bank of Korea (GDP and current account), Korean Ministry of Commerce, Industry and Energy (FDI), reprinted in 'South Korean Economy. Economic Data', Korean Economic Institute, Washington DC, November 2003. Sources for years 2003, 2004, 2005 and 2006 (GDP and current account): compiled by Department of Foreign Affairs and Trade, Market Information and Analysis Section, using latest data from Australian Bureau of Statistics, IMF and other international sources.

In May 1999 the government, under local and international pressure to get tougher with the *chaebol*, introduced two major policies: the Big Deal and reduction of corporate debt. The aim of the Big Deal was, once again, to enforce rationalisation of *chaebol* activities, to get rid of non-performing *chaebol* affiliates and to cut overcapacity in key sectors. Despite the *chaebol* agreeing to co-operate and pledging to cut their affiliates by half, they actually did little to achieve this. In fact the *chaebol* were striving to emerge from the Asian financial crisis with even larger empires than before 1997.

The second major policy at that time, cutting debt, was similarly circumvented. The aim was to force the top five *chaebol* to reduce their debt-to-equity ratios by December 1999 to 200%, but lack of *chaebol* co-operation forced repeated extensions of this deadline (Millett 1999). Instead of borrowing, the *chaebol* were supposed to access funds through the markets, for example, by pursuing foreign equity and selling their *chaebol* assets. By implication, to gain international market confidence they would need to remove their non-performing companies first, but, once again, the policy floundered when the *chaebol* chose to inflate their asset values. This may have meant the debt-to-equity ratio was lowered but not because debt had been reduced (Millett 1999). It was contrary to the intention of the reform. Between December 1998 and the end of June 1999 the Hyundai Group increased its debt by 6%, yet its debt-to-equity ratio fell from 450% to 340%. The *chaebol* sought other avenues for funds, such as job retrenchment and labour reform, which yielded windfall financial bonuses and reduced labour costs overall. They were supposed to aim for increased efficiency and profits, but instead expanded their empires, increased their debt obligations and fuelled the ire of the militant labour unions (Veale 1998:7).

Nevertheless, since 1997 corporate economic reform has made some progress. Foreign equity participation in these conglomerates has been increasing, and failed companies have been broken up and sold. France's Renault car producer owns 70% of Samsung Motors. General Motors acquired control of Daewoo Motors globally in 2001 when the bankrupt Daewoo was sold. By 1999 seven of the 30 largest *chaebol* had collapsed (Millett 1999). There has also been a reduction in the number of *chaebol* subsidiary companies. By 2001 more than 400 *chaebol* subsidiaries had been sold, many to foreign buyers (Colebatch 2001).

Anti-corruption campaigns continue to be waged by successive governments, especially regarding the perennial charges of illicit political funding by the *chaebol* in return for political kickbacks. These campaigns have had mixed success. In 2003 the accounting scandal in the giant trading company SK Global triggered a dramatic loss of confidence in South Korea's corporate governance (Pearson 2003:60). In April 2006 the Chairman of Hyundai Motors was charged with embezzlement and breach of trust regarding alleged slush funds to bribe politicians (Song 2006:24).

Lodging consolidated financial statements has been compulsory since 1999, and the rights of minority shareholders are gradually being acknowledged. Upgrading accounting practices to international standards and the appointment of independent auditors and external directors are just some of the changes that should increase the pressure on these companies to improve corporate governance and the degree of transparency of their activities overall. In the end the operations of the *chaebol* should approach a more balanced mix of foreign and local shareholders, debt with equity capital, and access to capital funds from a more developed local financial sector and from one more open to foreign investment (Table 2). Nevertheless, the government still hovers nearby, albeit more discreetly.

The state and private sector relationship shows how both contributed to the economic development process, as well as to the inherent structural problems that emerged after 1997. It seems that unbalanced growth contributed to South Korea's economic success as prominently as to the structural problems it generated. Balanced economic growth would not have generated such a fast-paced structural transformation of the economy over the decades. Moreover, economic development occurred before political and social development was attained and this facilitated its easy, but unbalanced, path. The government artfully utilised the rest of the world and the market to channel its vision for the economic development of the nation. This entailed unbalanced growth, but the consequences are evident today.

The Asian financial crisis stripped bare South Korea's economic problems, which were a direct consequence of South Korea's past model of economic development that had begun in the 1960s. While it was essentially a model heavily orchestrated by the state, the private business sector (together with the international economy) still played a predominantly constructive part. The growth years were fashioned by both state and market players; their contributions ebbed and flowed over the decades. At times the government failed just as succinctly as the *chaebol*.

The two sides continue to pose problems. The post-1997 reform process surges and stalls for reasons as much attributable to the state as to the market. The conditions of the international economy are also an important constraint, for economic reform will inevitably slow during a cyclical slump. The state and the market must undertake economic reform together; neither can achieve this on its own. Yet mutual dependence still exists. To that extent, as with the whole process of South Korea's economic development, neither camp alone (state nor market) can claim the ascendency. However, while the balance needs to be changed towards the market, the state still has a vital role to play in its economy—perhaps less interventionist than during the high-growth decades but somewhat more involved than the market model might advocate.

Case study of Hyundai

Some *chaebol* began in the late 19th and early 20th centuries and a few even survived Japanese colonialism, but most date from the 1950s and 1960s. The *chaebol* have always preferred to be family owned and operated and, in fact, until recently the original founders still held tight control of all firms within their global empires; they were keenly involved in all aspects of their corporations. This changed in 2001, however, with the death of Hyundai's Chung Ju Yung, who at 86 years of age had been the longest surviving founder of a *chaebol*. As typical of *chaebol*, the reins were then handed to his sons and nephews.

Throughout the decades various governments have tried unsuccessfully to dilute the complex family ownership structures, but since 1997 the *chaebol* have found such pressure increasingly harder to resist. This time it is not only the state's economic reform policy but, more importantly, the international markets that are pushing for change. It was certainly not unusual for the *chaebol* to be responsive to export markets but this time it is their own foreign investors to which they must become accountable.

The founding entrepreneurs of *chaebol* created huge global conglomerates on the basis of their tenacity, ambition, ingenuity and opportunism. Hyundai's origins go back to the 1930s, when the teenage Chung Ju Yung went to Seoul from his farm in the north. According to Clifford (1994:115), he soon found a job helping out at a rice mill in Seoul, where his first few nights were supposedly spent secretly learning to ride the shop's delivery bicycle. Then in 1940 Chung became involved in an auto repair shop in Seoul.

Like his *chaebol* counterparts, he was adept at exploiting the slimmest of opportunities. Some 28 years later, in 1968, when Hyundai was building the Seoul–Pusan freeway, President Park asked Chung if he knew anything about cars. On the strength of Chung's meagre experience with the auto repair shop, the President coerced him into producing passenger cars: 'You're building the road. Now we need the cars' (Clifford 1994).

South Korea's motor vehicle industry was thus launched and production began the following year in 1969 when Hyundai Motors started assembling knocked-down kits of the Ford Cortina model. By the early 1970s it was building its own South Korean automobile with a simple four-cylinder engine, technical assistance from Japan's Mitsubishi, and Italian and British design and production experts. Thus began what was to become the global car producer Hyundai Motors, which was reliant on foreign technology and expertise. Hyundai's Excel model is still based on technology from Japan's Mitsubishi (Eckert 1993:120).

Chung Ju Yung had, in the early 1960s, gained the attention of President Park Chung Hee by bidding—for the token amount of one Korean won—to rebuild the original Han River bridge, which was still in ruins after the war (Clifford 1994:115). So in 1973, when Park launched his heavy industrialisation drive, he chose Hyundai to build what would soon become the world's largest shipyard. Given Hyundai's inexperience in shipbuilding, Chung had great difficulty in obtaining foreign finance. It has been claimed that the President admonished Chung for not trying hard enough to raise funds and Hyundai was threatened with not receiving any more government favours if it could not deliver what the country needed (Clifford 1994:116). The government did, however, provide extensive financial guarantees to help Hyundai win its first ship order (Amsden 1989:276). In this case, as in others, the state would reward and support its entrepreneurs once they had met its challenges. Those not rising to the occasion usually suffered some form of state retribution (see Amsden 1989:15 for examples of this). The story of how the ships were pieced together while the shipyards themselves were still being constructed is testimony to Hyundai's boldness and clever adaptation of existing technology (Amsden 1989:276–7; Clifford 1994:116–17). But it is also indicative of the tight relationship that existed between the state and the *chaebol*.

Hyundai built its empire by being successful in exports and an avid overseas investor. The South Korean *chaebol* typically invested at an earlier stage in the product life cycle than would other nations. Thus, according to Porter (1990:471), Hyundai opened its first foreign assembly plant in Canada in 1989, less than ten years after its first significant foreign sales. At times, however, such haste meant poor data preparation on the economic prospects and conditions of the investment destination (Cho 1994:71).

With foreign investment Hyundai, not only chased lower input costs but easier access to markets by operating inside trade barriers. But Hyundai, like all *chaebol*, could also target the more difficult markets indirectly. For example, access to the United States came not only through Canada but also Mexico, and into the European Union via Poland. Offshore production by South Koreans existed throughout Asia and Latin America and was quickly drawn into eastern Europe after the collapse of communism. In 2003 Hyundai Motors India exported half of its total exports (from India) to countries such as Mexico, Columbia and some African nations. These nations paid in United States dollars, which meant Hyundai could mitigate problems caused by the fluctuating Indian rupee (FIT 2004). In 2003 China became the single largest destination for South Korea's foreign direct investment and Hyundai was a major contributor to the rising importance of China to South Korea (Pearson 2004:87). In fact, the 2003 winning soccer team in Beijing was the local 'Beijing Hyundai' club.

Chaebol excelled in the assimilation and improvement of imported technology, especially in machinery, electronics, shipbuilding and cars. They were adept at adaptation rather than creation of high technological products and production. Amsden praised them for 'learning by doing' (Amsden 1989:152–3). Indeed, the *chaebol* learned well from their Japanese rivals and have become reluctant to transfer technology to other Asian nations for fear of nurturing potential rivals. Hyundai Heavy Industries is today defending its position in the overcrowded global shipbuilding industry with new highly technological ships. These compressed natural gas vessels, which compress and carry natural gas at the normal temperature, can substantially reduce the costs of marine transport and storage. But this new invention has only been made possible because of Hyundai's American technological partner, EnerSea Transport LLC (Kim 2004).

The 1997 economic crisis meant profound changes to these eminent family dynasties—Hyundai has been forced to break up into component parts. Success internationally is mixed, especially with the excess capacity in the car industry globally. As a result of the Asian financial crisis, Hyundai Motors has been quick to expand by absorbing the ailing Kia Motors Corporation to become South Korea's largest car maker, but the tight family control lingers—the President of Kia Motors is the son of Hyundai Motors' Chairman, Chung Mong-koo (Song 2006:24). In 2000 Hyundai began a somewhat torrid alliance with Daimler Chrysler, which finally ended in May 2004 when the German company sold its 10.5% equity in Hyundai Motors (*Asia Pulse* 2004a). This was not before Hyundai, in September 2003, had urged Daimler Chrysler to drop a joint venture deal it had with Beijing Automotive Industries to produce cars in China. Hyundai's reason was that it had itself signed a contract with the same Chinese company a year earlier for a 50/50 auto assembly joint venture (Asia Pulse 2004a). This particular Chinese–Hyundai partnership had created the Beijing Hyundai Automobile Company Limited, which, in May 2004, produced its 100,000th car. In 2004 the plans were to produce 70,000 Sonata sedans and 60,000 Elantra sedans and to target 12% of the market share in the fiercely competitive mid-sized sedan market in China (AFX News 2004).

According to the *New York Times* (Maynard 2001), Hyundai Motor America, the United States operators of Hyundai, had suffered poor sales in the United States through the late 1980s and most of the 1990s. In 1998 a new chief executive, Finbarr O'Neill, was appointed and within a few years sales were soaring. Designs were improved, prices became competitive and new innovative customer services were introduced. So successful were these developments that Hyundai's customers at home claimed discrimination in favour of its American customers (*Asia Pulse* 2004b). Hyundai's response to improving its market share in America had been typical of the *chaebol* in moving up the value chain (*BizAsia* 2003), seeking ways to position itself more competitively and favouring its export market to the domestic one.

Hyundai's post-1997 corporate reform has had mixed success. To survive the Asian crisis, Hyundai, as with other *chaebol*, had to depend on international mergers—so, for example, Hyundai Semiconductor became Hynix Semiconductor Inc when desperation forced it to negotiate with foreign companies in order to raise funds to roll over debts. But negotiations with potential buyers can also stall when the South Koreans ask too high a price for assets. For example, Hynix and Citigroup's PE arm disagreed in April 2004 over the price of Hynix's non-memory division (du Mars 2004). Hynix could also survive by shedding its smaller units in order to restructure its debt. For example, China's BOE Technology Group Co Ltd bought Hynix's flat panel display unit in 2003 (du Mars 2004).

In the past the *chaebol* were always reluctant to dilute their family equity by integrating with foreign shareholders. Increased acceptance of foreign equity will not only reduce the penchant of the *chaebol* for debt funding, but also force them to be judged by international capitalists, to be answerable to all their shareholders.

chapter four

China: privatisation and enterprise restructuring in a socialist market economy

Russell Smyth

China is currently the second largest economy in the world on a purchasing power parity basis and the world's fastest-growing economy. Along with the United States, China is the world's major recipient of foreign direct investment, with almost US$500 billion flooding into the country since the beginning of the 1980s (Sun & Tong 2003). Since China's accession to the WTO, its influence as a major player in world business has continued to increase, such that it is now often referred to as the factory floor of the world.

China's success story as an emerging economic superpower is, in many respects, one of paradoxes. One paradox, at least for orthodox property rights theory, lies in the Chinese approach to economic reform. In spite of the existence of poorly defined property rights in state-owned enterprises (SOEs), a hallmark of China's economic approach is that it avoided large-scale privatisation in the initial stages of marketisation, preferring instead a piecemeal gradualist approach to reform (Wen 2003). Moreover, notwithstanding the recent increasing importance of private enterprise, for most of the market reform period, the driving force behind China's high rate of growth has been large SOEs in upstream industries, coupled with non-state collective township and village enterprises (CTVEs) in downstream industries (Nolan 1996). The distinguishing feature of the dominant *sunan (Southern Jiangsu)* model of CTVEs, which had its origins in Jiangsu province, has been its ambiguous ownership arrangements (Weitzman & Xu 1994; Chang & Wang 1994; Smyth 1997).

The paradox lies in the fact that China's reforms have been successful in spite of, or perhaps because of, their failure during most of the reform period to establish secure property rights. This stands in contrast to the experience of the transitional economies in central eastern Europe, which pushed through much more radical reforms (under the auspices of the World Bank and other lending agencies) that were designed to 'create' a market economy (Rapaczynski 1996). The reality is that these economies have gone backward, and have suffered from increased economic and social instability. For example, in Russia in the period 1992–96, following Yegor Gaidar's reforms, GDP decreased by 40% and industrial production by 50%. The level of prices increased up to 26 times, and increases in nominal wages were much slower than increases in the CPI (Kazakevitch & Smyth 2005). There is a growing academic literature that spells out the theoretical reasons for China's gradualist, mixed-ownership success. Tian (2000) shows that optimal ownership arrangements depend on the level of marketisation and that pure, private ownership is not welfare optimal with low levels of marketisation such as those that are typical of the initial stages of economic transition. Lau, Qian and Roland (2000) argue that maintaining state ownership of major enterprises in the initial stages of transition not only helped China to avoid the large falls in output that characterised the transition economies of central and eastern Europe, but also helped maintain public support for the reforms.

A second paradox is that while the Chinese leadership continues to speak the rhetoric of socialism, its commitment to gradual economic reform has seen a significant increase in the operation of market forces over time. When the economic reforms commenced in the late 1970s, there were few free markets in major cities for agricultural goods or small industrial goods. In contrast, there are now extensive product markets and (albeit imperfect) emerging capital, equity, labour, housing and futures markets. Even by the mid-1990s over 90% of retail prices and 80% of agricultural and producer goods prices (as a proportion of output value) were determined in the market (Wen 2003). This has changed the whole environment in which business operates, so that it is fair to say that the Chinese economy in the 21st century is far different than that which existed in the early 1980s, let alone when Mao Zedong was still alive (Wen 2003).

The changing nature of China's business environment is not just restricted to determination of prices. It also extends to ownership. China is in the midst of a major privatisation program, which, if fully implemented, might be the largest industrial ownership transformation ever undertaken—it will affect more than 200,000 SOEs and 100 million urban workers (Wei, Verela & Hassan 2002; Wei et al 2003). In March 2004 the National People's Congress approved an amendment to the Chinese constitution, which gives private property rights the same legal status as public property for the first time since the founding of the People's Republic of China. This change formally acknowledges a major change in Chinese thinking during the past few years—namely that owning private property and starting private enterprise is now not only encouraged, but considered vital for fostering economic growth (Sui 2004).

This chapter provides an overview of the changing nature of Chinese business since the 1990s. The next section reviews the progress with, and outcomes from, restructuring of China's state-owned sector. It also examines the debate about the role of the state in promoting business. Following this, the development and role of the non-state sector is examined, focusing on the changing contributions and significance of CTVEs and private enterprise. A case study of the D'Long investment group follows. Originally founded in Xinjiang Autonomous Region, D'Long developed into the largest private company in the merger and acquisition business in China and then in 2004 it went into liquidation in spectacular fashion. After the case study, the final section concludes the chapter.

Restructuring China's state-owned sector

Background to the current reforms

China's SOE reform has undergone four stages, which are well documented in the literature (see Choe & Yin 2000; Hay et al 1994; Lo 1997). These are the profit-retention reform (1979–83), tax-for-profit reform (1983–86), the contract management system (1987–92) and the corporatisation reforms (from 1992). This section focuses on reforms since the mid-1990s.

In a 1995 survey the State Assets Management Administration reported that the state-owned sector had about 300,000 SOEs (Cao, Qian & Weingast 1999). These can be divided into large, medium and small SOEs according to size.[1] Small and medium-sized SOEs are predominantly under the control of county and city governments, while large SOEs are under the supervision of the national government. In the mid-1990s, while large industrial SOEs were responsible for about two-thirds of profits and taxes and the net value of fixed assets, small and medium-sized industrial SOEs accounted for 95% of the total number of SOEs (Cao, Qian & Weingast 1999).

In the mid-1990s the financial performance of the state-owned sector looked poor. One of the main problems was 'cradle to grave socialism', where SOEs were responsible for a range of social welfare obligations. Between 1980 and 1994 enterprise expenditure on social welfare increased six times and in the mid-1990s it was roughly half of the SOEs' total wage bill (Huang, Woo & Duncan 1999). SOEs also had a number of redundant workers who could not be dismissed. In the mid- to late 1990s the State Commission for Economic Restructuring estimated that the number of surplus workers in SOEs was about half the total workforce (Morris, Sheehan & Hassard 2001:699). Estimates of what it cost SOEs to keep these surplus workers on the books varies between Chinese renminbi (RMB) 96 billion, which was twice as much as the total profits of SOEs in 1997 (about RMB45 billion), and RMB300 billion (Lee 2000:918). As a result of these extra costs of doing business, the profitability of SOEs over the 1980s and early 1990s fell dramatically, and from 1996 the consolidated state sector was a net loss-maker (Bonin & Huang 2001). This aggregate picture, however, masked differences between small and large SOEs, and the financial performance of large SOEs was better than small SOEs. Lo (1999) shows that total factor productivity growth has been higher in large SOEs than small SOEs and most loss-making SOEs have been small SOEs. In 1994, 90% of loss-making SOEs were small and 60% of small SOEs were making losses (Zhou & Shen 1997).

Fifteenth Party Congress

One of the watersheds in the reform of SOEs since the mid-1990s has been the Fifteenth Party Congress in 1997, which endorsed the slogan *zhua da fang xiao* (grab the big firms, let the small ones go). The slogan encapsulates two policies. 'Grab the big firms' suggests that large SOEs in strategic sectors are to remain under state ownership. The objective of 'grab the big firms' is to build large SOEs and SOE business groups that can compete in international markets. Following the Fifteenth Party Congress, the Chinese government announced preferential support for 120 large *qiye jituan* (enterprise groups), sometimes referred to as the 'national team' (Sutherland 2001), and for 512 key large SOEs—of which at least 74 were core members of the national team (XGTGZ 1999:325–33). These 512 key enterprises formed the backbone of the state-owned sector. While the 512 key enterprises amounted to just 1% of all SOEs, they were responsible for 55% of assets, 60% of sales and 80% of taxes in the state-owned industrial sector (Lo & Smyth 2005).

'Let the small ones go', the second part of the slogan, endorsed the disposal of small and medium-sized SOEs through various forms of privatisation. Privatisation had commenced in the early 1990s in pioneering counties such as Yibin in Sichuan, Shunde in Guangdong and Zhucheng in Shandong and had become widespread by the mid-1990s. The most common forms of privatisation have been *chushou* (sales) to private or foreign investors, *gongsizhi* (corporatisation) into a limited liability or stock company, and *gufen hezuozhi* (stock co-operatives), where shares are sold to workers (Cao, Qian & Weingast 1999). Surveys suggest that these methods have been responsible for over half of all privatisations (Lu 1997). Estimates suggest that soon after the Fifteenth Party Congress as many as 90% of small and medium-sized SOEs were privatised (Zweig 2001).

One problem with the reform process was that provincial authorities were grasping the biggest available firms, which were often small firms on a national scale, and were creating artificial enterprise groups by merging enterprises that had nothing in common in order to consolidate their power. This process was widespread (Shieh 1999) and was described by the well-known Chinese economist Wu Jinglian as an attempt by the authorities to 'forcibly weld sampans together to build an aircraft carrier'. Politburo member Wu Bannguo criticised this practice on the basis that it increased bureaucratic interference in smaller firms (Wu 1998).

A separate problem was that provincial authorities deliberately undervalued state assets before selling them in order to allow bureaucrats to gain by purchasing assets at a discount to their true value. This has focused attention on the growing problem of depletion of state assets (Smyth 2000a). At a conference in late 1997, former Premier Zhu Rongji admitted that the drain on state assets was as much as RMB150 million to RMB160 million per day (Smyth 2000a). Illegal personal gains from state asset stripping since the 1990s have also resulted in capital flight as corrupt officials shift the proceeds out of the country. Through the 1990s China's annual capital flight increased from US$10 billion to US$80 billion and was larger than annual foreign direct investment in this period, except for the years 1994, 1995 and 1996 (Zhang 2002).

Equity-for-debt swaps

Another significant development in the reform of SOEs in the past few years is the equity-for-debt swap scheme. The scheme was first announced in 1999 and came into operation in 2000 when the State Council promulgated regulations on the operation of asset management companies (AMCs). The four big state-owned banks each set up one AMC to handle bad loans. The four AMCs are Xinda (attached to the China Construction Bank), Great Wall (attached to the Agricultural Bank of China), Orient (attached to the Bank of China) and Huarong (attached to the Industrial and Commercial Bank of China). The purpose of the equity-for-debt swap scheme is to restructure China's large SOEs and clear up the bad loans of the banks. Estimates suggest that the proportion of non-performing loans of the state-owned banks was about 25% before the Asian financial crisis and 30% after the crisis (Li 1998). Yuan (1999) reports that in the mid-1990s the proportion of non-performing loans varied considerably between provinces, from 19% in Jiangsu province to 43% in Jilin province.

When the equity-for-debt swap scheme was announced, 2,000 of China's large and medium-sized SOEs applied (Steinfeld 2001). The State Economic Trade Commission (SETC) selected 601 mainly key SOEs in the initial round. The total value of the debt of the 601 enterprises involved in the swap was RMB400–500 billion, which was about 50% of the outstanding loans of the banking sector at the end of 1997 (Huang 2001). At the end of 2001, the official estimate of non-performing loans held by Chinese banks was RMB1.8 trillion (US$217 billion) or 25.4% of bank lending (Xinhua 2002). However, Ernst & Young estimates the total value of unprofitable loans to be US$480 billion or 44% of bank lending (Chandler 2002). A total of RMB1.4 trillion (US$170 billion) was transferred to the four AMCs in the first round (Tam 2002). In November 2003 the government announced a second bailout of the state-owned banks, consisting of asset injections and a further transfer of non-performing loans to AMCs in preparation for listing of the banks on the domestic stock exchanges (Stewart & Chan 2003).

The available evidence to this point, though, suggests that the equity-for-debt swap scheme has had little effect on improving the decision-making structures within the enterprises or the bad-debt problems of the banks (see Steinfeld 2001; Steinfeld & Hulme 2000; Smyth, Deng & Wang 2004a). The AMC provisions state: 'The AMC as a shareholder of the enterprise can send people to join the board of directors and supervision committee and enforce its rights as a shareholder' (AMC 2000:item 20). In theory the shareholders and the board sit at the top of the decision-making tree (PBNRC 1999). However, in practice it is the government that continues to appoint senior management in large SOEs, and outside shareholders cannot interfere in the day-to-day management of the firm. Even in cases where the AMCs own the majority of the shares, they will typically not interfere in the day-to-day management of the firm.

The equity-for-debt swap scheme has also done little or nothing to change the soft budget credit mentality prevailing in SOEs that run up huge debts prior to the swap. Steinfeld (2001), for instance, notes that it is common for the local branches of state banks to line up to extend new loans to SOEs that have participated in the swap. He notes that this reflects several factors. First, banks want to lend to firms that have undergone the scheme because they have been through an official vetting process and, hence, have the imprimatur of the state. Second, the debt-to-asset ratio in such firms has fallen, so the banks consider them safer bets. Third, because AMCs have large financial obligations to the banks, the banks do not want the firms with which the AMCs are involved to get into financial difficulties in the short term because of cash-flow problems.

Labour redundancies and social unrest

At the enterprise level these reforms have been accompanied by attempts to separate the social welfare obligations of SOEs and streamline the workforce. The policy of labour retrenchment in Chinese SOEs was first trialled in 1994 and was launched in 1997. Since that time the number of *xiagang* (laid-off) workers has become a major social problem. According to official figures 26 million workers were laid off from SOEs between 1998 and 2002 (Armitage 2003). Studies suggest that the burden of retrenchment has fallen heaviest on the disadvantaged. Appleton et al (2002) find that the risk of retrenchment has been higher for females, the less educated, the low skilled and the middle aged, who are precisely the people who find it most difficult to find re-employment. This has led to widespread protests, which have the potential to threaten social stability. In several cases abrupt announcements of redundancies have caused workers to go to local authorities to demand explanations for events and sometimes, when these have not been forthcoming, violent street protests have resulted (Morris, Sheehan & Hassard 2001). The plight of laid-off workers is being highlighted by leftist elements opposed to the reforms; they argue against privatisation and aim to stall the wave of reform (Zweig 2001).

The debate over the role of the state

The role of the state in promoting state-owned business in China is controversial. In the literature on China's reforms there are two contrasting views of the Chinese state. One is the strong state perspective and the other is the weak state perspective (see Ma 1999:320–3). The strong state perspective likens the Chinese state to an East Asian-type development state (White & Wade 1988; Unger & Chan 1996; Lo & Smyth 2005). Lo and Smyth (2005) argue that the *zhua da* policy of building big enterprise conglomerates is in the spirit of the East Asian or South Korean–Japanese model of late industrialisation. Several studies for a range of industries have argued that the Chinese state's active role in constructing enterprise groups represents an attempt at technological catch-up (see Nolan & Yeung 2001a; 2001b for pharmaceuticals and steel; Smyth & Zhai 2001 for petrochemicals; Smyth, Deng & Wang 2004b for shipbuilding). The argument is that the development path of conglomerates in late-industrialising countries has been different from that of industrialised countries (see Amsden 1992; Amsden & Hikino 1994). Large firms in industrialised countries first specialised in producing a narrow product line based on core competences and then diversified into related industries, but firms in late-industrialising countries have been forced to import and adapt foreign technology and to depend on learning through doing to compensate for the absence of core innovation.

In contrast, the weak state perspective argues that the chaos of the Cultural Revolution eroded developmental institutions, creating an 'erratic state' in the post-Mao period (Pye 1990). Breslin (1996) suggests that far from being a developmental state in the East Asian sense, China is suffering from 'dysfunctional development' characterised by bureaucratic incompetence, rampant corruption and centrifugal forces undermining the power of the centre. Authors such as McNally and Lee (1998) and Shieh (1999) argue that the Chinese government's attempt to build large enterprise groups is misguided because the relationship between state and enterprise is too close. These authors argue that this results in the same sorts of corporate governance problems that afflicted the Japanese and South Korean enterprise groups in the lead-up to the Asian financial crisis. China's accession to the WTO adds an extra dimension to the debate, with serious questions now being posed about whether China's large enterprises are ready to compete on a global 'level playing field'. Even traditional supporters of China's late-industrialisation program, such as Nolan (2002), have expressed grave doubts about whether China's firms are in a position to compete with the world's leading businesses.

The role of the non-state sector

For most of the market reform period, China's non-state sector has been dominated by the *sunan* model of CTVEs, which is famous for ambiguous property rights. CTVEs first emerged in southern Jiangsu in the 'Great Leap Forward' and developed rapidly from the mid- to late 1970s, filling gaps in China's haphazard planning regime. CTVEs prospered in light industries not included in the state plan and in goods that SOEs produced in insufficient amounts, such as textiles (Ho 1994; Smyth 1999). Throughout the 1980s and first half of the 1990s, it is widely acknowledged that CTVEs were driving China's high growth rate. The growth in real annual gross output value of CTVEs between 1985 and 1995 was just over 25% (Smyth 1998). At the start of the 1990s other models of non-state enterprises started to emerge, such as the private ownership Wenzhou model in southern Zhejiang, although in terms of gross output value CTVEs were still the most common form of ownership in the non-state sector. In 1990 CTVEs under the control of *xiang, zhen* and *cun* (townships and villages) produced 65% of the gross output value of the non-state sector, and in 1995 the comparable figure was still over 60%. However, in the mid- to late 1990s CTVEs were caught up in the wave of shareholding reform and most were converted into shareholding co-operatives or privatised. One news report suggests that as early as the end of 1996, prior to the Fifteenth Party Congress, 70% of CTVEs in Jiangsu had been transformed into joint stock companies, leases or options (*CICT* 1997:4; Smyth 1999).

While private enterprises in China have been legal since 1978, private entrepreneurs have long faced discrimination in obtaining credit, labour and material supplies. Private enterprises are also subject to various forms of informal and irregular *tanpai* (levies) imposed by municipal governments (Mok 2000). In an attempt to sidestep this discrimination, private enterprises would often register as 'collective enterprises'—a phenomenon known as 'wearing a red hat'. Woo

(1999) suggests that in the 1980s, in the private sector stronghold of Wenzhou, almost all private enterprises described their businesses as 'collectives'. The importance of the private sector, however, has grown over time and since the late 1990s private enterprises have replaced CTVEs as the most important form of ownership in the non-state sector. According to the State Administration for Industry and Commerce, in the decade between 1993 and 2002 the number of registered private enterprises increased from 238,000 to 2.4 million, the number of employees in private enterprises increased from 3.7 million to 34.1 million, and total registered capital increased from RMB68.1 billion to RMB2,475.6 billion (Zhang & Liu 2003). There are no longer any 'red-hat firms'. The increasing recognition of private enterprises led these firms to remove their 'red hats' and register as private enterprises.

In 1999 the National People's Congress passed a resolution that the private sector was to be regarded as a key part of the national economy, rather than just a supplement to the state-owned sector, but baulked at ruling that private property should have the same legal status as state-owned property (Lam 1999). In a concession to the party's left-wing and socialist rhetoric, in 2000 the state-run media were still preferring the term *min ban* (people-operated) enterprises rather than the term private enterprise (Smith, CS 2000:16), but at the Sixteenth Party Congress in 2002 Jiang Zemin broke with the past and stated that the time had arrived to welcome private entrepreneurs into the Communist Party. In March 2004 the National People's Congress went one step further than five years earlier and passed an amendment to the Chinese constitution to give private property rights equal status with public property. The amendment to the constitution states that 'private property obtained legally shall not be violated' and 'will be on an equal footing with public property' (Sui 2004; Min 2004).

The available evidence suggests that private firms still face discrimination in obtaining finance. There is evidence that the D'Long Group, once one of China's largest private firms and featured in the case study below, faced discrimination in accessing capital and that this was an important reason why it failed. More generally, in a 2004 survey of private entrepreneurs in Zhejiang province, which has China's most active private sector, 45.7% of respondents said their biggest obstacle was finding finance and 66.7% of respondents were of the view that it is 'very hard' for them to get loans from financial institutions (*BDU* 2004). The All-China Federation of Industry and Commerce and the Research Centre for Private Enterprises are using the latest amendment to the constitution to argue for increased efforts to solve funding difficulties facing private enterprises and to clamp down on overt discrimination.

Case study of the D'Long investment group

The D'Long investment group was established in Urumqi in Xinjiang Autonomous Region in 1986 by brothers Tang Wanli and Tang Wanxin.[2] Their first business, a colour photographic development shop in Urumqi, earned the seed capital of RMB1 million in the first year. The Tangs then expanded into fashion, noodle production, fertilisers and computer software. The big break came in 1993 when the Tangs invested in the embryonic mainland stock market and made tens of millions of renminbi within a few months (Pun 2003). Subsequently, D'Long developed into an investment conglomerate controlled by 33 private entrepreneurs, with a global presence in a broad range of businesses and with headquarters located in Shanghai. Prior to its collapse in 2004, it was one of the largest private enterprises in China; it employed 15,000 people worldwide and had a sales turnover in 2002 of RMB40 billion. In 2002 the Tang brothers were ranked 27th on the Forbes list of the wealthiest people in China, with assets of US$195 million (*AFX Asia* 2003a).

The D'Long Group had three major operations. The first was D'Long Strategic Investment Company, which, at the core of the D'Long Group, built group strategies, selected companies to acquire and developed measures to improve corporate value. It employed 200 researchers, all of whom had postgraduate qualifications in economics or business administration. About a third of the researchers acquired their degrees from foreign universities, another third of researchers were recruited from foreign firms and the rest had at least ten years of experience working in Chinese companies (*JoongAng Daily* 2004). The second major operation was D'Long Industrial Investment Company, which managed several private equity funds, and the third was a group of financial service providers (including Xinjiang Jinxin Trust and Investment Company and Xinjiang Financial Lease Company) in which D'Long held a majority stake.

In its range of interests the D'Long Group resembled the archetypal East Asian conglomerate, with a presence in such diverse product ranges as agribusiness, building materials, financial services, foodstuffs, mechanical and electrical equipment, and entertainment and tourism. It had a controlling interest in three companies listed on the Shanghai and Shenzhen stock markets; namely Xiang Torch, Xinjiang Tunhe and Shenyang Hejin.

The main products of Xiang Torch and Shenyang Hejin are mechanical and electrical parts and tools. Xiang Torch has a 40% market share of the auto parts market in China and is China's biggest exporter of braking drums to the United States. Its major international clients include Citroën, Sears, SVW and Home Depot. Shenyang Hejin is the leading supplier of nickel-based alloy materials, with a market share of 60%. Its major international clients include Black &

Decker, Makita and Bosch. Xinjiang Tunhe produces tomato-based products and fruit and vegetable juices, including 'Hui Yuan Juices', which is a leading brand name in China. Its major international clients for its tomato pastes and juices include Heinz, Petti and Spreada. Its supply of tomato paste products accounts for 85% of the domestic market and 6% of the global market, making it the second-largest tomato paste producer in the world.

A number of Chinese businesses have started to invest offshore. In 2002 Chinese outward foreign direct investment was worth US$2.9 billion (*Economist* 2003). While this amount is small compared with foreign direct investment into China, it is an increasing trend. A report published by consultants Roland Berger in July 2003 suggested that three-quarters of Chinese manufacturing firms surveyed had plans for overseas expansion (*Economist* 2003).

Prior to its collapse, D'Long had been at the forefront of the offshore push, which was reflected in some important foreign acquisitions. In 2000 D'Long bought Murray, a leading United States lawnmower and bicycle maker. In 2003 it bought a project to build a 70-seat passenger jet from a bankrupt German aircraft manufacturer, Fairchild Dornier. The project was still at the prototype stage and at the time of acquisition it was expected to cost US$1 billion to complete (*Gazette* 2003). In 2003–04 D'Long also attempted to acquire Grundig, the German home appliance manufacturer, but this proved unsuccessful (*SinoCast* 2004).

Some Chinese companies, of which Haier is a notable instance, concentrated on building up brand recognition in international markets (see *Economist* 2003). D'Long's view was that the problem with this strategy was that Chinese brands were associated with cheap prices and poor quality in international markets. Therefore, D'Long's strategy was different. Instead of building up its own name abroad, it focused on purchasing well known but ailing foreign brands. It retained their marketing distribution and research and development operations, but transferred the bulk of manufacturing to China to cut costs. The thinking was that foreign brands with Chinese input costs would offer larger profit margins. In the three years following D'Long's acquisition of Murray, D'Long closed two of Murray's three factories, fired top management and 650 workers, and moved the manufacture of low-end mowers to Jiangsu province. D'Long's president, Benny Li, is reported as saying that D'Long could halve the cost of a lawnmower if engines were made in China rather than the United States. The constraint, however, was that D'Long had to move slowly to avoid getting offside with the trade unions representing Murray's employees (*Economist* 2003).

The industries in which D'Long invested seem, at first sight, to have little in common. As such D'Long was criticised for being too diverse. For example, in 2003 D'Long, through Xiang Torch, bought controlling stakes in Chongqing

Heavy Duty Trucks and Shaanxi Heavy Duty Trucks to become one of the largest heavy-duty truck manufacturers in China. This move was criticised on the basis that D'Long lacked a comparative advantage in trucks and that competition in the truck-manufacturing industry was expected to become more intense, with expanded capacity of other domestic manufacturers and the entrance of international companies such as Volvo (*AFX Asia* 2003b).

D'Long, however, mimicked the strategy of other East Asian conglomerates, such as the Charoen Pokphand Group of Thailand, in investing in what it saw as industries with growth potential. D'Long's investment in the Fairchild Dornier jet project and related investments in the Chinese aviation market were good examples. In 2000 D'Long started leasing jets via its Xinjiang Financial Leasing operations and subsequently took a major stake in the Hongdu Aviation Industry Group (*SinoCast* 2003). The rationale was that the Chinese domestic airline industry was seen as having much growth potential as domestic living standards improved and people had more income to spend on travel. D'Long's involvement in the food and beverage industries was another illustration. China's juice/soft drink market was growing at an annual average rate of 19% and in 1999 was worth RMB40 billion. In 2000 D'Long's forecasts suggested that food and drink would grow into a RMB3 trillion industry in China by 2020. D'Long saw itself as getting in on the ground floor, where it would be well positioned to benefit from the growth.

Another similarity between the D'Long Group and the Charoen Pokphand Group was that the D'Long Group worked hard at forging joint ventures with the leading companies in the industries it entered. For example, it had successful joint ventures with global car-part manufacturers such as Delphi from the United States and ZF from Germany, and with multinational food companies such as Heinz and Petti. The philosophy of D'Long was consistent with the perspective of late industrialisation—that is, business groups add value through diversification because they are better able to imitate the functions of institutions in advanced capitalist economies (see Khanna & Palepu 1997).

However, in 2004 concerns started to surface about the business dealings of D'Long. In April 2004 Torch Automobiles, Shenyang Hejin and Xinjiang Tunhe issued statements noting that D'Long had been using the shares that it owned in the companies as collateral for loans. In June 2004 the People's Bank of China began an investigation into D'Long's complicated shareholding structure, which led in October 2004 to government-directed restructuring of the group and the appointment of the state-owned AMC, China Huarong Asset Management Corporation.

D'Long's collapse in 2004 reflected the culmination of several processes: regulators' increased scrutiny of the group's activities and financial structure, the People's Bank of China's own concern over loans outstanding to D'Long's companies, and a general tightening of bank credit because of the central government's attempts to reduce overheating in the economy (Hirson 2005). Initially Huarong attempted to sell D'Long in one piece, but was unable to find willing purchasers at a suitable price. As a consequence, throughout 2005 the majority of D'Long's assets were sold separately to state-owned firms in a process described in the Chinese media as the 'nationalisation' of D'Long's assets. Many observers have argued that a primary reason for D'Long's collapse was discrimination by the state-owned banks against private enterprises, which forced D'Long to leverage off its shareholdings in state-owned companies. As Hirson (2005:32) put it:

> Combined with the perception that D'Long collapsed because of the credit squeeze at private firms caused by 'macrocontrols', and the government's unwillingness to save the group, D'Long is taken by some observers as a symbol of the unequal treatment that private firms in China receive relative to their state-owned peers.

Improper business practices within D'Long also played a role. Indeed Hirson (2005) argues that D'Long's behavior illustrates how lack of access to capital by private firms, coupled with China's weak regulatory environment and poor corporate governance arrangements, creates incentives for market manipulation and misuse of a company's financial assets. In December 2004 Tang Wanxin and 60 D'Long executives were charged with corruption and embezzlement. In April 2006 Tang Wanxin was sentenced to imprisonment for eight years and fined RMB800,000 (about US$100,000) after being found guilty of illegal banking and stock market manipulation.

Conclusion

The Chinese economy has come a long way since market reforms were first introduced in the late 1970s. China can now rightly be regarded as an emerging economic superpower, whose influence will continue to increase now that it has joined the WTO. The challenge facing the Chinese government is to deal effectively with its ailing state-owned sector. The focus of the *zhua da* policy has been to build large state-owned conglomerates in strategic sectors that are capable of competing in international markets. Whether these conglomerates have caught up with the world's leading businesses and are now able to compete on the global 'level playing field' is a serious issue for China's industrial strategy. The available evidence from extensive fieldwork suggests that China's large firms are not ready to compete (Nolan 2002). A related issue facing China's policy makers in attempting to make the state sector more competitive is how to best deal with the mounting number of laid-off workers. This is not only an economic issue, but increasingly a humanitarian issue, given the size and scope of the problem. This issue is also linked to the growing problem of maintaining social stability. It is difficult to see how China's high growth rate can be maintained if violence continues to escalate.

Traditionally the non-state sector has been dominated by CTVEs, but since the late 1990s private enterprises have become more important. While the status of the private sector is now recognised in the Chinese constitution, private entrepreneurs still face discrimination in raising capital vis-à-vis the state-owned and collective-owned sectors, although this is starting to change. The initial success of large privately owned conglomerates such as the D'Long Group shows the potential for private enterprise in 'socialist' China, including active participation in restructuring the state-owned sector. D'Long Group's offshore activities also highlight the trend towards China's large non-state and state-owned businesses moving offshore. While the focus of the world's business community is rightly on opportunities for inward investment in China, this is a trend that can be expected to increase as the Chinese economy continues to mature. The collapse of the D'Long Group, however, provides a telling tale. At one level the collapse is testament to the problems besetting debt-dominated East Asian conglomerates. However, at another level, it shows the potential negative fallout confronting private enterprises in China, which have difficulties accessing state-owned loans. As the private sector in China continues to grow, this is an important lesson for the future.

Notes

1 The official Chinese definition of large, medium and small differs by industry (see Lo 1999 for details). In practice it is common to designate the largest 1,000 SOEs as 'large' and refer to all the others as small (see Cao et al 1999).
2 Unless indicated otherwise, all information on the D'Long Group in this section is from information supplied by the firm at an interview at its Shanghai headquarters in November 2003. The fieldwork in Shanghai was conducted in collaboration with my colleagues, Chris Nyland and Cherrie Zhu. I thank them for allowing me to use information gathered in our joint work in this chapter.

chapter five

India: energy and the role of the state and private sectors in a rising giant[1]

Marika Vicziany

India has been emerging as a major economic power for some time, but it has taken the international business community a while to recognise this. The judgments of international business began to shift from 1991 onwards, when the Indian government declared a new liberalising policy of economic reform. After 1991 questions about the size of the domestic Indian market were beginning to enter into business speculations about the potential pent-up demands of almost one billion people. The positive reassessment of India's potential received a boost from the rapid development of the Indian information technology customised software industry, which emerged within six years (1995–2001) to become a world leader. It has been suggested that perhaps India is indeed a lucky country—it appears to have entered into a new growth era based on clean information technology and other service industries in contrast to China, which, in becoming the new leader of manufacturing, is lumbered with dirty and polluting industries (Vicziany 2005a).

India is increasingly regarded as a 'good bet' for international business because of the extensive linkages that exist between Indian and United States business. It has been noted that in the information technology, electronics and other high-technology sectors of the economy of the United States, well-educated Indian labour has made a significant contribution. The extensive Indian diaspora, which arrived in the United States as migrants and students during the past 50 years, now finds itself at the top of the management ladder in United States companies, non-government organisations, and government departments and agencies (Cohen 2001:116–77). This international network provides India with many 'natural' advantages in developing business opportunities between the United States, the world's largest economy, and India, an emerging Asian giant.

It has taken the United States and European Union governments even longer than the business community to appreciate the role that India will play in the Asian region and globally. It was not until India tested nuclear weapons in 1998 that governments began to ask what had suddenly given India the capacity to explode a nuclear device? India's nuclear capacities are merely further evidence of the extent to which India has developed unique technological capacities as part of its long-term industrialisation since the end of British rule in 1947—but this is only now being understood, with the United States government again paying attention to India's special needs, including a new agreement to transfer to India advanced civilian nuclear technology (Joint Statement 2005).

These reassessments by international business and foreign governments of India's potential mark a significant shift away from the negative stereotypes that used to dominate analysis of the Indian subcontinent. Those images were focused on mass poverty, illiteracy, religious and social violence, and terrible inequality. All these contributed to the view that India was essentially an unstable polity. In addition to these negative images, the international business community appeared to be repelled by corruption, red tape, the lack of respect for timetables and deadlines, bureaucratic intervention in business and by nepotism. It was frequently suggested that the Indian business world was based on family connections rather than merit or talent. Few authors challenged these negative perceptions until the mid-1990s.[2] Clearly these unfavourable images of India have now been overthrown, but is the new optimism perhaps too glowing? The conclusion to this chapter identifies the chief, long-term problems that will persist in India regardless of the speed of its economic growth, middle-class prosperity and technological brilliance.

The bulk of this chapter, however, focuses on the factors driving India's economic successes since independence by looking at two of India's most powerful companies. The first case study concerns the high-performing Oil and Natural Gas Corporation (ONGC, previously Oil and Natural Gas Commission) of India, a state-owned company; the second study deals with Reliance Industries as an example of the dynamism of the private corporate sector. These two giants played a critical role in developing India's energy infrastructure and their long histories allow us to track how the Indian economy has evolved to assume its new economic prominence. The case of Reliance Industries focuses on the period up to 2005, for in that year the company divided after bitter feuding between the two brothers whose father established the firm decades earlier.

To begin with, however, some brief words about India's energy problems are needed. The question of reliable energy sources is one of the first logistical issues that all foreign and domestic firms face when setting up ventures in India. Electrical blackouts are common in Indian cities and towns, leaving swathes of urban areas in the dark for between 30 minutes and five hours. Companies respond to these difficulties by setting up generators that kick-in automatically when the main electricity supply fails. Another option is to establish businesses in special industrial parks set up by local governments. These industrial zones have guaranteed electricity supplies. If a business takes the form of a large manufacturing concern, a third possibility is to build a small electrical plant as part of the basic business infrastructure. Fourth, some states in India suffer less electrical failures than others, so these attract a disproportionate amount of investment. Having said all this, the bulk of businesses in India take their energy needs from large public and private suppliers—the two most prominent of these are discussed in this chapter. The energy question is certainly irritating and sometimes frustrating, but none of this detracts from the vast appeal of the Indian market, which sustains a huge population and an increasingly wealthy middle class of some 300 million and more people.

International firms have also been attracted to India by its English-speaking culture, respect for international contracts, timely payment of international bills and debts, and its talented workforce. Even Bollywood, long ridiculed for producing insanely romantic and escapist movies, has become the darling of the global film industry.

India's economic success and new energy problems

The great paradox of becoming a successful economic giant is that success brings with it new concerns, and one of the most pressing in India is the country's rapidly growing energy deficits. India has been the world's 11th largest economy for over a decade (Cohen 2001:27), with the result that energy supply has become an ever more urgent question, exceeded in Asia only by China's energy problems.[3] Given the size of the Indian economy and its projected high growth rate for the next five decades, it is hardly surprising that in June 2004 the then-British Prime Minister Tony Blair suggested that India should be brought into the G8, one of the world's most powerful economic groups (Vicziany 2005a:210). This proposal recognised that India, and its many problems, has an impact on the global economic and business environment.

Table 1 shows Indian economic growth during the past 50 years. Before 1980 it was fashionable to talk about India's modest growth of below 4% as the 'Hindu rate of growth', a term invented by Professor Raj Krishna to capture the contrast between India's relatively low growth during the 1950s and the high expectations that had led to the formulation of India's state planning system in the 1940s. Thereafter, economic growth began to pick up to almost 6% in the 1980s and 1990s. By the early 2000s the GDP growth rate seemed to be trending towards 7% or 8%. International agencies such as Goldman Sachs and domestic organisations such as the Confederation of Indian Industries now predict that Indian economic growth is likely to persist at between 6% and 8% per annum for some five decades (Vicziany 2005a:211–21). This assumes that the growth rate will not be disrupted by social violence stemming from the persistence of mass poverty.

Table 1: Average GDP growth rates (%) of the Indian economy, 1950 to 2004

	Agriculture	Industry	Transport/ trade	Finance	Public administration	Total GDP
1950s	3.2	6.3	5.4	3.0	3.7	3.9
1960s	2.6	5.6	5.0	3.4	5.3	3.7
1970s	2.0	4.0	4.9	4.0	4.0	3.2
1980s	3.8	7.0	5.8	9.8	6.0	5.7
1990s	2.7	5.4	7.8	8.5	6.8	5.7
2003–04	8.6	6.7	10.9	6.4	5.9	8.1

Source: figures are calculated from *Table 1.6 Annual growth rates of real GDP at factor cost by industry of origin* (GI 2005: S–10).

Table 1 shows that the chief driving forces behind India's accelerated economic growth are industry, transport/trade and finance. Agriculture has also picked up, and India has developed a thriving agri-industrial base. Sustained growth will ensure that India becomes a major global power, but it will also place tremendous pressure on India to find sufficient energy for all its diverse needs.

The current and projected economic growth rates are now driving Indian governments to consider new technology to save fossil fuels, including the building of hydrogen-driven cars (Jha 2005:1). Other alternative energy sources that continue to be developed in India are gobar gas[4] and wind and solar power. These new energy sources will relieve pressure on the Indian economy by providing individual households with more fuel options, but alternative energy has not yet taken the form of a technology that can be applied to modern industry. Hence India will remain dependent on the conventional sources described in

Table 2. Estimates by the Gas Authority India Limited (GAIL) show that between 1965 and 2003 India's use of conventional energy increased more than six times from 388 million barrels (measured in terms of oil equivalents) to 2,383 million barrels (GAIL 2005a). Despite this large increase, the structure of India's primary energy consumption remains backward relative to world trends that have seen a shift to gas and nuclear energy (Table 2).[5] India, by contrast, remains heavily dependent on coal for electricity, yet increasing the productivity of the coal sector remains deeply problematic.[6]

Table 2: Components of primary energy consumption in India in 2005

	% of total energy consumption	
	World	India
Hydroelectric	6.3	5.2
Nuclear	6.5	1.4
Coal	25.5	55.8
Gas	24.3	7.8
Oil	37.5	30.0
Total	**100.0**	**100.0**

Source: GAIL 2005a.

India's capacity to shift away from coal as the primary source for electricity has been constrained by limited domestic oil supplies and the high cost of oil imports. In 2004 total Indian output of crude oil was half of what was imported: 32 million metric tons compared with 60 million metric tons respectively (GAIL 2005a; GAIL 2005b). The import bill on foreign oil is great: depending on annual prices, India spends between 15% (for instance, in 1998–99 when international prices were low) and 31% (such as in 2000–01 when international prices were high) of its total import bill on energy imports of both crude oil and refined petroleum products (GAIL 2005a:7). This import dependency exposes India to economic fluctuations: for example, during the first half of 2004 crude oil import costs increased by 56% (Domain-b 2004). Moreover, India's import dependency is growing despite exploration and discoveries of oil fields in India's territorial waters. In the years between 1990 and 2001, India's imports of both crude and refined products increased almost threefold, from 29 million metric tons to 83 million metric tons (GAIL 2005a:8). The driver behind these growing aggregated imports reflect India's insatiable demand for crude oil—while imports of refined products dropped significantly in response to increased domestic capacity, dependency on crude oil jumped to about '71% of the total domestic consumption in FY 2002' (GAIL 2005a:9). According to Muni and Pant, the collapse of Indian oil self-sufficiency is worse than the GAIL figures suggest if projections to 2006–07 are included: self-sufficiency will drop from 55.6% in 1990–91 to 23.5% by 2006–07 (Muni & Pant 2005:15).

The dependency on oil imports will worsen as the Indian economy enters the long-term growth period that has been projected by Wilson and Purushothaman 2003. Shifting some energy consumers away from oil towards natural gas will help to relieve the problem but not resolve it. India has its own onshore, natural gas outlets, so one benefit of this shift has been an increase of about 65% in the production of natural gas (GAIL 2005b:3), in contrast to total crude oil production that has remained relatively unchanged in recent years. Another strategy has been for India to diversify the countries from which it imports energy.

Strategies for diversifying India's imports of oil and gas

Like China, the government of India has adopted a realist strategy for sourcing energy imports in a manner that does not expose the national economy to dependence on the oil fields of the increasingly unstable Middle East. In early 2005 the Indian government contracted the Iranian government to supply eight million tons of liquid natural gas between 2005 and 2030 (Dawn 2005; Domain-b 2005c). This gas is to be carried in tankers, but the status of this deal is ambiguous. The United States has indicated its unwavering opposition to any contracts that bring Iran into the normal arena of global commerce. Iran was identified in President Bush's State of the Union Address in 2000 as one of the rogue states that formed the 'axis of evil' (Bush 2002). The status of an alternative gas pipeline from the gas fields of Iran to India via Pakistan is equally controversial. The pipeline project was championed by Mani Shankar Aiyer, India's Petroleum Minister, but increasingly ran counter to the foreign policy objectives being promoted by Indian Prime Minister Manmohan Singh. In June 2005, during Singh's visit to Washington, it became clear that the pipeline project was in jeopardy, with the United States willing to export civilian nuclear technology to India. By late 2005 the Petroleum Minister had been replaced, thereby making it easier for India to collaborate with the United States in strengthening its economic boycott on Iran. Economic collaboration between India and the US increasingly depends on the latter exporting civilian nuclear technology to India; Australia too is now considering the export of uranium to India to increase the nuclear energy option.

Another example of India's adherence to realist paradigms is its willingness to consider investing in Russia's largest oil plant, Yukos (Blakely 2005). The need for economies of scale is also sinking in, as India faces growing competition from vast United States and Chinese oil firms (Domain-b 2005a; 2005b). The driving force behind all these initiatives is the Indian government's realisation that by 2020 India will have to import 85% of its crude oil needs, a 15% increase over the current situation. In tons, the picture is worse than this because the total volume of crude oil imports is predicted to increase by more than 250% (Jha 2005:1). Other state-initiated joint ventures have been undertaken to diversify India's oil supplies—some of these are addressed below.

India has always been a mixed economy, with both state and private sector firms sharing in the development process. However, the relationship between these two sectors has changed over time, as the first case study below shows. ONGC is one of India's leading companies, and it remains firmly in the hands of the central government. The history of ONGC contradicts the simplistic picture that has been drawn of the Indian 'licence permit Raj', which dominated Indian political economy between 1950 and 1991.

The 'licence permit Raj' is a concept that stresses the extent to which the Indian economy was regulated, especially after the nationalisation of many companies and banks in the 1980s and the withdrawal of the foreign multinationals. The central government managed the economy in many ways: through nationalisation of domestic and foreign companies; by controlling licences and permits to the private sector; through price controls and subsidies; via tight controls on the foreign sector; and through the principle of 'indigenous availability' and high tariffs, which pressured Indian industry to buy Indian crude and intermediate inputs and only resort to cheaper, high-quality imports if domestic supplies did not exist. Importing components or raw materials alone could involve an Indian firm in negotiations with no less than a dozen government departments (Mathur 1994:106). The business of getting permits was so complex that only well-heeled companies were able to sustain the effort; such companies then used their access to scarce supplies by selling them to smaller firms that did not have the capacity to court the officials. In addition to the controls imposed by the central government in New Delhi, there were also regional-level controls imposed by state governments in the provinces. District level governments also had their rules and regulations.

The history of the old regime or the 'licence permit Raj' is well documented in the secondary literature. This chapter, by contrast, considers one of the Indian government's success stories—the achievements of ONGC. In doing so, it is hoped that this case study will also encourage a reassessment of the role of the state in the economic development of Asia because, at the present moment, there is too much triumphalism in the literature celebrating (perhaps prematurely) the superiority of market forces over all other forms of macro-economic management.

Case study one: ONGC—a public sector company

It has become fashionable to assume that market mechanisms and private enterprises are always superior to state-owned enterprises as forms of economic organisation. In the Indian context, the preponderance of 'sick industries' contradicts this proposition. The term 'sick industries' describes private sector companies that are bankrupt but have been rescued and absorbed by the state sector. In other words, despite a long history of state support and subsidies, many of India's private sector companies failed to prosper. The state has historically played the role of rescuing these companies in order to shore up employment. As a democracy, no Indian government has been prepared to sacrifice winning the next election for a tougher policy against corporate failure and inefficiency. The history of India's sick industries certainly blurs the lines between what constitutes the private and government sectors.

The history of state-owned enterprises in India, however, is not much more impressive. Many of them have also failed, especially when a state corporation has been formed on the basis of amalgamating ruined private sector firms. The National Textile Corporation is a good example of the latter. Formed in 1968 on the basis of 16 ruined private textile mills, by 1995 it had some 119 former private mills under its umbrella (MT 2006). According to the 2003 report on public sector units by the Comptroller and Auditor of India, there were 366 public sector companies controlled by the central government, of which only 139 or about 38% were profitable; the rest were all running at a loss (CAGI 2003:vi). Half of the revenues earned by the minority of companies that *did* make a profit (including ONGC) were under the Ministry of Petroleum and Natural Gas, one of India's best-performing public sector industries for many decades. On the negative side of the government's performance were the losses incurred by 97 of the 227 financially non-viable public sector units. These were so serious that the equity value of the firms was negative and the chances of the government recovering hefty loans given to the firms were very low (CAGI 2003:vi).

The high percentage of non-performing government companies at the central level was matched by the equally dismal performance of companies managed by state governments. Together, this large, cumbersome and ailing public sector has been behind the momentum for disinvestment of public sector equity. Beginning in 1991, economic reforms involved a disinvestment process that saw the bundling up of small allotments of equity capital from a range of high-, medium- and low-performing companies. Not surprisingly, the speed of disinvestment was abysmally slow, given the reluctance of the public to purchase bundles that included loss-making shares. Moreover, the early policy was to sell only minority ownership, which meant that the management of the public firms remained in the hands of government-appointed directors, thereby exposing the managerial process to bureaucratic red tape and 'toplessness'—the quaint Indian term for public sector units that do not have chief executive officers because the political process involved in the appointment of top management has not been resolved to the satisfaction of the competing political parties that wield power in New Delhi.

Taken together, the disinvestment process has not inspired confidence amongst potential buyers of state-owned companies. As a result, since 1999 the disinvestment of public sector firms has focused on strategic sales of large volumes of equity to established Indian private sector firms (GI 2005:40). The benefit of strategic sales is that management of the company shifts into private hands. The process by which strategic sales were initially instituted was heavily criticised for lacking sufficient transparency and for being driven more by the requirements of boosting the Indian government's cash reserves rather than generating rational economic reforms. In 2003–04 the disinvestment policy was refined further to enable strategic sales to occur alongside the sale of equity to smaller investors via the share market. One of the most popular sales by this method was the public offer of Maruti Udyog Ltd, the maker of India's popular Maruti car (GI 2005:40).

ONGC as a showcase public sector firm

ONGC is one of India's most highly regarded and successful companies and is typically used as an example of state efficiency in response to critics of the public sector. As noted before, the state-owned petroleum sector has been profitable and annually generates about one-fifth of government revenues (GAIL 2005a:9). Table 3 summarises some of the important achievements of ONGC.

Table 3: Achievements of ONGC

Indicators	ONGC
Awards	Biggest Wealth Creator Award, India, 19 January 2005 (based on long-term Indian company performances by Motilal Oswal Securities)
	Global Finance Magazine, November 2004 survey, Best Oil and Gas Company
	Financial Times, number one in Global 500
	Forbes 400—number one
Profits	When partially privatised, shares oversubscribed six times
	Platt Energy Business Technology Survey 2004—most profitable oil/natural gas firm globally
	Highest profit in 2003–04 of Indian rupees (Rs) 86.64 billion; net worth Rs400 billion
	Holds 57% of all hydrocarbon fields in India Capital value—9% of total Bombay Stock Exchange
Production	Rapid growth continues: 2003–04 added 49.06 million metric tons of reserves to its total
	Managerial brilliance—reformed Mangalore Refinery and Petrochemicals Limited in 12 months
	One of 30 international firms with daily output of more than one million barrels
	India's largest exploration company—found five of six oil and natural gas basins of hydrocarbons
	Cumulative output of 660 million metric tons so far of crude and 350 million metric tons natural gas from 115 fields
Capacity	Largest deepwater exploratory project in the Sagar Sammriddhi Project; daily cost is US$0.75 million
	Owns and operates 15,000 kilometres of pipelines, of these 3,800 under water
	Plans to double reserves by 2020, that is, by six billion tons, of which four billion in the ocean; plans to raise extraction rate from 28% to 40%
Contribution to national economy	Zero debt
	17th company in world by market capitalisation on July 2004—Rs1 trillion
	Annual return to government revenue of Rs168 billion
	84% of Indian gas and oil production; largest producer
	One-tenth of total Indian refining capacity

Source: ONGC (2005).

The track record of ONGC is even more impressive when placed into historical context. Before independence in 1947, India only had two oil companies, Assam Oil Co and the Attock Oil Co, in eastern and north-western India respectively, and, as with iron and minerals, the British colonial government did not believe that India had any reserves worth worrying about. It did not suit the British to concern themselves with India's energy potential because they had no plans to industrialise a mere colony. Moreover, the raw materials and components that India needed were imported from Britain or its dependencies or trading partners. India's role as the economic fulcrum for the British Empire trade via the multilateral payments system is well known (Saul 1960:58); Indian industrialisation was ruled out because of imperial priorities.

Independent India's Industrial Policy Resolutions of 1948 and 1956 reversed colonial indifference by giving prominence to India's industrialisation. Those early documents included the need to build an oil industry (ONGC 2005). As happened with the iron and steel industry (Harris 1958), Indian delegations travelled abroad to study the petroleum industries in the advanced countries and by the mid-1950s strategies for an indigenous modern oil sector were in place. This reflected the broader vision of the government of India, which was inspired by the development strategies of the Soviet Union. The Soviet Union had emerged after the Second World War as a global superpower, and this had been possible partly because heavy and basic industries received massive investments of state-owned capital. Vladimir Ilyich Lenin's (1922) words were taken seriously in India: the oil industry was seen by Indian economists and politicians as a critical component of the 'commanding heights' of the economy and, as such, needed to be a state sector monopoly. The OPEC oil crisis of the 1970s reiterated the lessons of reducing dependence on unreliable market forces, whether international or national. The result was that by 1981 the oil industry of India was fully nationalised: the foreign oil companies withdrew from the Indian market and did not re-enter until the 1990s in response to the deregulation of the Indian economy, which began with the policies formulated by Manmohan Singh (prior to becoming a politician, he had been an academic advocate for market liberalisation).

By 1959 ONGC was established as a statutory body charged with the responsibility of building an oil industry in all its various dimensions. Its first great success was the discovery of Bombay High in 1977, one of India's most productive oil fields located off the western coast of India. Bombay High was the first of many other high-yielding offshore oil and gas reserves, all of them located within India's territorial waters. By 2000 ONGC had drilled 1,528 wells, of which 44% were for oil and 5% for gas (SEEN 2002). Taking ONGC's total production into account, this public sector giant still produces between 90% and 95% of India's crude oil and natural gas (Sridhar 1998).

The Oil and Natural Gas Commission was renamed the Oil and Natural Gas Corporation after it was converted into a limited company in 1994 as part of the new disinvestment policies introduced after 1991. The first disinvestment occurred in 1993 and the second when the company offered shares to its employees. Further rationalisation and privatisation followed. The current situation is one in which 15.89% of the ownership of ONGC is in private hands. It should be stressed, however, that the state remains the dominant partner in ONGC and controls over 80% of shares. Another dimension to the new rationalisation process has involved ONGC developing a strategic partnership with GAIL. GAIL also experienced some limited privatisation when 2.5% of the asset value was sold to the private sector a few years ago (ONGC 2005). A third component of the liberalisation of India's state-controlled oil industry was the decision in 1994 to give the Reliance–Enron consortium two of ONGC's potentially most productive medium-sized oil fields—the Mukta and Panna fields alone brought in a return US$440 million during the first year of operations. Another field, the Ravva, was given to Videocon and Command Petroleum, and also proved to be profitable, especially because none of these private sector firms had made any initial investment in the exploration or development of these fields. ONGC, in other words, passed on the benefits of its own success to the private sector.

The economic and strategic importance of ONGC

ONGC plays a critical role in helping to diversify India's dependency on oil and gas imports. It has done this by becoming a part owner of a number of major oil and natural gas fields in Africa and central Asia during the past decade through its international subsidiary ONGC Videsh Limited (OVL). From its inception ONGC has long been involved in international oil and gas explorations in partnership with foreign governments and companies, but in 2003 the pressure to diversify the sources of Indian energy compelled it to become a part owner in an oil and natural gas field in the Sudan. The Indian government purchased its share in the Greater Nile Petroleum Operating Company when Talisman, a Canadian firm, came under intense financial and political pressure to withdraw its investment, partly in response to human rights abuses in Sudan's civil war (Smith, C 2000; HRW 2003:385–436). India now holds a 20% interest in this company (the Chinese National Petroleum Corporation and Malaysia's Petronas company each hold a 40% share).

OVL is also in charge of a project to upgrade the capacity of the Port Sudan refinery and build a 720-kilometre pipeline. These investments brought OVL's interests in the Sudan up to the value of US$1.6 billion, which represents about 14.55% of total foreign investment in the whole of the African continent (Harsch 2004:8). As evidence of its determination to reduce dependency on foreign control over energy imports, the Indian government insisted that when OVL starts earning a profit from these investments, the profit should be remitted to India in the form of 'equity oil exports' (Ranjan 2003). The expected annual return to India is about 3 million metric tons (MMT) of oil per annum, which represents about a quarter of total output in that oilfield (Menon 2002). Table 4 summarises some of OVL's other oil and natural gas investments abroad. All of these are driven by the same strategic imperative to import '20 million tones of equity oil per year by 2020 and 60 MMT by 2025' (ONGC 2005).

Further evidence of India's expanding global oil and natural gas interests has been the opening of some 100 Indian Oil Corporation petrol stations in Sri Lanka. Sri Lanka, like India, is dependent on energy imports but, unlike India, lacks the infrastructure for exploration and exploitation. According to the Indian Petroleum Minister, India is 'building an energy bridge' to Sri Lanka (Ariyadasa 2003) but, in fact, Indian interests are much wider than this and include placing Sri Lanka into India's sphere of international influence. Indian investments in Africa are also driven by long-term strategic interests, and began with the first Indian Prime Minister Jawaharlal Nehru, who refused to line up with the United States or Russia during the Cold War and became a leader of the global non-aligned movement in the 1950s and 1960s. Today India retains a strong interest in the economics and politics of the African subcontinent—Indian soldiers are involved in peacekeeping activities in Africa (Harsch 2004) and India has persuaded the Sudanese government to support its bid to be an observer at various international Islamic conferences (Malhotra 2003).

Table 4: OVL's oil and natural gas investments globally in 2002

Country/nature of Indian interest O—oil; NG—natural gas	Total value of investment by OVL	Expected return to India	Total estimated reserves
Sudan/O	Greater Nile Oil Project, 25% stake or US$750 million	12 million tons per annum, currently of which 3 million tons per annum to India	150 million tons
Sudan pipeline project	1st ONGC foreign engineering project		
Sudan	24% share in Blocks 5A and 5B		Production to begin in 2006–07
Vietnam: green fields/NG	Production-sharing contract Rs9 billion = 45% share ONGC; partners are BP and Petro Vietnam	Total output 7.5 million cubic metres gas	Commenced January 2003
Sakhalin	Production-sharing contract 20%—US$2.77 billion Largest foreign contract in Russia; largest foreign investment by India	2.5 million tons of oil per annum in three years plus gas	Production commencement 2005–06
Burma	Shwe gas field Block A1 20% share	Total reserves of 4–6 trillion cubic feet gas	
Iraq	Exploration contract 100%		
Libya	Exploration contract 49%		
Iran	Exploration contract 40%		
Syria	Exploration contract 60%		
Other oil fields being considered include fields in Indonesia, United Arab Emirates, Nepal, Venezuela, Algeria			

Source: The data in this table were collated from Menon (2002); ONGC (2005); Muni & Pant (2005:26 fig 1).

Case study two: Reliance Industries—India's largest private sector company

The second case study in this chapter focuses on India's largest private sector business house, which has started to challenge the old dominance of public sector giants such as ONGC. The recent discovery by Reliance Industries, for example, of a major gas basin in the Krishna–Godavari basin is said to contain reserves that are 40 times larger than those of Bombay High, which is controlled by ONGC (Balse 2002). The story of how Reliance Industries rose so rapidly to challenge ONGC is the focus of this section.

The traditional Indian business character of Reliance Industries

Reliance Industries is a diversified conglomerate, which, much like South Korea's chaebol, produces a wide range of products including textiles, petrochemicals, oil/gas and, most recently, telecommunications services. By the end of 2004 Reliance Industries' profit levels exceeded US$1 billion, making it one of the largest of the top 150 global firms. It is the first Indian firm to reach this size and profitability. In recent years, the growth indicators for Reliance Industries have been a microcosm of India's general economic growth: for example, between 2000 and 2004 net sales grew by 30.52%, operating profits by 26.32% and exports by 61.39% (II 2004:6).

Despite its modest beginnings, Reliance Industries was well positioned to emerge as India's most modern company because its founder, Dhirubhai Ambani, started the business by focusing on synthetic fibres at a time when Indian textile manufacturers were preoccupied with natural cottons. Synthetic fibres took Ambani into the petrochemicals sector and eventually into oil and gas exploration, the construction of a cracker and refinery, and ultimately into offshore investments in Europe, Yemen and elsewhere. The Ambani story provides almost a classic textbook case study of how to develop backward and forward economic linkages. By 2001 Dhirubhai Ambani's family wealth of US$7.4 billion made him the third-richest Indian globally (Dhawade 2001). In the following year, just before his death in mid-2002, Ambani was listed by Forbes as the 138th-richest billionaire of 500 in the world, with a total personal value of US$2.9 billion (Rediff 2002a). The Reliance Industries story is a remarkable tale of an economic transition that captures India's transformation from being a 'licence permit Raj' before 1991 to an increasingly market-oriented, private sector economy after that date. But, as noted below, the meteoric rise of Reliance Industries could not have been achieved without considerable support from the Indian government—especially Congress Party governments.

Contrary to popular rumour, Dhirubhai Ambani (1932–2002) was not poor or illiterate but was, rather, the son of a Gujarati schoolmaster. He completed higher secondary school and went to Aden, as many other traditional Indian entrepreneurs had done in the past to learn about international trade. His first job there was as a petrol pump attendant. When he returned to Bombay in 1957 he had only Rs50,000 to invest in his first trading/export company, a textile firm called the Reliance Commercial Corporation (Stewart 2004; Rediff 2002c). Eight years later, the Reliance Textiles Industries Pte Ltd was established to begin production of the textiles in which his company traded. In 1973 he incorporated his first company in Karnataka under the name of Mynylon (Stewart 2004). This was followed in 1977 by merging Mynylon and Reliance Industries and trading under a single name, namely Reliance Textile Industries Ltd (Stewart 2004). The rapid growth of Reliance Industries in the 1970s and 1980s was closely linked to state patronage and the support of the Indian Congress Party, as was typical of the growth of other large firms during the 'license permit Raj' era.

A traditional feature of Reliance Industries was that it was run like a family business, despite its enormous size and the fact that Dhirubhai Ambani only had two sons. Until late 2004 Anil and Mukesh Ambani had a famed relationship, which appeared to represent the ideal type of sibling business. The two brothers divided their respective skills and roles amicably, with Mukesh being regarded as the hard-headed investment brain and Anil as the friendly public relations expert. There seemed to be little of the rivalry and division that had befallen other large Indian firms based on family participation and capital pooling. In November 2004 this all changed when the two brothers had a massive and highly public falling out, a mere two years after their father's death. In June 2005, the brothers divided Reliance Industries after their mother stepped into the fray to prevent things from turning ugly. The division cuts across the different interests that the Reliance firm had in India's energy sector;

The petrochemicals and oil/gas sector is now controlled by Mukesh Ambani while Reliance Energy is in the hands of Anil Ambani. Sibling rivalry was also reflected in the different political loyalties that the two brothers had: Mukesh has always supported the family's traditional favourite, the Congress Party, but Anil threw in his lot with the Samajwadi Party and in 2004 entered the upper house of the Indian Parliament (the Rajya Sabha) as one of its representatives (Bobb & Bhupta 2004:41).

These political connections have always allowed Reliance Industries to harvest significant state patronage to support its growth and to do so by minimising its exposure to market risks. Again, the analogy with the South Korean chaebol is striking. Amongst the support Reliance Industries received from the state are the following: access to concessional institutional finance from public sector banks and long-term lending and investment institutions; tight controls on the growth and output of public sector petroleum companies to ensure the success of its Jamnagar refinery; restricted funding to competitor companies such as Essar; a refusal to allow cheap imports by Royal Dutch Shell; and continuous revision of investment norms in refineries by public and private sector companies in order to privilege the position of Reliance Industries (for example, during the 1980s and 1990s the Petroleum Ministry issued new guidelines proscribing the import of cheap 'second-hand refineries', a decision of enormous benefit to Reliance Industries).

Another traditional aspect of Reliance Industries is the relatively small public shareholder base on which it is built. According to one report, in August 2004, only 13.75% of the company's shares are owned by the Indian public; the rest are owned by companies, joint ventures, foreign investors, financial institutions and non-resident Indians (II 2004:1). This is indeed a surprising statistic, given that one of the most innovative aspects of Ambani's empire building was his capacity to utilise the Indian share markets as no other firm had done. Ambani's financial entrepreneurship took him into rural India, where small investors were able to buy Reliance Industries shares via the local post offices. The result was that by the 1990s the annual general meetings of Reliance Industries were so large that the Bombay football stadium had to be hired in order to seat the attendees (McDonald 2002). By 1999 Reliance Industries had about five million shareholders, making it one of the largest shareholder gatherings in the world (Rediff 2002c). Despite this, the capital value of the shareholder base by the Indian public has remained quite small. Ambani's financial flair took Reliance Industries into international financial markets when the company floated shares on the New York Stock Exchange in 1992.

Taken together—the origins of Reliance Industries, its historical links with the Congress Party, its dependence on family control and the small public shareholder base—the business house of Reliance Industries shares more in common with other large, traditional family business of India rather than with the new kinds of companies that have emerged since the 1980s. The growth of the Indian middle class during the 1970s and 1980s saw the rise of new firms based on new sources of wealth and skills, as Khanna (1987) has argued. This new wealth, much of it driven by the successes of India's Green Revolution, facilitated investment in business by professionals, retired army personnel, bureaucrats frustrated by the failure of the civil service to recognise their entrepreneurial skills, non-resident Indians, newly rich peasants and others. In particular, the new technology companies, like Hindustan Computers Limited, were founded as a result of the common professional interests of the partners rather than family connections (Khanna 1987:57). The same is true today of the large information technology-servicing giants such as Infosys. In origin and function, Reliance Industries differed from all of these—its growth path was based on Indian textiles and in this regard alone it is not merely a typical example of early Indian industrial entrepreneurship but also a good example of early modern Asian entrepreneurship during colonial times (see Chapter one). The important difference was the focus of Reliance Industries on synthetic fibres and textiles, an intermediate industrial product that had the potential to link Reliance Industries directly to India's petroleum sector.

The other characteristic that marks out the Ambani family from other large, traditional firms was its willingness to move into the opportunities thrown up by the liberalisation of the Indian economy after 1991, in particular the deregulation of oil and gas exploration, extraction, processing and distribution. Having built up a large asset base in synthetic and natural textiles, Reliance Industries was in a position to make the enormous capital investment needed in these heavy industries—by 2002, for example, the company had total assets worth Rs550 billion and net profits of Rs46 billion (Rediff 2002b:2).

The deregulation of the Indian oil industry has been a slow process, but the Ambani approach has been distinguished by the family's readiness to leap into the market whenever an opportunity presented itself. Deregulation of oil refining began in 1999, but it took another four years to deregulate the marketing of oil in 2003. By 2004 Reliance Industries, together with foreign multinational competitors, was given a licence to sell petroleum products (BL 2002; Equityequation 2002). In a strange way, the Reliance Industries enterprise had returned to the very origins of Dhirubhai Ambani's first insight into the world of business when he worked petrol pumps in Aden.

Conclusion

A close examination of the emergence of India as an economic power reminds us of the contradictions inherent in that development. State sector public enterprises have been in serious difficulties for a long time, yet ONGC stands out as an impressive financial and managerial success long before the liberalisation of the Indian economy was announced in 1991. That liberalisation process has been fraught with complexities and, despite encouragement to the private sector, ONGC continues to dominate the Indian oil industry. At the same time, India's private sector had been growing vigorously long before 1991. The example of Reliance Industries was cited here because its growth both precedes and post-dates liberalisation. Moreover, the growth of India's most successful private firm depended heavily on state patronage before and after 1991. In other words, the lines that divide the public and private sectors in India are not as sharply drawn as many pro-market liberalisers seem to think; nor does 1991 represent such a sharp discontinuity in Indian economic development.

Although not discussed in this chapter, a critical fillip to India's long-term growth was the Green Revolution, which provided India with a reliable food base and also generated rural wealth in states such as Punjab and Haryana, which became the surplus food-producing states. The White Revolution (the name given to India's new milk and dairy sector) in Rajasthan, Maharashtra and elsewhere builds on that success. And a new red wine revolution is emerging in western India, with the appearance of many vineyards that cater to the changing palates of modernising Indians. To some extent, the growth of the agricultural sector in the early 2000s reflects these successes and the emergence of agri-industries. New technology and marketing institutions in rural India have contributed also to the expansion and diversification of the Indian middle classes. It is this group in particular that has pulled the Indian economy into the orbit of global business by its wealth, its professionalism and its international labour mobility.

But despite all these positive developments, many have missed out on rural and urban prosperity. Current concerns about a different kind of 'Red Revolution' in the backward rural provinces of Bihar, Madhya Pradesh and eastern Uttar Pradesh remind us that India's failure to address persistent mass poverty (which affects about 30% of the total population) could threaten current and projected optimism. My own assessment is that despite fears of a Maoist insurgency spreading across central and eastern India and linking up with left-wing terrorism in Bangladesh and Nepal, the Indian economy will continue to grow and the poverty of one in three Indians will be tolerated in the same way that the United States, the world's most powerful and successful economy, still tolerates the mass poverty of poor whites and blacks (Vicziany 2005a:230–1). Even India's fastest-growing industry, the information technology sector, cannot absorb the surplus labour that has accumulated in recent years, let alone the displaced labour of the future (Vicziany 2005b:154–165).

But one thing unites the Indian rich and poor and that is the emerging energy crisis. Nobody can do without energy any more than they can do without water. To address this problem and ensure ongoing economic growth, Indian responses will need to be placed into the context of the emerging security architecture of the Asian region. Given the rise of China, the re-emergence of Japan, the re-engagement of the United States with South Asia, sanctions by the United States against oil- and gas-rich Iran, and the instability of Iraq, Afghanistan and Pakistan, India's energy strategies will continue to be driven by realist paradigms, which will require the diversification of energy supplies. Public sector enterprises, such as ONGC, will continue therefore to play a major role in India's economic growth, regardless of the dynamism of the private sector. At the same time, a dynamic private sector will provide a check against state inefficiency; if the public sector oil companies fail to meet the national needs identified by government, the speed of privatisation can always be accelerated.

Notes

1. I am grateful to Kannan Srinivasan, who has reported on the Indian energy sector for some 20 years, for his comments on this chapter.
2. For some exceptions, see the collection of essays in Vicziany 1993.
3. Despite rapid growth in India and China, demand for energy by the United States remains the highest in the world, putting vast pressure on global resources and also on its foreign economic and defence policies. In particular, as Morse and Richard note, imports of oil will continue to grow, making the United States 'the single most important force in the oil market' (Morse and Richard 2002:16–31).
4. Gobar gas is methane gas that is generated by a process of anaerobic combustion, in which cow dung and water are mixed and kept in an airtight container from which the gas and residual sludge is drained for usage in nearby facilities. In 1978 Vicziany visited a large Sikh temple on the outskirts of Agra, where lighting and cooking fuel was generated by this process; the effluent supplied the temple vegetable gardens with organic, liquid fertiliser.
5. Table 2 underestimates the energy problems of India because data about biomass as a source of fuel has not been included. Biomass, in particular the burning of wood for fuel, constitutes the most important energy source for rural families, who account for some 70% of all households.
6. Attempts to modernise the extraction of Indian coal have not been very successful despite the model provided by the White Industries project in Piparwar: see Vicziany 1998: 484–533.
7. I am grateful to Kannan Srinivasan for checking this information in Mumbai, 2006.
8. I am grateful to Kannan Srinivasan for these details. Forbes.com (2005), 'India Reliance group's Ambani brothers reach deal on dividing business empire', 19 June http://www.forbes.com/finance/feeds/afx/2005/06/19/afx2099903.html
9. The Green Revolution succeeded in massively increasing Indian grain yields as a result of the use of high yielding variety seeds, fertilisers, weedicides, pesticides and irrigation.

chapter six

Vietnam: the search for a socialist market economy

Keith Trace

Vietnam's post-colonial economic revival has lagged behind the rest of Asia—for instance, decolonisation occurred almost three decades after Indian independence. This is hardly surprising. Vietnam had been at war for most of that time, and the opportunities for indigenous entrepreneurial growth were seriously constrained. No other former colony in Asia had suffered as much devastation of people and resources:

> in the South, 9,000 out of 15,000 hamlets, 25 million acres of farmland, 12 million acres of forest were destroyed, and 1.5 million farm animals had been killed; there were an estimated 200,000 prostitutes, 879,000 orphans, 181,000 disabled people, and 1 million widows... (Young 1991:302).

As a consequence, the development of the Vietnamese economy has been slow and difficult. Not only had the infrastructure of Vietnam been compromised, so had its next generation of children: bombing campaigns using Agent Orange resulted in a plague of birth defects.[1] Following the reunification of Vietnam in 1976, the government of the new Socialist Republic of Vietnam imposed its Soviet-style central planning system on the South.[2] With hindsight, the post-1976 planning system performed poorly, leading to a series of economic crises in the late 1970s and early 1980s. In turn, these crises forced the government to adopt a more pragmatic approach to economic policy. However, the tentative reforms of the central planning model tended to throw up problems in unreformed areas of the economy. By the mid-1980s it had become apparent that more thoroughgoing reform was necessary if Vietnam was to emulate the success of its Southeast Asian neighbours.

A policy of renovation (*Doi Moi*) was formally adopted at the Sixth Party Congress in December 1986. While the 1986 reforms were limited in scope, and elements of the old system—notably the setting of physical production targets—remained in place, the creation of a more permissive economic environment, coupled with the removal of internal trade barriers, was sufficient to encourage economic growth. However, Vietnam suffered a series of reverses in 1988. Bad weather and poor economic management led to famine in the North, while the economy experienced a substantial trade deficit and inflation rate of over 300%.

These difficulties strengthened the resolve to reform, and a series of dramatic changes was introduced in March 1989. The budget deficit was brought under control. Restraints on domestic and international trade were lifted. The banking system was reformed and a central bank—the State Bank of Vietnam—was set up to oversee the monetary sector. The Vietnamese currency, the dōng, was devalued sharply, bringing the official rate closer to the market rate. Most subsidies to state enterprises were abolished and firms were given the freedom to set prices for their products. Households rather than communes were to form the basic unit of production in agriculture. By 1992 the Vietnamese economy had made a substantial transition towards a market economy.

As the World Bank (2001b) has noted, the *Doi Moi* and succeeding reforms were extraordinarily effective in galvanising the energy of millions of Vietnamese citizens, who diversified and expanded production rapidly, setting up many micro-household enterprises, as well as private small and medium-sized enterprises (SMEs). Foreign firms were encouraged to invest in majority-owned joint ventures or in wholly foreign-owned enterprises. The immediate effects were striking. GDP rose by 8% in 1989, while agricultural output rose by 7.5%. Within a few years the country switched from being a major rice importer to being the world's third-largest exporter. The annual rate of inflation fell from 308% in 1988 to 35% in 1989. The growth spurt of the early 1990s was remarkable in that it created opportunities for many of Vietnam's poor.

The reform program was effectively put on hold for a brief period in the mid-1990s. Conservative forces within the Communist Party voiced concerns that the speed of change towards a market economy threatened to end the Party's monopoly of political power, while other Party members were concerned that Western influences were leading to a breakdown of social cohesion, especially in Ho Chi Minh City. Decisions taken at the Eighth Party Congress (EIU 2000:23) lowered the target rate of economic growth, forbade Party members to engage in small, household businesses (but did not prevent them from engaging in 'private economic activities') and rejected the privatisation program envisaged by reformers (while expanding the 'pilot' program of equitisation). The ruling troika—Du Muoi, Le Duc Anh and Vo Van Kiet—were re-elected. In effect, reform was temporarily put into the 'too hard' basket, awaiting the retirement of the older generation, which had led the country in the war of national liberation.

In the late 1990s the main emphasis was on stabilising the economy, with the leadership favouring incremental rather than progressive policies. During the East Asian recession (1997–99), the government of Vietnam adopted a cautious economic stance, giving priority to the attainment of macro-economic stability rather than taking risks in order to achieve higher rates of growth. This approach proved successful. Contrary to fears expressed in late 1998, Vietnam avoided the serious balance of payments, fiscal and banking crises that affected some of its neighbouring countries. By 2002 remarkable progress had been made in macro-economic management. Vietnam had also made some progress in structural reform, although the structural indicators remained far from ideal.

The World Bank has argued that, prior to the Asian Financial crisis (1997–99), Vietnam's main strengths lay in macro-economic management and in policies for social inclusion. In both respects, Vietnam vastly outperformed the average low-income country. Its indicators actually were similar to those of the most successful 20% of countries in this group (WB 2002). According to the World Bank, Vietnam's main weaknesses lay in its structural policies and governance, in which its performance was no better than the average low-income country.

The creation of a market economy with a socialist orientation

Under the *Doi Moi* reforms, Vietnam began the transition from a centrally planned economy to a market-oriented economy based on price signals. While the goals and objectives of the two economic systems are broadly similar, the strategies for achieving those goals differ markedly.

Under central planning, the planners attempt to control the economy by setting objectives, production targets and prices for every sector. The information requirements for such planning are immense, and experience in many countries suggests that the process usually fails to deliver the desired outcomes. In contrast, the government of a market-based economy does not allocate resources according to predetermined production plans and targets. Instead, market forces determine what goods and services are produced, while the interaction of supply and demand determines prices for the majority of goods and services. The role of government is to create a framework within which economic activity can take place. It does so by implementing laws and introducing appropriate institutional structures, including pro-competition economic regulation.

In the period since the 1992 constitution was adopted by the National Assembly, far-reaching institutional reforms have been enacted and an impressive legal edifice covering many aspects of public and private rights has been created.

However, the institutional and legal changes have significant shortcomings and there is a danger that a renewed expansion of economic activity may outpace the legal and institutional framework.

Since the institutional and legal structures appropriate for a market economy are very different from those that are required by a centrally planned economy, old rules and institutions need to be replaced with a set of new ones. Institutions critical to the smooth functioning of a market economy include:

- a legal and juridical system that is capable of protecting property rights and ensuring contract enforcement;
- an independent judiciary and legal transparency;
- accounting and legal services that reliably scrutinise corporate performance; and
- a regulatory framework that enables a market economy to function efficiently, affording protection for consumers.

A comprehensive review of Vietnam's legal system (usually referred to as the Legal Needs Assessment) was conducted in 2001–02. The assessment identified five key areas requiring action: legislative and law-making reform; judicial reform; effective and efficient implementation of the existing law; improvement of legal information and transparency; and legal education and training. The key principles underlying the assessment (and enshrined in the constitution) in December 2001 are that state institutions and bureaucrats should be permitted to do only what is specifically permitted by the law, while citizens should be able to engage in any conduct that is not explicitly prohibited.[3] Many of the reforms identified by the assessment, such as the introduction of a competition law and the revisions of the bankruptcy law, are already on the legislative agenda.

Vietnam's industrial structure and enterprise reform

State-owned enterprises

During the pre-1986 period, state-owned enterprises (SOEs) dominated Vietnam's industrial scene. With the exception of petty trading, private ownership of productive facilities was forbidden prior to the reforms of the late 1980s and 1990s. The state-owned industrial sector includes enterprises owned and operated by the central government, as well as locally owned and managed state enterprises, run by People's Committees, at provincial, district or ward levels. In 1990 there were approximately 12,000 SOEs, of which about 3,000 large- and medium-scale enterprises were owned and controlled by the central government, and 9,000 medium- and small-scale enterprises were owned and controlled by provincial and local governments.

Production targets set for SOEs were not based on the perceived needs of the market, as determined by observed demand, but on detailed plans formulated by bureaucrats in the state planning commission. The state supplied raw materials, met the firms' salary bills, set output quotas and marketed the finished products. In theory, at least, managerial responsibility was limited to the production processes within the enterprises.[4] The efficiency of most SOEs was generally acknowledged to be low. Many SOEs operated unprofitably and the sector consumed an unduly large portion of investment.[5] As a result, the reform of SOEs came to be regarded as an essential element of the overall reform agenda.

Under the comprehensive reform program adopted in 1989, the autonomy of SOE management was broadened considerably. Managers were authorised to adjust product mix; procure inputs and market outputs; introduce new production technology; borrow funds; invest resources generated by the enterprise; acquire assets; lease and divest assets; set wages, salaries and benefits subject to the agreement of the Ministry of Labour; hire and fire employees; and allocate after-tax profits.

Recognising that the reform of the state enterprise sector was fundamental if the economy was to be transformed into a market system and also that SOE reform was vital if macro-economic stability was to be maintained, the government set out to restructure government-owned firms. By the end of 1993 the number of SOEs had been reduced to around 7,000. Over 2,000 SOEs, most of which were locally controlled, had been liquidated, while a further 3,000 SOEs had been merged with other government-owned enterprises. The reduction in the number of SOEs was achieved by eliminating operating subsidies, subjecting SOEs to market forces in a liberalised and increasingly competitive economy, and permitting the liquidation of unprofitable enterprises. The World Bank (1994:38) noted that the adverse social effects stemming from mergers and liquidations were minimised by the existence of an adequate social safety net and by the expanding opportunities for employment in the non-state sector.

The post-1992 approach to SOE reform in Vietnam differs from that in other Southeast Asian countries. The main instrument, introduced in 1992, is equitisation, a form of privatisation in which all or some of the state's interest in an enterprise is sold in the form of shares. Directors and employees are given preferential treatment in the allocation of these shares. No individual may purchase more than 30% of the equity of a given company.

Other mechanisms have also been used to restructure the state sector. Small SOEs have been sold, leased or assigned to their workers at a negotiated price. Potentially viable enterprises have been merged into larger enterprises to gain economies of scale, while non-viable enterprises have been liquidated.

The speed of the industrial enterprise reform program has waxed and waned over time. The number of SOEs was reduced from over 12,000 in 1990 to about 6,300 in 1992, mainly as a result of the liquidation of locally owned enterprises. Between 1993 and 1997 the reform program stalled, with few SOEs equitised, merged or otherwise disposed of. Only 17 firms had been equitised by December 1997. From 1997 onwards, as the equitisation mechanism introduced in 1992 gained momentum, the process gathered strength, with 363 firms being equitised between 1997 and 2000. However, resistance to equitisation by party leaders, managers and employees of SOEs remains strong. The main problem is that most SOEs have substantial outstanding debt and so are unattractive to investors.

How well have the equitised enterprises performed? Some enterprises have been outside the state sector long enough to assess their performances. A recent study by the Vietnamese Central Institute of Management examined the performance of 422 enterprises equitised prior to 2001. The study found that sales in such companies were growing at almost 20% a year, employment at 4%, wages at 12% and assets at 21%. Respondents considered that firm performance had improved substantially since equitisation (cited in WB 2002:25).[6] The World Bank (2002) argues that the findings are more positive than anticipated, but notes that this may be due to the fact that the best-performing enterprises were the first to be equitised.

The private sector

The private (non-state) sector consists of informal family businesses (private households), co-operatives and private firms. Small family enterprises began to appear in Vietnam in the late 1970s, especially in Ho Chi Minh City. The growth of the formal private sector was made possible by the *Doi Moi* reforms. Under the December 1990 *Law on Private Enterprises* and *Law on Companies*, Vietnamese were allowed to own private companies for the first time since 1975. The number of private companies grew rapidly in the 1990s. In 1991 there were 450 private firms, employing 21,000 workers. By 1995, 12,500 firms had registered with the government. Roughly half of these firms were located in Ho Chi Minh City.

A further significant shift in policy favouring the private sector occurred with the enactment of the *Enterprise Law (2000)* and the formal endorsement of the private sector following the Fifth Plenum of the Ninth Party Congress (March 2002). Since the enactment of the law, the growth in the number of registered private enterprises and the output of the private sector has been spectacular. Between January 2000 and October 2002, almost 50,000 new enterprises were registered, the vast majority of which are fully privately owned. Three-quarters of all enterprises registered in Vietnam in 2002 had been set up between 2000 and 2002. The industrial output of the private sector grew by almost 19% in 2001, compared to a growth of 13% in the state sector.

Several features of private sector growth are worth noting.

- First, despite rapid growth, less than half of manufacturing GDP is produced by private firms, with domestic private enterprises dominating the sector. The approximately 600,000 micro-enterprises in manufacturing, together with the private SMEs, account for 28% of manufacturing GDP.

- Second, the domestic private sector is by far the most labour intensive. In 2001 household enterprises and SMEs employed more than 64% of industrial workers, compared with the 24% of industrial workers employed by SOEs.

- Third, the largest private SMEs in manufacturing are highly export-oriented. There are approximately 450 private manufacturers that each have more than 100 workers and that operate mainly in labour-intensive sectors like garments, footwear, plastic products and seafood. On average these SMEs export around three-quarters of their production.

- Fourth, foreign-owned enterprises accounted for a fifth of manufacturing output in 1991. Most foreign investment is in the production of import-competing goods in capital-intensive sectors.

The playing field in Vietnam remains tilted in favour of public sector enterprises. The government appears determined to ensure that SOEs remain dominant in a number of industrial sectors, including the production of machinery for agriculture, forestry and fisheries and the production of electronic equipment, information technology, cement, various consumer goods and processed foodstuffs. Private firms face discrimination in factor markets. For example, private firms lacking land-use rights or other forms of collateral have to rely more heavily than SOEs on extended families or personal connections to access capital. In general, as discussed further below, the banking sector's loan policies are skewed towards SOEs.

Factor markets

By the mid-1990s the transition from a centrally planned economy to a market economy was well advanced in product markets. However, market forces played a less-important role in the factor markets, especially in the market for land.

The labour market

A large, rapidly growing, relatively well-trained yet inexpensive labour force is one of Vietnam's main competitive strengths. Vietnam's population was approximately 80 million in 2002, and the country had an estimated labour force of 38 million. The annual rate of growth of the labour force is around 1.9%. Although access to higher education has been limited, the introduction of near-universal primary education has led to high literacy rates.[7] Approximately 16% of Vietnam's labour force is considered to be trained or skilled. The upgrading of labour force skills is a priority concern of government.

The *Labour Code (1994 as amended)* sets out the rights and obligations of employers and employees. It covers such areas as working hours, labour agreements, payment of social insurance, the laws relating to overtime work, strikes and termination of employment contracts. In general the law provides for an eight-hour working day and a 48-hour working week. An employer and employee may agree that overtime be worked, but this must not exceed 200 hours a year. With effect from October 1999, government offices, administrative agencies and sociopolitical organisations implemented a 40-hour working week. The Labour Code applies not only to Vietnamese working for domestic firms, but to Vietnamese citizens working for foreign-owned enterprises and to foreigners working for Vietnamese enterprises and organisations.

Banking and the capital market

The financial sector in Vietnam comprises state-owned banks, joint-stock or shareholding banks, credit co-operatives and finance companies. In 2003 there were six state-owned banks (five commercial banks plus the Bank for the Poor), 50 joint-stock banks and 29 licensed foreign banks, including joint-venture banks and branches and representative offices of foreign banks.

Since the late 1980s, major changes have occurred in the structure, operations and regulation of the Vietnamese banking sector. The *Law on Credit Organisations*, which came into force on 1 October 1998, defines a wide range of products that can be offered by banks, ranging from traditional financial products to fund management and insurance services. The new law encouraged entry to the industry. While the four largest state-owned commercial banks still account for over 70% of the total assets in the system, their operations are now complemented by joint-stock and joint-venture banks. Also, security market regulations permit domestic banks to participate in the securities market. The World Bank has noted that the large state-owned commercial banks have gradually evolved from specialist policy lending vehicles to more commercially oriented financial intermediaries. This trend accelerated in 2001 and 2002 (WB 2002).

In 1998 the government outlined a comprehensive reform and restructuring program intended to improve the efficiency of the commercial banking system. The program envisaged:

- the restructuring of joint-stock banks through mergers and closures, with the aim of reducing the number of joint-stock banks by 50%;
- transforming state-owned commercial banks into independent businesses;
- improving and strengthening the supervision and inspection of commercial banks and creating a 'level playing field'; and
- establishing bank-based asset-management corporations as a tool for resolving problems stemming from non-performing loans.

Despite reform and partial deregulation of financial and banking services, a truly 'level playing field' has yet to be achieved. For example, barriers to entry to the banking industry remain high, with the State Bank of Vietnam tightly controlling the granting of banking licences. The banking sector remains focused on providing the credit requirements of SOEs. As of September 2002, loans to SOEs constituted 50% of the loan portfolio of state-owned commercial banks (WB 2002:27). In general, joint-stock banks cater for the needs of privately owned firms, while foreign banks provide financial services to multinational corporations operating in Vietnam.

The Economist Intelligence Unit (2000:26) has noted that Vietnam's banking system remains fragile. The deposit base of the system is small (equivalent to 20% of gross national product), the four large state-owned commercial banks have a large number of non-performing loans (many associated with SOEs) and the regulatory structure remains weak.

Creating a market for land

Land reform is an integral part of Vietnam's economic reform process. Commencing in the 1980s, the reform of rural land holdings contributed to the sustained growth of the rural economy, which has been a marked feature of the period since the *Doi Moi* reforms. Vietnam's land is considered to be the property of the people, and is managed by the state. Since 1993 the right to use land has been assigned to individuals and firms by means of land-use certificates, which allow the holder long-term use of designated land. The holder of a land-use certificate has conditional rights to transfer, exchange, lease, inherit (individuals only) and mortgage the land-use right. The World Bank regards the allocation and distribution of land-use certificates to most agricultural land as one of Vietnam's major achievements and as the basis for a major increase in agricultural production (WB 2002:41). Land-use rights in the form of certificates that can be traded or mortgaged represent a major step towards an efficient property market. They offer holders secure property rights and can be used as collateral.

The creation of land-use rights created large transitory economic rents. Economic rent is normally defined as that portion of earnings in excess of the minimum amount needed to attract a worker to accept a particular job or a firm to enter a particular industry. Economic rent typically arises in situations of scarcity, whether that scarcity is natural or artificial. In the case of land, economic rents arose because of the arbitrary way in which land-use rights were awarded. Economic rent arose either when land-use rights were awarded to individuals, who could then build houses for their own use or sell the rights to do so, or when land-use rights were given to SOEs, which could use the rights as their share of the capital in joint ventures with foreign investors.

Vietnam's land and property markets remain relatively underdeveloped. Many Vietnamese citizens have yet to secure land-use certificates or tenure contracts. As late as 2002, only 18% of households in urban areas and 50% of households in upland areas held valid land-use certificates (WB 2002:42).[8] Although the number of land transactions has increased significantly over the past decade, commentators agree that the majority of transactions—perhaps 70–85% in urban areas—are informal. While land-use rights may be used as collateral to obtain loans, it has been estimated that 85% of house purchases are financed by family savings.

The market for land, especially in urban areas, is highly distorted, limiting ownership options for the poor. The Co-operation Program on Land Administration Reform has estimated that the 2001 land price in prime city-centre locations was about US$4,000 per square metre, while the price of land one kilometre from the centre of the cities averaged almost US$2,500 (cited in WB 2002). According to the World Bank estimates, the (2002) price of land on the edge of Hanoi and Ho Chi Minh City was close to US$450 per square metre, higher than the country's average annual per capita income.

Foreign investors may acquire land either by leasing it from the state for the duration of a project or by way of a Vietnamese partner in a joint venture or business co-operation contract leasing the land from the state and contributing the value of the land-use rights to the project. In contributing the land, the Vietnamese partner is effectively capitalising the value of future rental payments. The maximum lease period is generally 50 years, although in special cases this term may be extended to 70 years. The foreign investor may only use the land for the designated purpose but can mortgage the land-use rights to banks operating in Vietnam.

In general, the evidence suggests that the market for land is highly distorted. Vietnam lacks an efficient market for one of the key factors of production.

Technology transfer

Intellectual property rights falling within defined categories—inventions, utility solutions, industrial designs, trade marks and appellations of origin—are accorded legal protection in Vietnam. In general, in awarding rights relating to intellectual property, Vietnam adopts similar criteria to those adopted in developed economies. For example, to be patentable, an invention must have worldwide novelty, contain an inventive step and have practical applicability. Protection of a trade mark may be obtained either by registration in Vietnam or through the international convention known as the Madrid Agreement. If the latter course is adopted, the trade mark must still pass the same substantive examination in Vietnam.

The Civil Code specifies the types of written works, artistic works and performances that are protected by copyright. Vietnam is not a member of the Berne Convention, so foreign authors may only benefit from copyright if their works are created in Vietnam or if their works are first published in Vietnam.[9]

Until comparatively recently, implementation of these policies has been relatively lax. Unauthorised copies of consumer products have been freely available in the shops and markets of Ho Chi Minh City and Hanoi, leading to frequent complaints from Western firms. Over time the policing of trade marks and industrial designs appears to be tightening.

There are three mechanisms by which foreign technology may be transferred to Vietnam. The technology may:
- form part of the capital contributed by a foreign investor to a joint-venture enterprise or a business co-operation contract;

- be sold to a Vietnamese firm, including an enterprise set up under the laws on foreign investment; and
- be licensed to a Vietnamese firm.

Vietnamese law requires that technology transfer takes place on the basis of a written contract detailing the object of the transfer, price and terms of payment, details of the transfer, duration and timing of the contract, undertakings made by the parties to the contract, and provision for training and dispute resolution. The Ministry of Science, Technology and the Environment is responsible for approving contracts relating to technology transfer (see Freehill, Hollingdale & Page 2002:19–20).

Foreign investment

Prior to the *Doi Moi* reforms, foreign direct investment was virtually unknown in Vietnam. Not only did the government adopt an extremely cautious stance towards foreign direct investment, but foreign investors regarded such investments as highly risky.

The *Law on Foreign Investment 1987* (amended in 1992, 1994, 1996 and 2000) opened the door to a rapid influx of foreign capital. Between 1990 and 1995 the annual inflow of foreign capital grew from US$600 million to US$3 billion, with the result that cumulative registered investment grew ten-fold from US$800 million to US$8 billion. Alternatively, the growth in foreign investment can be measured by the number of investment projects. Since the passing of the Law on Foreign Investment, there have been 3,770 licensed foreign investment projects, with more that US$41 billion registered capital. Leaving aside projects that have expired or been withdrawn, 3,047 active licensed projects, with total registered capital of US$38.9 billion, existed in 2003.[10]

Three main forms of investment are allowed under the Law on Foreign Investment: joint ventures, wholly foreign-owned enterprises and business co-operation contracts.

Joint ventures: under Vietnamese law a joint-venture enterprise is a legal entity (with limited liability) established by a joint-venture contract between one or more Vietnamese partners and one or more foreign partners. The foreign partners in a joint venture are required to contribute at least 30% of the venture's legal capital.[11] There is no ceiling for the foreign capital contribution, although the Vietnamese partners generally contribute at least 30% of the legal capital, often in the form of land-use rights. Profits and risks are distributed among the partners in proportion to their legal capital contributions.

Wholly foreign-owned enterprises: under Vietnamese law, a 100% foreign-owned enterprise is a legal entity set up by one or more foreign investors, with limited liability separate from that of its parent company. As in the case of joint ventures, the legal capital of a wholly foreign-owned enterprise must be at least equal to 30% of the total investment capital. The investors can adopt any form of control and management consistent with the business charter approved by the Investment Licence Authority at the issue of the investment licence.

Business co-operation contracts: a business co-operation contract is an agreement between one or more foreign investors and one or more Vietnamese partners to co-operate in operating defined business activities. This form of investment does not imply the formation of a new legal entity. The parties involved are free to decide on the nature and limits of their co-operative agreement.

Build – Operate – Transfer contracts were approved under the amended *Law on Foreign Investment 1992*, with the Build–Transfer and Build – Transfer – Operate forms being added in 1996. Under the Build – Operate – Transfer form, the investor constructs a plant or facility and operates it for a specified period, after which the facility is transferred to the state without compensation. Under the Build – Transfer – Operate form, title is transferred to the state immediately on completion of construction, but the state allows the investor to operate the facility for an agreed period of time to enable the investor to recover its capital. Under the Build–Transfer form, ownership of the facility is transferred to the state on completion of construction and the state compensates the investor, usually by granting the investor land-use rights or the right to construct and/or operate another facility (MPI/PC 2003:33).

Foreign trade

Over the past 15 years Vietnam has substantially liberalised foreign trade. Tariffs have been reduced, a large number of quantitative restrictions have been abolished and the foreign-exchange rate regime has been liberalised. In 2006 Vietnam remained committed to continued trade reform under the auspices of the ASEAN Free Trade Area (AFTA), the Asia–Pacific Economic Cooperation and various bilateral trade agreements, although the pace of reform appears to have slowed.

Prior to the *Doi Moi* reforms, foreign trade was in the hands of a small number of foreign trading corporations, with effective monopolies over imports and exports of designated commodities. Import volumes were determined by the projected gap between domestic production and domestic demand. Export volumes were set at levels necessary to finance planned imports.

Under the *Doi Moi* reforms, almost every aspect of the trading regime was liberalised to some degree. Restrictions on the establishment of foreign trading corporations were relaxed, leading to a rapid increase in the number of enterprises allowed to engage in trade, from about 30 in 1988 to over 1,200 by the end of 1994 and 16,200 in 2001. While all registered firms, regardless of ownership, are allowed to engage in foreign trade, some restrictions remain. For example, regulatory requirements imposed by ministries prevent private firms from exporting rice or importing fertilisers. Similarly, some producer monopolies (such as coal production) include monopoly trading rights.

Vietnam's tariff schedule was rationalised in 1992 and simplified in 1999, following Vietnam's accession to AFTA. Although Vietnam has met its commitments on tariff reductions under AFTA, it has been able to place a number of products on the General Exception List, effectively excluding them from tariff reductions. The list includes alcoholic beverages, vehicles with fewer than 15 seats, and motorcycles with a capacity of less than 250cc (WB 2002:16). The effective protection rate—an indicator of inefficiency—is as high as 599% for domestic-oriented production of motorcycles, 366% for sugar, 241% for tea and 181% for clothing. Not surprisingly, a substantial share of public and private investment is directed towards these sectors. In effect scarce resources are drawn towards those types of manufacturing that are flourishing under protection, imposing welfare costs on Vietnamese society. As the World Bank has noted, Vietnam has been able to liberalise its trade regime while maintaining a policy bias in favour of domestic market-oriented industries, particularly those dominated by SOEs (WB 2002:16).

Quotas and targets, the basis of the central planning system, have been progressively eliminated. By early 2003 quantitative restrictions on imports (with the exception of sugar and petroleum products) had been eliminated. Most of the quantitative restrictions on exports have also been abolished. The exceptions are textiles and garments and a list of sensitive items. Bilateral quotas on textiles and garments are allocated through an auction process.

Major steps have been taken to liberalise foreign-exchange markets, including the phasing out of the foreign-exchange surrender requirement by the end of 2003. Some restrictions on international transfers and payments remain.

Case study: upgrading the infrastructure

In general Vietnam's infrastructure is in poor physical shape, requiring a massive injection of investment to bring the facilities up to a standard required in a market economy. For example, the number of Vietnamese with access to electricity is lower than the average for neighbouring countries, and transmission and distribution losses are high because of the run-down condition of the 'poles and wires'. Similarly, the majority of the population, especially in rural communities, does not have access to safe water supplies. According to a master plan for water supply up to the year 2015, about US$1.7 billion worth of investment is required to bring water access up to acceptable levels (Freehill, Hollingdale & Page 2002:10).

The transport sector illustrates many of the infrastructure problems faced by Vietnam. The victim of 40 years of war, as well as post-war neglect due to shortage of funds, transport infrastructure (equipment and vehicles) is dilapidated and operational efficiency is low. While the national road network is extensive, central and provincial government budget allocations have been insufficient to maintain, let alone improve, road surfaces. Major highways are narrow and extensively potholed. Existing bridges are in need of repair and new river crossings are needed urgently (WB 1994). The railways, coastal shipping and ports are also in poor physical shape. Overall, the transport sector is characterised by old equipment, deficiencies in maintenance, inefficient operations, numerous bottlenecks and lack of integration between the modes, as well as by a serious mismatch between transport infrastructure and the emerging pattern of industrial and urban growth.

The present transport system reflects the priorities of the colonial period, as well as the devastation of the Vietnam War and the austerity of the post-war planning era. During the post-war era (1976–86), the transport system evolved to serve the needs of a planned and substantially self-sufficient economy. Priority was given to internal transport needs and, within that, to the movement of primary products (coal, rice) and passengers. Transport markets were regulated, with planners favouring rail and coastal shipping, while according road haulage a low priority. Given the acute shortage of capital, funds were insufficient to repair existing facilities, let alone improve system efficiency.

The Vietnam National Railways (Vinarail) system is in poor physical condition; maintenance of the tracks has been inadequate, while locomotives and rolling stock require replacement (Trace 1996). More specifically, the following problems need to be considered:

- track capacity: available track capacity is barely adequate for today's reduced traffic;
- conditions of the track: while improvement of the main Hanoi–Ho Chi Minh City line has been accorded high priority by Vinarail, it remains in poor physical condition. The rate of sleeper replacement is low. Old rails (lighter than 38 kilograms per metre) are being replaced

by 43-kilogram per metre track, but the carrying capacity of the track remains low by standards of mainline railways in developed countries. The Ministry of Transport, Communication and Post has estimated that over 300 turnouts (points) require urgent replacement on the Hanoi–Ho Chi Minh City main line;

- separation of road and rail: between Ga Hoa Hung (the main station in Ho Chi Minh City) and Ga Trang Bom (to the east of the satellite town of Bien Hoa), the Hanoi–Ho Chi Minh City main line crosses 40 roads: only five of these crossings take the form of a bridge, 15 are level crossings with 'secure barriers', and the remaining 20 crossings are unprotected;

- encroachment onto railway reserves: within city limits, buildings encroach on rail reservations, limiting train operating speed;

- condition of locomotives and rolling stock: as of August 1991, Vinarail had 497 locomotives (123 steam, 374 diesel). Only 332 were said to be in 'operational condition' (180 of the 332 were out of use because too few trains operated to employ them). The large number of locomotive types makes for high maintenance costs. Vinarail possesses a relatively large fleet of passenger coaches, though many await repair, and the system operates few modern, air-conditioned carriages. Freight wagons are small in size and poorly maintained;

- small trains and limited train loads: the condition of tracks, locomotives and rolling stock limits the number of passenger carriages or freight wagons. Train size and train loads are small by comparison with other rail systems;

- signalling and communications: according to the Ministry of Transport, Communication and Post, as late as 1994, 92% of the Vinarail network was operated by the primitive and labour-intensive token block system (MTCP 1994). Under Vietnamese conditions, with long sections of track, the system limits the number of train paths along a typical single-track line to 16 per day. In contrast, a semi-automatic block system would cater for 24 trains per day and an automatic block system would cater for 40 trains. A semi-automatic block system is gradually being extended along the Hanoi–Ho Chi Minh City line.

The post-1986 shift towards an open market economy led to marked changes in the pattern of both production and consumption. In turn these changes gave rise to rapid growth in the demand for transport services and new patterns of demand in transport markets. Responding to these pressures, the government partially deregulated the transport sector in 1988–89, allowing shippers greater freedom to choose their modes of transport (WB 1994). This new freedom changed the pattern of transport usage; measured in terms of tons carried, rail lost heavily, inland water transport lost marginally and road transport gained substantially. The major loser, rail, lost about 40% of its freight traffic over the period 1988–94. By 1994 Vinarail was technically bankrupt, with a US$1.1 million annual deficit in operating costs. In that year Vinarail's capacity was about four times in excess of the annual transport load of 2.6 million tons of freight and 10 million passengers.

The government of Vietnam issues bonds for nationally important infrastructure projects, but there remains a substantial gap between the funds that can be raised from the issue of bonds, budget appropriations and overseas development aid and the annual spending required on infrastructure. For this reason, the government has looked to the private sector, including foreign investment. Private participation in infrastructure projects may give rise to substantial benefits, lead to increased efficiency in investment and operations, provide access to private finance, and allow the government to divert money away from spending on infrastructure and into high-priority social programs in health, education and poverty alleviation.

Decision 62/2002, which sets out a list of national projects calling for foreign investment capital over the period 2001–05, includes a number of infrastructure projects. However, relatively few infrastructure projects have been funded by foreign investment, partly because a number of limitations apply as to the approved form of foreign investment. For example there has been no significant foreign investment in the rail sector. A January 2002 master plan for the sector suggests that the cost of required investment in below-track infrastructure for 2002–10 is Vietnamese dong (VND) 23,530 billion and that a further VND62,870 billion is required for above-rail investment (new locomotives and rolling stock). Funding of this magnitude will have to depend in part on foreign investment. Decision 62 lists two rail investments for which Build–Operate–Transfer funding was sought during 2002–05—construction of a new double-track line between Bien Hoa (near Ho Chi Minh City) and Vung Tau, and a new line from Bien Hoa to Trang Bom.

In other sectors there has been one completed Build–Operate–Transfer project for water supply to Ho Chi Minh City. Several other water-related Build–Operate–Transfer projects have been approved but none has so far been implemented. At present, telecommunications projects may only take the form of a business co-operation contract. A business co-operation contract or a joint venture is required for oil and gas and mining projects and also for construction of ports and airports.

The challenges ahead

During the early and mid-1990s, Vietnam's transition from a centrally planned economy to a market economy with socialist characteristics was remarkably successful and the country experienced a rate of economic growth that equalled or exceeded the average rate for the East Asian region. The *Doi Moi* and later reforms galvanised the energy of millions of Vietnamese citizens, who diversified and expanded production rapidly through micro-household enterprises, as well as privately owned small and medium-sized businesses.

After an economic slowdown during and immediately after the East Asian crisis, during which government policy gave priority to macro-economic stability rather than economic growth, the economy resumed relatively rapid economic growth in 2001. According to the World Bank, the improved growth rates of the past three years are partly the result of a series of policy measures, including measures aimed at encouraging private sector development and trade liberalisation. However, there is general agreement that further reforms are necessary if growth is to continue over the medium to long term.

A number of commentators see Vietnam as being at a crossroads. Will the country opt for further reform (if so, will the reform program be fast or slow?), leading to success in creating a market economy with a socialist orientation? Alternatively, will the country reject further reform, allowing vested interests to capture economic rents and promote private wealth generation rather than the public interest?

A number of challenges lie ahead. The first is the need for further progress in economic reform. The government of Vietnam has introduced a number of initiatives aimed at accelerating the transition to a market economy. However, reform is proceeding at different rates across the economy, creating various bottlenecks that threaten future growth. For example, as the World Bank has noted, relatively rapid progress in liberalising foreign trade appears at odds with the slowdown of state enterprise reform (WB 2002:i). Similarly, despite the enactment of the Enterprise Law, the formal domestic private sector is tiny and relatively fragile. Growth in this sector is critically important if the 1.2 million new entrants to the labour force are to be given productive employment. The playing field still appears to be tilted against the private sector, with access to factor markets more readily available to SOEs than to private sector firms. Many private sector firms lack land-use rights or other forms of collateral, having to rely on personal connections and personal relations to raise capital.

A second priority relates to the implementation of reforms already in place. Putting into effect the government's commitments and initiatives to accelerate the transition to a market economy is a major task for a country whose administrative capacity is limited, especially as decisions are increasingly implemented at the regional and local level. The alignment of the commitments and initiatives of the central government with the grassroots policy implementation at the provincial and local levels is one of the major challenges facing Vietnam.

A third priority relates to institutional change and improvement in the quality of governance. Vietnam has an excellent record in macro-economic management, but there is a danger that economic growth may outpace the capacity for institutional change. Secure property rights, an independent judiciary and legal transparency are needed to keep attracting investment and generating jobs. Similarly, public expenditure management needs to be overhauled. As the World Bank (2002) has noted, processes for prioritising expenditure remain ineffective. Capital and recurrent expenditure budgeting needs to be integrated within a single framework.

Fourth, Vietnam's infrastructure is in poor shape. Rapidly increasing road traffic volumes, coupled with a lack of funds for maintenance, let alone new road construction, has led to the deterioration in the condition of many roads. The rail system is in a run-down condition, needing large expenditure on both track and rolling stock. Electricity production, transmission and distribution systems all require substantial investment. The expenditure required on infrastructure is such that foreign investment and foreign aid must necessarily play a major role in the future.

Notes

1. Children of United States soldiers have also suffered from birth defects and cancers as a result of a parent's exposure to Agent Orange during the war (Young 1991:325–6).
2. The North had adopted a Soviet-style central planning system in 1954. At the time of reunification, Vietnam had been devastated by two decades of war and was cut off from trade and investment flows as a result of the United States *Trading with the Enemy Act*. Vietnam's isolation was emphasised by a series of embargoes imposed by various OECD countries following Vietnam's invasion of Cambodia (Kampuchea) in 1978.
3. An extended discussion of the legal edifice underlying Vietnam's reforms is contained in World Bank 2002.
4. In practice the inadequacies of the planning system meant that Vietnamese managers—like their Soviet counterparts—had to engage in various extra-legal activities to ensure, inter alia, that their firms had the necessary raw materials to meet output goals.
5. A precise estimate of the share of capital absorbed by the state sector is difficult to obtain due to problems in the valuation of assets.
6. According to the World Bank (2002), quantitative responses were obtained from 31% of the enterprises and qualitative responses from a further 38%.
7. The Vietnamese Living Standards Survey (1997–98) found that 89% of the population over ten years old was literate—86% of females and 94% of males. Literacy in urban areas (94%) is slightly higher than in the countryside (88%). The highest literacy rate is found in the Red River Delta region of northern Vietnam, where 98% of the men are literate.
8. The World Bank (2002) notes also that while 90% of agricultural land users have been granted certificates, the demand for their amendment or re-issuance has grown due to the informal consolidation of previously fragmented land parcels.
9. A bilateral copyright agreement between Vietnam and the United States offers protection to United States authors and publishers.
10. There has been a large gap between the value of foreign direct investment approved by the Government of Vietnam and the level of foreign direct investment actually realised. The high failure rate (only 30% of approved foreign direct investment translating into actual investment in 1995) is attributable to inertia within the Vietnamese bureaucracy and excessive initial optimism on the part of foreign investors.
11. Legal capital is akin to equity capital. Under Vietnamese law the legal capital of a venture must be at least 30% of its total investment capital. Reduction in legal capital is not allowed during the life of the venture (see MPI/PC 2003:31).

chapter seven

Thailand: financial institutions and regional trade

David Treisman

By the middle of the first decade of the 21st century, Thailand, Southeast Asia's resurgent 'tiger', had risen from the ashes of financial devastation that had swept the nation and the region in the wake of the financial crisis of the late 1990s. Thailand's recovery is largely thanks to its dynamic interplay between the state and the role of business in its domestic and foreign markets. This should not be of much surprise to scholars of Asian economic development, in which *dirigisme* (state control of economic affairs) has played a fundamental role in the economic development of the region since 1945. However, the modern Thai economy can trace its economic development lineage back almost two centuries, during which its regionally unique experience of continued, progressive leadership, slow policy implementation, benevolent monarchs and a non-colonial-based outward-looking business environment (Treisman 2004) have led to it being the second-largest economy within ASEAN, with a GDP of US$143,303 million (ASEAN 2005).

Since the 1960s Thailand's economy has transformed itself from an agrarian-based export-led economy (in which 95% of exports were agricultural) to a mixed but predominantly manufacturing-based export-led economy (by 1990, 31% of exports were agricultural) (Muscat 1994:227). In an effort to maintain Thailand's positive economic momentum, policy makers of the 1990s turned towards the expansion and formation of Thailand's sectors of comparative advantage; namely tourism and banking. Thai policy makers during the 1990s believed that the expansion and development of these two sectors were the next steps in promoting economic prosperity. The Thai economy by 1990 was seen by the business community as being a stable, developing economy whose positive economic indicators were a testament to its structural adjustment policies (Muscat 1994). The tourism sector benefited from this stability and its inherent relationship to the property development and real estate sectors created a positive outlook. Thai policy makers felt that this positive outlook and stability could be utilised to expand and promote the banking sector. The expansion of the Thai banking sector was particularly spurred on by the sentiment that a regional financial void would be created once Hong Kong was handed back to mainland China in 1997 and that a correctly positioned Thai banking sector could challenge Singapore for supremacy within the Asian region (Hanfley 1992).

The purpose of this chapter is to provide the reader with an overview of the Thai business environment through the analysis of Thailand's financial liberalisation and its subsequent impact on the economy. This chapter begins with a brief background analysis of the Thai economy, before turning to an analysis of the reforms of Thailand's financial institutional framework during the 1990s. The chapter then explores the rationale behind Thailand's aspirations as a regional banking hub, the economic impact of the financial reformation, and the economic conditions within Thailand preceding and following the 1997 financial crisis. The chapter concludes with a contextualisation of Thailand's financial liberalisation through the analysis of the case study of Citibank Thailand in order to demonstrate the nature of the Thai business environment.

Thailand's economic development in historical perspective

Modern Thailand can trace its lineage back to the formation of the Bowring Treaty in 1855 (Muscat 1994). The present Thai political economy has developed in a relatively unique manner compared to the rest of Asia. Thailand, unlike many other states within the region, has never had to endure a period of colonisation by Western powers, has always encouraged private ownership (especially land), has never experienced any major food shortages, has a largely homogenous ethnic group, and has maintained the influential role of its uninterrupted monarchy in the governance of the state. The Thai state remains heavily reliant on its technocrats for the formation of much of its policies. Thai politics tends to be dominated by consensus decision making and, as such, policy implementation tends to be longwinded. However, the reliance upon technocrats for the formation of economic policies has kept the policy procedure dynamic, and thus has allowed it to readily cater for the needs of the market, while concomitantly allowing for direction by the state. Thailand's economic policy process tends to operate between traditional East Asian *dirigisme* and laissez faire (Treisman 2004).

The development of the Thai financial institutional framework is reflective of the state's overall economic development and implementation of economic policy: it has been dynamic and incremental. Changes to the financial institutional framework took a major leap forward in the 1990s when the Thai polity expanded and promoted the banking sector. Until the 1990s Thailand's financial institutional framework pertaining to the banking sector was largely dominated by the Bank of Thailand and the Financial Institutions Development

Fund (FIDF) (Treisman 2004). The Bank of Thailand was formed in 1942 in order to stabilise the war-time economy and since its inception has competently performed the tasks of a central bank, largely independent of any vicissitudes in the political climate.

The market for finance in Thailand grew considerably in the 1970s in accordance with the overall growth and development felt throughout the economy. In 1975 the Stock Exchange of Thailand was founded in order to provide an institutionalised means of access to capital for the private sector, and was prompted by the rapid growth in the size and scope of banking and financial institutions across the country (Muscat 2004).

During the 1980s most of the development of, and changes to, Thailand's financial institutional framework largely fell under the government's broader structural adjustment policies, which were focused on monetary and fiscal discipline through the cutting of unnecessary expenditure, restructuring of the tax system, and stimulation of private savings through the strengthening and creation of new financial institutions. The purpose of these structural adjustment policies, along with subsequent support from the IMF, was to reorient the economy (under a less-favourable international environment) in order to curb growing external debt and domestic inflation and to improve the overall efficiency and adaptability of the economy to external shocks (Muscat 1994).

However, by 1983 a financial crisis was forming in the Thai market and several financial institutions required liquidity support. The government eventually came to the aid of financial institutions through soft loan facilities arising from the creation of the FIDF (Rajan 2001). The FIDF was formed in 1985 (following the 1983–84 financial crisis) in order to provide liquidity support to these ailing financial institutions (Rajan 2001) and to prevent possible social unrest (Muscat 1994). The FIDF has since shaped much of the market's reaction to a change (or lack thereof) in the financial institutional framework by the state. The FIDF is a mechanism of the Bank of Thailand and its function does not require the implementation of any substantial reforms in the operations of financial institutions and allows for more timely liquidity assistance through its acceptance of a wider range of assets as collateral and its ability to supplement Bank of Thailand's assistance (Rajan 2001). The FIDF has thus created a perception in the market that the state implicitly guarantees to intervene in the market to prevent the collapse of any financial institution.

The latter half of the 1980s proved to be prosperous for Thailand. Moves towards implementing its structural adjustment policies were paying off and Thailand was experiencing considerable economic growth, which elevated it to the status of being the fifth Asian tiger economy. The positive economic performance of the economy and the implicit undertaking of the government to bail out ailing financial institutions led to a suspension of much of the financial market reform processes proposed in the 1980s (Muscat 1994).

The financial reforms of the 1990s

By the 1990s Thailand had been very successful in its economic growth (see Tables 1 and 2) and development and in transforming its economy from an agricultural-based economy to a mixed, export-led economy (Muscat 1994) in which, as indicated in Table 3, manufactured goods increasingly dominated exports.

Table 1: Thailand's GDP, 1984, 1994 and 2004

	1984	1994	2004
GDP US$ billions	41.8	144.5	163.5

Source: World Bank 2005.

Table 2: Thailand's average growth in GDP, 1984–2004

	1984-94	1994-2004	2004-08
Average % GDP growth	9.6	2.2	6.2

Source: World Bank 2005.

The Thai leadership decided that the next step in Thailand's economic development would require the further liberalisation of its financial market. Based upon this decision, in May 1990 the then-Prime Minister Chatichai announced that Thailand was moving to formal adherence to Article 8 of the IMF's Charter (General Obligation of Members), and specifically Article 8(3) of the Charter (Avoidance of Discriminatory Currency Practices). By adhering to Article 8, Thailand would gain considerable economic prestige, as only the developed member-states of the IMF had such status at that time. Article 8 required Thailand to eliminate controls over foreign-exchange transactions and capital movements. The Bank of Thailand began to implement a liberalisation program in order to achieve Article 8 status. Several changes in the financial institutional framework were required to achieve Article 8 status while not reducing Thailand's high levels of economic growth. Several reform measures were implemented to achieve these goals (Treisman 2004).

Table 3: Thai exports by industry, 1993–2004

(Millions of US$)

	1993	1994	1995	1996	1997	1998	1999	2000	2001	2002	2003	2004
Agriculture	4,390	5,173	6,466	6,627	5,998	5,074	4,890	4,958	4,798	5,159	6,644	8,007
Fisheries	2,210	2,713	2,872	2,517	2,327	2,171	2,079	2,307	2,031	1,640	1,757	1,778
Forestry	16	23	32	40	42	33	64	86	94	147	189	263
Mining	228	272	309	412	536	427	364	793	595	707	920	1,256
Manufacturing	29,855	36,851	49,442	45,646	48,182	44,857	49,273	59,765	55,467	58,384	68,705	84,780
Labour-intensive products	8,298	9,736	10,937	9,068	8,394	7,369	7,599	8,204	8,052	7,933	8,159	9,221
High-technology products	15,907	20,098	26,572	27,650	30,596	29,835	33,266	42,448	38,203	40,246	47,575	61,192
Resource-based products	3,411	4,143	5,191	5,359	5,352	4,693	5,257	5,649	5,577	5,859	6,607	7,202
Samples & other unclasified goods	357	314	509	6,39	1,151	1,750	1,705	1,772	2,155	1,974	1,702	1,455
Re-exports	70	83	95	103	196	149	126	94	96	145	132	162
Total exports	37,126	45,430	56,725	55,984	58,431	54,460	58,501	69,775	65,236	68,156	80,049	97,701

Source: Bank of Thailand 2005.

One such major reform occurred through the formation in 1992 of the Thai Securities Exchange Commission (SEC). The introduction of the SEC went a long way to removing overall responsibility for, and authority over, the financial wellbeing of the state from the Central Bank. The introduction of the Securities and Exchange Act meant that the Bank of Thailand was assigned the task of supervisory authority over the finance business, while the SEC was assigned the task of supervisory authority over the securities business. The assigning of these supervisory tasks was in line with those of developed financial markets. However, in most developed financial markets these supervisory roles complement policy implementation by both institutions. In the case of Thailand, the lack of adequate financial reform pertaining to the operations of financial institutions meant that the supervisory roles of the Bank of Thailand and the SEC overlapped. This overlapping, and the suspension of the reform of financial institutions mentioned above, meant that often a policy implementation by one institution did not complement the other's policy. Thus the introduction of the SEC, with a supervisory capacity, led to complex financial policy implementation by the Bank of Thailand and the SEC that did not allow for the optimal level of efficiency between the Thai financial market and its financial institutional framework. This policy complexity did not, however, deter investment in, and operations by, the market, which maintained a belief in the state's FIDF-based implicit guarantee to bail out financial institutions in distress (Treisman 2004).

The attraction of international financial flows was still on top of the state's agenda and was believed to be instrumental in the expansion and promotion of its banking sector and the establishment of Thailand as Asia's new regional financial centre (Treisman 2004). Thus, in order to attract international financial flows, in 1993 another major change in the Thai financial institutional framework occurred with the introduction of the Bangkok International Banking Facilities (BIBF). The BIBF is an institution utilised to encourage the flow of foreign capital into the Thai financial market. BIBF would offer operating incentives to institutions, such as reduced taxes, and would also operate as guarantor for foreign investors. The introduction of BIBF led to the successful development of Thailand's offshore-banking business, which, in turn, provided the Thai economy with the capital it needed to further its economic growth and development (Rajan 2001).

The changes to the financial institutional framework implemented in the 1990s proved to be very successful for the state. The government's stated policy was to seek economic growth and development at similar levels to those Thailand had experienced in the 1980s. The required foreign capital to encourage economic growth and the sustained foreign financial flows were secured through the liberalisation of Thailand's financial market as the state sought the status of Article 8 recognition (Treisman 2004).

The Thai financial market had shown considerable positive growth since the state's implementation of its liberalisation policies. However, the Thai financial market still lacked the adequate financial depth required by its financial institutional framework in order to allow it to meet the operational demands necessary to sustain its high growth rate (Treisman 2004). Thailand's financial institutional framework had developed considerably and concomitantly with the economy since the mid-1970s. The government's steps toward greater liberalisation of the Thai financial market appeared to have paid off and it was well on the way to Article 8 recognition. However, the entire financial liberalisation process implemented in the 1990s was built upon a poor financial institutional framework whose need for change was identified in the 1980s (Muscat 1994). A negative shift in Thailand's export-led economic growth could undermine the economic gains made through its financial liberation process. Such a negative shift in growth did occur in 1996 and soon the economic gains of Thailand's financial liberation process almost disappeared. Thailand would soon be plunged into a severe financial crisis that would threaten the entire economy with financial failure (Treisman 2004).

Thailand as a regional financial hub

Thailand's aspiration to become a regional financial hub, independent of and directly challenging Asia's other financial hubs (namely Singapore and Hong Kong), appears quite peculiar. The motivation for the creation of a Thai-based financial hub arose from political desire and economic rationality. Thailand's Article 8 recognition would be a prestigious move towards formal acknowledgment of its economic success by the international community (Treisman 2004). The formation of a financial hub in Thailand was not, however, dependent on its Article 8 recognition. Banking in Thailand has always been dominated by its need to provide financing for trade (Treisman 2004). Post-Cold War dynamics and the subsequent changes in the East Asian political economy led to the opening of Indochina's controlled economies, and Thailand was well positioned, as Indochina's main trading partner, to take advantage of the opening of markets in Laos, Cambodia, Burma and Vietnam. Many Thai banks had an established presence throughout Indochina and the Thai baht quickly rivalled the United States dollar in these markets as the common unit of exchange. As development priorities and trade would dominate the economic policies of Indochinese states, the Thai polity and business community felt that it was well positioned to act as a facilitator of the international financial flows to these states (Hanfley 1992). Table 4 and Figure 1 demonstrate that Thailand's growth in exports to all four countries positioned Thailand's financial institutions very well to benefit from its role as a facilitator for Indochina's international financial flows for trade and development.

Table 4: Thai exports to Indochina, 1993–2004

(Millions of US$)

	1993	1994	1995	1996	1997	1998	1999	2000	2001	2002	2003	2004
Cambodia	180	262	335	363	317	301	354	352	469	517	686	724
Laos	175	293	357	364	385	374	410	385	413	397	456	581
Burma	154	239	349	320	416	348	396	510	356	323	439	609
Vietnam	117	257	471	581	549	592	573	849	801	948	1,261	1,878
Total exports to Indochina	626	1,051	1,512	1,628	1,667	1,615	1,733	2,096	2,039	2,185	2,842	3,792

Source: Bank of Thailand 2005.

Figure 1: Total Thai exports to Indochina and Burma, 1993–2004

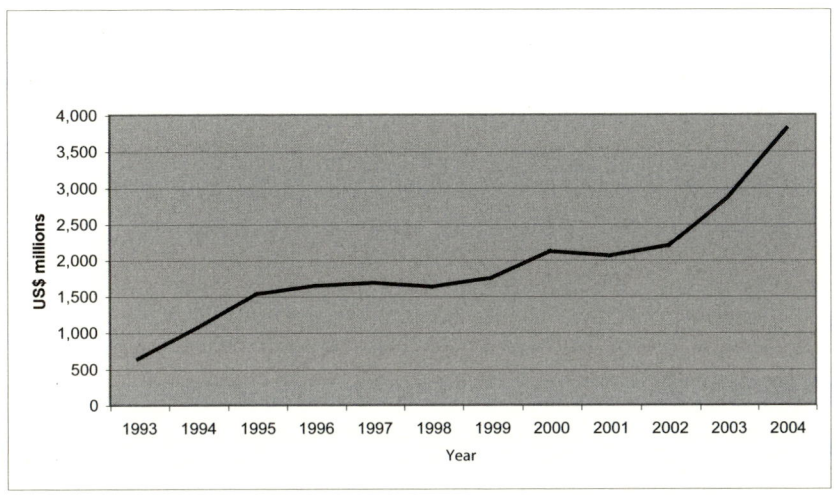

Source: Bank of Thailand 2005.

The Thai authorities did recognise several limitations to a strategy of engaging Indochina, the most significant of which were Thailand's insufficient financial institutional framework, the lack of financial skilled labour and the need for additional international financial institutions, especially banks (Hanfley 1992). Article 8 recognition would formalise much of the exchange control liberalisation Thailand had achieved and define the government's approach to its further financial market liberalisation and strengthening of its financial institutional framework. The BIBF was the government's answer to the need to attract more international financial institutions and its subsequent operation became the means with which Thailand's financial-skilled labour shortage could be addressed (Treisman 2004). The fiscal incentives created by the BIBF, the implicit undertaking by the government under the FIDF to bail out financial institutions in distress and the burgeoning opportunities of Indochina made Thailand a very attractive environment for investment by international financial institutions.

Would all these incentives and opportunities create a regional financial hub that could rival Hong Kong and Singapore? Thailand was a more competitive environment for financial services and did not have similar limitations to those the Singapore government had placed on its internal banking operations. Thailand was not a shipping hub for the region like Hong Kong and Singapore. However, the Bank of Thailand was keen to allow Thailand's financial liberalisation to encourage its banking sector to grow from a regional substitute for banking to a more formalised extra-regional banking hub (Hanfley 1992). The Bank of Thailand's outlook on the growth of its banking sector and the creation of a banking hub made sense, especially in light of various factors: its financial services were dominated by its financing of trade for export; exports and the economy's export-led growth were high and did not appear to be likely to decline; and Thai businesses, as indicated in Figure 1, were successfully operating in the economies of Indochina and Burma. Fundamentally, the Bank of Thailand had seen an opportunity to utilise Thailand's current and future potential for trade as a means with which to exploit a market opportunity for its financial services and thus allow it to gain a comparative advantage in the region.

The impact of financial reforms on market conditions

Thailand's financial market reforms and liberalisation during the 1980s and early 1990s appeared to have taken hold and were producing positive results. The introduction of the FIDF gave the market an implicit guarantee that the government would provide liquidity support for financial institutions. The introduction of the SEC, although creating additional regulatory complexity, demonstrated the government's commitment to a stronger institutional framework and the introduction of the BIBF had fostered a burgeoning international banking facility.

These financial market reforms and liberalisation, coupled with the structural adjustment policies of the 1980s and the concomitant sustained economic growth, had made Thailand an attractive market for investment by both domestic and foreign investors. The economic gains of liberalisation held true until 1997, when the Thai financial system experienced a sudden collapse (Treisman 2004). It is widely argued that the Thai financial crisis arose through the poor management of Thailand's economic conditions by the state, and this, coupled with derivative operations, allowed for the spread of the crisis to the rest of the Southeast Asian region (Steinherr 2000). While Thailand's role in the Asian financial crisis is not the main focus of this chapter, it should be noted that the economic environment and the subsequent impact of this economically catastrophic event is indicative of the manner in which business was conducted in Thailand. In light of the discussion on the financial institutional framework and in order to understand the economic conditions surrounding the Thai financial system, economic conditions that made Thailand so susceptible to a financial crisis in 1997 are analysed.

Capital flows conditions

Thailand, like the rest of Asia, received significantly increased amounts of capital inflows during the 1990s. Thailand's current account ran an average deficit of 7.5% for the period 1990 to 1996 (Rajan 2001:16). This current account deficit was not seen by investors as a major concern, as Thailand's net private capital inflows were the main cause of the deficit. The high levels of net private capital inflows were a direct result of the state's financial market liberalisation policy, and in particular the formation of the BIBF, which created considerable fiscal incentives for foreign investors (Rajan 2001).

However, 75% of net capital flows consisted of short- and long-term credits, currency deposits and other accounts receivable and payable (Rajan 2001:20). These capital flows are largely regarded as being the most volatile form of capital flows, as their nature allows them to be utilised in a multitude of short-term financing operations. In the case of Thailand, these capital flows allowed for the 'rebooking' of intra-company loans in which companies transferred their existent foreign direct investment in order to maximise the benefits derived from the tax advantage offered to companies under the BIBF (BT 2005). Concomitantly, portfolio investment decreased, thereby reducing the net capital inflows. This reduction in the net capital inflows meant that more money was being lent in the economy through BIBF-based institutions than was being borrowed, creating a current account deficit (Rajan 2001).

Credit conditions

The net capital inflows, over the same period, had a significant 'knock-on' effect in the banking sector. Capital inflows are usually mediated through domestic banking institutions (as was the case in Thailand) and the growth in Thai bank credit grew by 20% annually from 1990 to 1995 (Rajan 2001:23). This meant that the Thai banking sector had more funds available to lend to the domestic market. The increase in credit available in the economy saw a rise in investment-driven economic growth. The credit available to the market continually increased, as most banks believed that they could elevate their status through increased lending levels (Rajan 2001). This led to significant amounts of investment in less-than-efficient projects (projects with a negative net present value) and in economic sectors prone to speculative booms, which ultimately created maturity mismatches throughout the financial market.

In Thailand such speculative sectors existed in the real estate and property development sectors. An IMF report estimated that in 1996 around 33% of loan portfolios of Thai financial institutions were in real estate and property development sectors (Rajan 2001:24). However, this underestimates the real exposure of financial institutions to credit risk in these two sectors. The indirect exposure of Thai financial institutions was significant. Substantial amounts of loans made by financial institutions to manufacturing and export-oriented institutions were passed on to subsidiaries operating in the real estate and property development sectors. This 'passing on' of loans led to considerable exposure by Thai financial institutions to credit risk in the real estate and construction sectors, as the lending by financial institutions in these sectors well exceeded the lending limits stipulated by the Bank of Thailand (Rajan 2001).

The importance of real estate and property development

Real estate and property development sectors have always played a central role in the Thai economy and thus have been popular for both domestic and foreign investment. By the 1990s these sectors were especially popular with investors for several reasons (Treisman 2004).

- Good returns from property development: the stated government policy was to achieve economic development, which traditionally requires some degree of real estate and property development. With Thailand's high growth rates, stemming from the 1980s, real estate and property development were seen as 'safe' investments with sustainable returns.

- Confidence in the country's land-based collateral system: land and land ownership have always been fundamental to the development of private ownership in Thailand. Thus lending and borrowing within the economy has developed in a way that provided for the offering of land as collateral. However, as this system has been in operation for the past 200 years, often the intrinsic value of land could not be accurately measured in order to advance adequate financing.

- Lax prudential supervision: Central Bank regulation prevented banks from investing all of their available capital into the real estate and property development sectors. However, there was no prudential supervision that required Thai banking institutions to perform adequate credit-risk analysis of potential customers. The lack of prudential supervision and the desire of many Thai banking institutions to gain a greater status saw lending (to many debtors operating in the real estate and property development sectors) merely based upon name and personal guarantees.

Thailand had found itself in an economic quagmire. The government's financial liberalisation policies had gone a long way in maintaining the extraordinarily high growth rates of the 1980s well into the 1990s. The need to attract foreign capital to further economic development was being fulfilled through various government-backed incentive schemes. Thailand's financial market appeared to be performing well. However, underlying these positive indicators were several factors that had, by 1996, resulted in the concentration of the financial market's operations in the real estate and property development sectors (either directly or indirectly). The attractiveness of Thailand's market to short-term capital flows, the continual extension of credit to the domestic market that exceeded the net capital inflows, and the poor financial institutional framework made Thailand ripe for a financial crisis. As the financial market continued to operate and as foreign banking institutions furthered their involvement in the Thai financial market, a financial crisis loomed ever closer. In 1997 the financial crisis came to Thailand when the regional economic downturn saw Thailand's export market contract, and the real estate and property development bubbles burst. The complete collapse of the Thai economy loomed (Treisman 2004).

Post-crisis institutional change and economic conditions

Once the initial effect of the financial crisis had run its course, the Thai polity initiated a revamp of the prudential and legal framework surrounding the banking and financial sectors. Prudential requirements focusing on capital adequacy, loan classification and provisioning rules were introduced in order to bring the prudential constraints of the banking and financial sectors in line with those of international best practices. These new prudential requirements imposed a considerable capital reserve requirement (as compared to previous requirements) and the banking and financial institutions were given various timetables in which to implement the reforms, the last of which expired at the end of 2000. The government, fearing the new prudential control would create a credit crunch throughout the financial market, implemented a timetabled introduction of the new prudential controls. The government also ensured that the process surrounding the implementation of the prudential requirements was made public in order to reassure the market of its commitment to financial reform (IMF 2000).

The Bank of Thailand also relaxed its foreign ownership limitations by allowing foreign entities to acquire more than a 50% ownership stake in banking and financial institutions. This new relaxation would last for a period of ten years, after which any new foreign purchases would be capped at 49% ownership. It was the intention of the Bank of Thailand to facilitate the sale of Thailand's suspended, bankrupt banking and financial institutions through the relaxation of foreign ownership (IMF 2000).

Several new laws that created changes in the financial institutional framework were enacted, including most notably (IMF 2000):

- the Financial Institutions Law, a law aimed at unifying the existent laws surrounding banking and financial institutions;
- the Deposit Insurance Law, which was aimed at introducing a legal framework for the insurance of banking and financial institutions and was implemented in order to remove the precedent created by the government's implicit guarantee of banking and financial institutions' operations; and
- a New Central Bank Act, which was aimed at improving the accountability and independence of the Central Bank and extending the authority of the Central Bank over the banking and financial sector.

By the end of 2000 it appeared that the changes to Thailand's financial institutional framework had begun to take effect, and confidence in the banking and financial sector was on the rise. The Thai government approached the reform of the financial institutional framework by fostering market stimulation and thus limiting its role in controlling individual banking and financial institutions. The process was not complete by 2000 but showed encouraging prospects. It was recognised that until 2000 the reform processes did little to address the need for debt restructuring in banking and financial institutions or to mitigate the state's reluctance to ensure the enforcement of property rights, especially in regard to non-performing loans (IMF 2000).

By the end of 2002 (five years after the crisis started) Thailand's vulnerabilities to external shocks had been reduced. Reduced vulnerability was indicated by the currency surplus in the Bank of Thailand's forward book at the end of 2002. However, domestic 'fundamental' problems still existed. Government debt was higher than pre-crisis levels and exposure to credit and market risks by banking and financial institutions was still high and could have been devastating had an economic slowdown or increase in interest rates occurred. Foreign-based debt was still considerable; however, hedging of currency risk was being undertaken by domestic banking and financial institutions. Capital adequacy of banking institutions remained a concern for the market; 2002 was the first financial year since the crisis that banks showed a profit, and international rating agencies upgraded some of the investment ratings of Thai banking institutions above their previous speculative levels. Non-performing loans were still a large burden on the banking and financial sector, as the legal framework for dealing with non-performing loans remained weak and considerable administrative delays in the processing of non-performing loans persisted (IMF 2004).

Non-performing loans from the 1997 financial crisis still remain a major feature in Thailand's financial market, and the debt restructuring of small and medium enterprises is still a concern. Progress in post-crisis reforms in other areas such as corporate governance is moving ahead, although it remains slow. Despite these concerns and the slow and tedious policy implementation, Thailand has bounced back as a popular market for foreign direct investment and was ranked in a 2005 survey of multinationals as the third most-popular destination for investment by Asian investors and the 20th most-popular destination for investment by Western investors (WBG 2005). Thailand's success, resilience and adaptability to domestic and foreign economic environments are largely attributed to its competitive and dynamic business sector and its forward-looking and market-oriented policy makers (*China-Asean.net* 2001). Thailand's economy remains broad-based and robust, and high education and wage levels and growing wealth make Thailand a strong market within the region (*China-Asean.net* 2001). The Thai government has set its targeted GDP growth rate for 2005–08 at 6.6% per annum (WBG 2005:36). Should these figures be maintained, Thailand will be well on the way to becoming the world's eighth-largest economy by the year 2020 (China-Asean 2001).

Case study: Citibank Thailand

Citibank Thailand is a wholly owned subsidiary of Citigroup, an international banking group based in the United States. Citibank's operations in Thailand began in 1968 and have since undergone several acquisitions, expansions and mergers. Citibank's Thai operations began much later than most of its other Asian-based operations, which date from 1902, and the scope of Citibank Thailand's services has developed and expanded in conjunction with the demands placed on the banking sector (Citibank 2005). Citibank's involvement in Thailand is indicative of the government's strategy for the introduction of skills, services and sector development through foreign direct investment.

Citibank's international business strategy usually sees the establishment of a host-based corporate banking operation, which is then expanded to include services such as consumer banking. In the case of Thailand, Citibank offered both corporate- and consumer-banking services from the beginning. Early Bank of Thailand regulations prevented Citibank from establishing more than one branch (Nguyen 1995). Despite this severe limitation, Citibank turned a profit on its mortgage loan products and through its successful exploitation of one of its niches in the Thai market—credit cards. Citibank Thailand was the first bank to offer consumer credit products and has subsequently become the market leader for consumer credit in Thailand (SFD 2004).

In 1995 Citibank identified that the then-unregulated Thai credit card market was a major source of potential revenue (Sivasomboon 1995). Citibank's success in the Thai credit card market is largely attributed to its 'driftnet' marketing approach in which it targeted recent graduates and young workers as customers through database telemarketing, personalised services and remote automation. Citibank's approach was so successful that by 1997 it had managed to secure 40% of the total Thai credit card market (Treerapongpichit & Bunyamanese 1997).

Citibank's success in Thailand is not limited to its dominance in the credit card market. It owes much of its success in Thailand to its self-regulation through the use of United States banking practises in a business environment in which the developing financial institutional framework traditionally suffers from lags in policy implementation. Citibank Thailand, like the entire Thai banking sector, was hit by the 1997 financial crisis but managed to capitalise on the movement of capital in the Thai financial market to foreign banks through its lending in the repurchase market, which offset the slowdown in its long-term mortgage growth (SFD 2004). Citibank's ability to weather the crisis through self-regulation enabled it to successfully introduce revolving credit products to the retail market in light of the changing market conditions. These revolving credit products fell outside the Bank of Thailand's restrictions on foreign bank operations and provided Citibank with an unregulated mechanism to secure more retail customers in a market that was then categorised as being volatile (Treerapongpichit & Bunyamanese 1997).

In 1997, under the post-crisis reforms to dismantle restrictions on foreign ownership of Thai financial institutions, Citibank Thailand explored the acquisition of First Bangkok City Bank. Citibank's interest in First Bangkok City Bank was encouraged by the government and hailed by most analysts as being a step in the right direction to reforming Thailand's financial institutional framework. Citibank's success and continued involvement in the Thai market was expected to introduce new capital, skills and techniques to the market and to encourage further financial reform and improve overall performance of the financial sector (*Agence France-Presse* 1997).

Successful self-regulation and exploitation of niches within the Thai market have allowed Citibank Thailand to maintain its position as Thailand's largest foreign bank and market leader for consumer credit in Thailand (SFD 2004). In a period of two years (1995–97), Citibank Thailand was able to shift its Thai revenue-generating streams from mortgage loans to credit cards and treasury operations. In 2002 Citibank Thailand generated the majority of its annual profits from its treasury operations (SFD 2004), of which it held approximately 40% of the market and $US11 billion under custody (EII 2002)

Citibank Thailand has managed to maintain its levels of non-performing loans at between 10% and 20%, and has stated that it is developing mechanisms to manage good and bad assets and that it intends to expand its operations in support of Thailand's export market. Corporate banking is seen by Citibank Thailand's management as its growth area and will be the main contributor to its expected 5–6% per annum revenue growth (SFD 2004). This expectation is consistent with the expected growth of the Thai economy and regional trade with Indochina and with the expansion of the economy anticipated by 2020.

Citibank Thailand operations provide an example of the mutually beneficial relationship that the Thai state tends to seek with foreign multinationals. Citibank Thailand has introduced new skills and technology to the economy and banking system through its operations and employs approximately 1,400 individuals in its Thai operations (Citibank 2005). These positive externalities for the Thai economy were achieved while Citibank Thailand experienced positive rates of private return on its investment.

Citibank's Thai operations benefit from a regulatory environment in which the developing financial institutional framework suffers from policy implementation lag but remains welcoming of foreign investment in an economy that is as dynamic as it is productive. Citibank's predominance in the banking and financial services sector places it in a strong position to take advantage of Thailand's growing exports to Indochina and the region. This is consistent with an expected expansion of the Thai banking sector, concomitant to the continued expected growth of the Thai economy.

Conclusion

Thailand's 'tiger' economy is largely a testament to the interplay between economic adaptability and dynamic and incremental policy implementation. Thailand's strengthening of its financial institutional framework in the 1990s, its attempts at Article 8 recognition in May 1990 and the formation of a Thai-based financial hub are indicative of this interplay, which led to, most notably, the introduction of the SEC in 1992 and the BIBF in 1993. The development of the financial institutional framework during the 1990s was successful in attracting foreign financial flows and foreign financial skills to Thailand.

Thailand's banking and financial services sector has always been dominated by the use of financing to support Thailand's trade. Thailand's economic transformation since the 1960s, its export-led economic growth and changing regional economic conditions in Indochina provided the Thai state and its banking sector with the opportunity to exploit regional market conditions pursuant to the formation of a regional Thai-based banking hub.

Thailand's financial liberalisation, driven by Article 8, and its sustained economic growth led to precarious market conditions, which developed into a financial crisis in 1997. By 1997 Thailand's current account was running a deficit, which was created by multiple short-term financing operations and long-term foreign direct investments; this subsequently increased the credit risk within the economy as more capital became available for investment by the domestic market. Increased levels of available capital led to the increase and concentration of investment in the real estate and property development sectors.

In the post-financial crisis period, several reforms were implemented, most notably the revamping of Thailand's prudential and legal framework pertaining to its banking and financial sector and the decrease in the limitations of foreign ownership of Thai banks. Thailand's economic growth has since recovered and exports look positive. However, non-performing loans are still a major concern in the banking sector. Reforms have been slow and tedious but Thailand still remains a popular market for foreign investment and is set to be the world's eighth-largest economy by the year 2020.

Citibank Thailand's experience demonstrates the environment in which foreign businesses operate in Thailand. Citibank Thailand's growth and operations have expanded with the demands of the economy. Much of Citibank's success in Thailand is due to its positioning in the market, which has ensured its domination in the provision of Thai consumer credit. Self-regulation based on international standards has, over time, seen Citibank Thailand through several lags in policy implementations and the 1997 financial crisis, and has laid the foundation for its now-prosperous treasury operations. Citibank Thailand is an example of the mutually beneficial relationship the Thai state seeks with foreign multinationals. It has introduced new skills and new technology to the Thai banking sector, while maintaining positive returns that have placed it in a strong position to benefit from Thailand's growing exports to Indochina and the region.

chapter eight

Indonesia: an improving business climate

Robert Rice

The purpose of this chapter is to briefly review the main factors that have been affecting Indonesian economic development recently. The emphasis is on the role of the state in business, the factors affecting the role and development of private businesses, opportunities for business, and positive and negative factors affecting the business climate. Some suggestions for improvements in government policies are also made.

The role of the state in business over time

According to mainstream economic development theory, the principal role of the state is to establish an environment in which private individuals, families and enterprises can experience increasing prosperity over time. This role includes the formulation and enforcement of laws, regulations, policies and programs to achieve this in terms of overall macro-economic and micro-economic performance. The state also has an important role supplying directly and indirectly public goods and services such as law and order, defence, much physical infrastructure such as ordinary roads, public health services, basic education, etc. This is because, if left alone, the private sector will supply much less than is socially optimal. The Indonesian constitution of 1945 is quite explicit about some of the roles of the state. Article 33(1) states that sectors of production that are important for the country and affect the life of the people shall be controlled by the state, although there is some debate in Indonesia as to whether control requires ownership or not (Rice 1983). With the increase in petroleum prices in the latter part of the 1970s, the Indonesian government invested heavily in state enterprises, especially in the heavy industry sector. Since the nationalisation of Dutch banks in the 1950s, the banking sector has been dominated by state banks. The banking sector was liberalised in the 1980s, resulting in a rapid growth of private banks, including foreign-owned banks.

In the mid-1980s the government changed its development strategy from an inward-looking strategy, which was heavily dependent on government investment, to an outward-looking private sector-led strategy. This resulted in rapid private sector-led growth of labour-intensive manufactured exports; exports of weaving yarns, textiles and textile products increased from US$240 million in 1985 to US$2,834 million in 1996 (the year before the economic crisis began) and exports of ready-made clothes increased from US$339 million to US$3,591 million (BPS 1988; 1998). However, the increase in national income from the private sector relative to the state sector was realised mainly through the rapid growth of the private sector, not the privatisation of state enterprises.

Although the IMF and World Bank have encouraged the government to privatise state enterprises, this was resisted partly because of the Indonesian constitution and partly for other reasons, including the protection of vested interests. An additional factor was the desire of the government (led by the then-Minister for Science and Technology BJ Habibie) to develop strategic industries, such as the aircraft, shipbuilding, armaments and steel industries (Rice 1998). In Indonesia private manufacturing industries are owned mainly by Sino-Indonesians and foreigners, not by indigenous Indonesians. Because the government could not be seen to be heavily subsidising Sino-Indonesian and foreign-owned industries, a politically attractive way to promote large, important manufacturing enterprises was through the development of state enterprises.

The Indonesian constitution also emphasises the role of co-operatives and family-oriented enterprises in the economy. This, plus the fact that larger enterprises are dominated by non-indigenous people, has resulted in government policies that favour, to varying degrees, co-operatives and smaller indigenous enterprises, which unfortunately (and in spite of strong ongoing official support) have never had an important role in the economy—except as an inefficient costly vehicle for the distribution of agricultural inputs to small farmers, the purchase of farm commodities and the distribution of agricultural credit. However, especially in the mid-1980s, private sector development (including privately owned larger enterprises) was facilitated and encouraged by the government, resulting in the rapid growth of the manufacturing and plantation agriculture sectors. During the latter years of the Suharto government, crony enterprises close to the ruling Suharto family (especially Suharto family-owned enterprises) were heavily subsidised and given monopolies and other privileges by the Suharto government, which resulted in massive inefficiencies and wastage of government funds. This enormous misuse of power was a major cause of the economic crisis of 1997. The abuses of power under the Susilo Bambang Yudhoyono administration are far less than during the latter Suharto years.

The economic crisis beginning in August 1997 resulted in a large, unintentional increase in state-owned enterprises because privately owned banks failed and were taken over (including their bad debts owned by private firms) by the Indonesian government through the Badan Penyehatan Perbankan Nasional (Indonesian Bank Restructuring Agency). The crisis also made the government dependent on loans from the IMF and World Bank, which resulted in these institutions obtaining commitments from the Indonesian government to privatise many of the old and newly acquired state enterprises. However, partly because of a lack of government commitment to this privatisation and partly because the revenues generated from the privatisation were well below expectations, privatisation has proceeded much more slowly than expected.

After getting off to a slow start, the government, through the Indonesian Bank Restructuring Agency, has now made much progress in selling the shares of the private banks that it acquired. The table below shows the percentages of shares the government owned after recapitalisation of the private banks and in mid-June 2004. Most of the shares of these banks are now privately owned and they are able to operate freely as privately owned banks.

The privatisation of the banks owned by the government *before* the crisis has been much slower. As of February 2004 the government still owned 99% of Bank Negara Indonesia (Kenward 2004:33).

Table 1: Government ownership of shares in private banks

Banks	% of shares owned by the government	
	after recapitalisation*	mid-June 2004**
Bank Central Asia	92.80	5.04
Bank Niaga	97.15	21.52
Bank Danamon	99.00	20.50
Bank International Indonesia	93.63	20.78
Lippo Bank	59.53	2.64

Sources: * *Laporan BPPN*, 31 December 2003 ***Media Indonesia*, 15 June 2004.

Factors affecting the role and development of private business over time

In comparison with the Northeast Asian countries, Indonesia is still a land of relatively abundant natural resources, which, combined with its low-cost diligent labour and quite favourable policies towards business (including foreign investment), results in many investment opportunities. The country can roughly be divided into two areas: Java, Madura, Bali, Lombok and Nusa Tenggara (Area one), where the population–natural resource ratio is very high; and the rest of the country (Area two), where population is relatively low, especially in Kalimantan and West Papua. Manufacturing is the sector with the greatest potential in Java and Madura—especially labour-intensive manufacturing for export and some manufacturing for the quite rapidly growing domestic market. With increases in the supply of skilled and educated persons and technological know-how in the country, opportunities for skilled labour-intensive and more technology-intensive industries will grow, but realisation of these opportunities is hindered by the weak higher education and technical school systems. In Area one there are still considerable opportunities for technology-intensive and skilled labour-intensive agriculture, such as the growing of flowers and other high-value crops.

In Area two the potential is greater in agriculture (especially tree crops, fishing and some forestry), mining and manufacturing (to add value to locally produced raw materials, such as by processing marine products, wood processing downstream beyond sawmills, manufacturing products based on palm oil and so on).[1] Although much of the non-renewable mineral wealth has been exploited, there are still substantial coal reserves with a sulphur and ash content of less than 1%, and copper and gold reserves. However, decentralisation, security and social problems, and illegal mining in some areas, increase the cost and risks of investment (EAAU 2000). Some of Indonesia's tropical rainforests have been converted from being renewable to nearly non-renewable resources in the form of coarse grass (*alang-alang* or *Imperata cylindrica*) because of the destructive logging methods used. This has resulted in a shortage of logs relative to the production capacity of wood-processing industries.

Although the opportunities for the development of plantations such as oil palm have rapidly been realised in Sumatra during the past 25 years, there is still a large potential, especially in Kalimantan and West Papua. The East Asia Analytical Unit in 2000 concluded that 'investment opportunities in agriculture are promising, especially in agri-industry':

> Investment opportunities exist in producing and processing estate crops like sugar and palm oil milling; developing fisheries such as shrimp farming; capturing, producing and processing fish based on deep sea fisheries and aquaculture; and raising livestock such as sheep and cattle by integrated animal husbandry... Significant opportunities also exist in downstream processing of agricultural products (EAAU 2000:178).

The low rate of investment in Indonesia, however, reveals that the investment climate is poor. Gross domestic fixed capital formation as a percentage of gross national product decreased sharply from 30.4% in 1996 and 29.2% in 1997 to

26.9% and 21.8% in 1998 and 1999 respectively. It then increased to 23.5% in 2000 and decreased steadily to 22.7%, 21.2% and 20.6% in 2001, 2002 and 2003 respectively, in spite of government efforts to improve the investment climate (calculated using data from Bank Indonesia). This is the major factor causing the moderate rates of economic growth of 3.7% in 2002 and 4.5% in 2003, which have been consumption-led (WB 2003a:5). Direct investment as shown in the balance of payments financial accounts was US$4,677 million in 1997, negative from 1998 to 2001, US$145 million in 2002, and –US$591 million in 2003. Both domestic and foreign direct investment projects approved by the government are also far below pre-crisis levels, but increased from 2002 to 2003 as shown in Table 2.

Table 2: Domestic and foreign direct investment projects approved by the government

Year	Domestic[1] Rp billion/US$ million	Foreign US$ million
1996	100,499/42,912	29,776
1997	119,756/40,568	33,127
2002	25,262/2,728	9,744
2003	48,485/5,657	13,207

[1]Domestic investment is probably increasingly underestimated because regional autonomy allows local governments to approve domestic investment proposals. The United States dollar figures are derived from the Indonesian rupiah (Rp) figures by dividing them by the average rupiah exchange rate per dollar for each year, calculated using data from Bank Indonesia (2006). The average exchange rates per US$1 for 1996, 1997, 2002 and 2003 were Rp2,342, Rp2,952, Rp9,261 and Rp8,571 respectively.

Source: calculated using data from Bank Indonesia.

Positive and negative factors affecting the investment and business climates are discussed below. Many of these are discussed in depth in Basri and Eng (2004). James Castle undertook a survey of officials representing 27 of Indonesia's 30 provinces in September 2002. This survey found that bureaucratic corruption was the most important perceived obstacle to foreign direct investment in Indonesia, followed by stability of policies and transport infrastructure. He notes that 'all of these have more to do with behaviour and operational issues than legislation or policy statements', and also points out some anti-foreign sentiment in the bureaucracy (Castle 2004:80–1). Despite this, the business climate has improved under the Yudhoyono presidency, which began in 2004. It must be remembered that rapid growth was possible from 1970 to 1996 in spite of serious legal deficiencies and widespread corruption, and therefore we can anticipate that rapid growth will return regardless of ongoing (but reduced) legal deficiencies and corruption. Such optimism depends on improvements being made to the business climate as discussed below. The Chinese experience also demonstrates that high growth rates are possible in spite of high levels of corruption and widespread deficiencies in the legal system. The following section addresses the positive and negative factors impacting on Indonesia's prospects for economic and business growth.

The positive factors

Improving macro-economic policies

Generally during the past 37 years, including the post-1997 period, the Indonesian government has implemented reasonably effective macro-economic policies, including conservative monetary and fiscal policies. This has resulted in a declining and low (by Indonesian standards) rate of inflation of just over 5% from the beginning to the end of 2003 (Kenward 2004:17), although the 'period from mid-2000 to late 2001 was characterised by an uncertain and unstable macroeconomy, as well as political instability' that adversely affected investment (Bird 2004:102). After wide fluctuations during the post-crisis period, in 2003 the rupiah appreciated from around Rp9,000 per US$1 at the beginning of the year to around Rp8,200 in June 2003, and then gradually depreciated to around Rp9,000 in August 2004. In 2003 the growth rate remained steady at 4.5% based on revised GDP numbers—a big improvement over the late 1990s but still not high enough to lessen the rate of unemployment (WB 2004b:1).

Before the IMF-supported program assisting Indonesia came to an end in December 2003, the government issued Presidential Instruction No 5 of 2003—'A package of economic policies before and after termination of the co-operation program with the International Monetary Fund'—known as the White Paper (BI 2004:196). In June 2004 the World Bank concluded that the implementation of the package had been impressive—over three-quarters of the measures committed to had been implemented on time, or had only experienced minor delays. It included various macro-economic stability, financial sector restructuring, and investment, exports and employment policies (WB 2004b:9).

Concern has been expressed, however, about some of the micro-economic aspects of the White Paper. Ray notes that it 'calls for Indonesia to strive for self-sufficiency in key agricultural commodities such as corn and soybeans, and talks of setting tariffs, in effect, to enable the relevant industries to compete' (Ray 2003b:260). The steel, ceramic, agricultural, fishery, mining and pharmaceutical sectors are included in the first phase of the harmonisation of import tariffs in accordance with changes in competitiveness (KMKBPRI 2004).[2] Castle comments on this as follows: 'the overall thrust of the paper is towards control and intrusion rather than facilitation or streamlining. The section on labour is particularly discouraging in this regard' (Castle 2004:82).

More favourable attitudes towards foreign investment and free markets

Although Indonesians coming out of the colonial era were generally wary of foreign investment and the liberal economy, attitudes towards foreign investment and a freer market economy have become much more favourable over the years. There is certainly a much greater appreciation now of the large benefits that can accrue to a nation from foreign direct investment, as evidenced by the Malaysian and Singaporean experiences.

Improved investment regulations

Instead of listing the business fields open to foreign investment, the Badan Koordinasi Penanaman Modal (Indonesian Investment Board) has now introduced a policy that is more favourable—all fields are open to foreign investment except for four lists of business fields in which foreign capital is closed or restricted. These lists are:

- List I—business fields absolutely closed for investment;
- List II—business fields closed to investment in which a part of the shares are owned by foreign citizens and/or foreign business entities;
- List III—business fields open to investment under condition of a joint venture between foreign and domestic capital; and
- List IV—business fields open to investment under certain conditions (BKPM 2000).

The business areas that are closed or restricted but likely to be attractive to some foreign investors are as follows:

- List I—industries producing alcoholic drinks and casino and gambling facilities;
- List II—concession for natural forests; contractors in the field of lumbering; and trading and trade-supporting services except large-scale

retailers, wholesale trading, exhibition/convention service providers, quality certification service providers, market research service providers, warehousing services outside seaports and after-sale services;

- List III—electricity production, transmission and distribution; shipping; processing and provision of potable water for public use; medical services; telecommunications; and regular/non-regular commercial airliners; and
- List IV—fishing of demersal fish; industries producing wood pulp; plywood and rotary veneer industries; sawn-timber industries; petroleum and natural gas drilling services; power plant businesses; restaurants; and some others.

In addition to these, two restrictions on foreign investors in Indonesia may be of concern. First, a foreign direct investment company can be granted a foreign investment licence of only 30 years, with an additional 30 years being permitted by the government if the foreign firm makes a commitment to additional, new investment (ICG 2004). Second, foreign-owned and Indonesian companies are not allowed to own land (only Indonesian citizens are entitled to own freehold land). Instead there are three types of rights to use land:

- *Hak Guna Bangunan* or the right to build on the land, which is generally valid for 30 years and renewable for 20 years;
- *Hak Pakai* or the right to use the land, which is generally valid for ten years and renewable for ten years at a time; and
- *Hak Guna Usaha* or the right to conduct business on the land, which is generally valid for 35 years and renewable twice, each time for 25 years (Ng et al 1998:302).

There is now some discussion of allowing foreigners to own land.

Ongoing recovery of the financial system

It is well known that the Indonesian banking sector was devastated by the 1997 Asian financial crisis, with both government-owned and many domestic, privately owned banks being rescued by the government at great cost to the Indonesian people. As discussed above, considerable progress has been made in privatising presently owned state banks, but the process needs to be hastened in order to improve banking efficiency, improve services to the private sector, and to free the government from possible future colossal financial losses from scandals and mismanagement of state banks. For several years banks were unable to perform their intermediation functions effectively. However, from 1999 to November 2003, the loan–deposit ratio of Indonesian commercial banks increased from 0.262 in 1999 to 0.330 in 2001 and to 0.437 in November 2003, even though it was still below the average of 0.75 during the pre-crisis period (BI 2004:113, 121). The amount of credit extended also steadily increased from Rp277.3 trillion in 1999 to Rp358.6 trillion in 2001 and to Rp475.7 trillion in November 2003, but is still much less in real terms than when it was Rp306 trillion in March 1997 (BI 2004:121; 1997:Table 46).

Bank Indonesia justifiably claims that banking-sector improvements are attributable to the banking policies adopted, internal banking reforms and improvements in various macro-economic indicators such as inflation, the exchange rate and interest rates. Its policies aim to enhance the recovery of banking intermediation, with special attention to expanding credit to micro-, small- and medium-scale businesses (BI 2004:111). Bank Perkreditan Rakyat (rural credit banks) are an important part of the government's strategy to facilitate micro-, small- and medium-scale businesses. However, the number of rural credit banks decreased from 7,764 in 2000 to 7,703 in 2001 and to 7,479 in 2003. There is still a need to increase the number of rural credit bank branches because there are still some areas underserved by banking services (Rice 2004:83–6).

International trade liberalisation

Indonesia has undertaken much international trade liberalisation during the past 20 years, with the result that, on average, import duty rates are low—this results in greater demand for imports and a weaker rupiah, which encourages exports. Import duty rates on raw materials and components are generally low. If an enterprise needs to import intermediate inputs for export production, it can obtain duty-free imports by locating production in a bonded zone or by applying for a restitution (drawback) of import duties paid on goods and materials (BKPM 2000). In addition, 'an investment Tax Allowance in the form of taxable income reduction [by] as much as 30% of the realised investment spread in 6 (six) years' and other tax allowances are granted to domestic and foreign investors (BKPM 2000).

Possible recovery of competitiveness in labour-intensive manufacturing

From the mid-1980s until the early 1990s, Indonesia was very successful in developing labour-intensive industries for export goods. This was facilitated by various changes in policies to aid production for export, together with the low wage rates paid for relatively well-disciplined, hard-working labour, especially in Java.

In the mid-1990s, and recurring during the past several years, three factors adversely affected the business climate for labour-intensive industries, with the result that some of them closed down (see Basri 2004 for a discussion of changes in revealed comparative advantage of manufacturing industries, 1985–2001). The causes of these business collapses can be reversed by the government if it has the political will.

The first cause was the rapid increase between 1989 and 1997 in real minimum wages, which increased over 170%, compared with an increase in the real average wage in Indonesia of approximately 10% (SMERU 2001:40). The 1997–98 economic crisis saw labour costs in manufacturing fall sharply to about 60% below the 1993 level; from mid-1998 to mid-2003 these labour costs steadily increased to about 70% above the 1993 level, greatly decreasing Indonesia's competitiveness in labour-intensive manufactures (WB 2004b:4). The increase in the average provincial minimum wage slowed down in 2004, increasing 11.1% from Rp414,715 in 2003 to Rp460,892 in 2004, but was still over 6% in real terms.

Producing labour-intensive products for export is a competitive business. Therefore, even though real wage rates are quite low in Indonesia, private sector investment is discouraged by the risk and uncertainty created by the Indonesian system of setting minimum wage rates. These rates are set through the political process at the district government level, with the final decision being with the provincial governors of the provinces, meaning that they are influenced by political factors and are not closely tied to underlying economic fundamentals (DM 2003). The wage rate uncertainty and risk would be greatly decreased if minimum wage rates were directly tied to the rate of inflation.

A very important industry which has lost competitiveness is the garments industry. A recent in-depth study of this industry found that, given Indonesia's labour productivity, its labour costs are still competitive in the Asian region. However, lack of new investments since 1992 has had an adverse effect on labour productivity, in contrast with the ongoing high levels of investment in China (Aswicahyono, Atje & Thee 2004). The study also discussed other ways of increasing Indonesia's competitiveness, including climbing up the technological ladder. Technology-intensive industries, however, cannot use the large pool of unskilled Javanese labour. Labour-intensive industries in which Indonesia has a comparative advantage (such as garment making) must not be abandoned just because the existing policies are deficient. My view is that garment production is just too important an industry in terms of both employment and income to be allowed to fail because the government is unwilling to make the necessary policy changes to increase the industry's competitiveness. Without these large, labour-absorbing industries, it is hard to see how Indonesia can generate the employment it needs. The alternative of natural resource extraction can never generate much additional employment in Java, and shifting the labour force into more technology-intensive industries will take years to materialise.

Other aspects of Indonesia's labour market contribute to the country's lack of industrial competitiveness. The administrative costs of hiring and firing Indonesian labour are very high. All enterprises must obtain permission from a government agency to dismiss labour and must provide compensation according to the labour protection law of 25 February 2003: 'Although less unfriendly to business than the previous regulatory framework, on key dimensions the new law still looks uncompetitive compared to practices elsewhere in the region' (MacIntyre & Resosudarmo 2003:148). Compared with Ministerial Decree No 150/2000, it continues to require employers to pay workers' wages when they strike legally, and it continues to provide for generous payments upon severance of employment (RI 2003). The increased militancy of trade unions, especially during the reformation of the post-Suharto era, has been a growing concern for those concerned with the business climate. The payment of workers while on strike is one of the factors contributing to rising costs and falling national competitiveness.

On the positive side, because Indonesia is a huge country there are many areas where investment can be made, with some areas being much more favourable than others, despite the statutory requirement to pay minimum wage rates. If we look at areas favourable for export-oriented manufacturing close to major harbours, we find the minimum wage rate in 2004 was high in the city and *kabupaten* (shire) of Tangerang (Rp660,000 per month), in the city and *kabupaten* of Bekasi, just east of Jakarta (Rp670,000), in the city of Surabaya (Rp550,700) and just east of Surabaya in Kabupaten Sidoarjo (Rp550,550). In the city of Semarang, however, the minimum wage rate was only Rp440,000, and Rp430,000 in Kabupaten Semarang, south of the city (DM 2005). Foreign capital might be encouraged to invest in the low-wage regions.

Bank Indonesia mentions various problems confronting businesses, including a serious erosion of Indonesia's comparative advantage in especially cheap labour. However, rather than recommending ways in which this comparative advantage might be regained, it concludes that 'a different approach is needed, oriented more towards the utilisation of natural resources and technology-intensive industries in line with the paradigm formulated in *Propenas*' (BI

2004:12–13).[3] My view is that, given the serious unemployment problem, especially in Java, facilitation of the growth of labour-intensive sectors must be given a high priority for many years to come.

Less danger of unfair competition from the political elite

If we compare the business climate at the present time with, say, the late 1980s under President Suharto, one major improvement is that it is much less likely (if you are a successful business enterprise or are in a potentially highly profitable business field) that a member of the Suharto family or closely connected conglomerates or present-day powerful government officials will use their power to negatively affect your business, including making regulations that disadvantage you. Well-known examples of government regulations favouring those close to the Suharto family included the monopoly over the export of citrus fruits from West Kalimantan to other parts of Indonesia, the clove monopoly, the favouritism towards the Timor car firm, bans on firms setting up hotels in certain areas, and the government subsidisation of Simpati Airlines.

The negative factors affecting Indonesia's business climate

Regional autonomy and decentralisation

Paradoxically, the new decentralisation of the Indonesian economy, which began in 1999, has increased business uncertainty. With the passage of Law 22 (on regional government) in 1999, Law 25 (on the financial balance between the central and regional government) in 1999—both effective 1 January 2001—and related legislation, various uncertainties faced by private businesses have increased. This legislation has increased the power of district level (municipal and *kabupaten*) governments to regulate economic activity. Entrepreneurs wishing to set up firms must now discuss their business plans with the appropriate district government office and obtain approval before beginning the venture. These 'consultations' have given local governments the opportunity to demand new forms of payments from enterprises. Large firms, in particular, have been subjected to such extractions—for example, the Tanjung Enim Lestari Pulp and Paper factory in Muara Enim Kabupaten in South Sumatra (author's case study 2002). Such demands as these are not likely to cause the closure of large existing plants, but they will certainly discourage new investment.

Decentralisation has given rise to hopeful expectations, but the impact of the new laws should not be exaggerated. For example, on 15 October 2004, Laws 32 and 33 of 2004 replaced Laws 22 (1999) and 25 (1999). This change is likely to have only a small positive effect on the business climate because the division of responsibilities between the district and central government are basically unchanged, although the power of the provincial governments relative to the district governments has increased. The increased powers of the provincial governments should enable them to better co-ordinate and facilitate economic development and should also have some positive effects on the quality of district government budgets, which now must be approved by the provincial governor, as well as by the district parliament. Budgets must also be approved by the Minister of Home Affairs (*Undang-Undan* 2004:108–11).

With decentralisation and regional autonomy, the expectation was that district governments would be more concerned than provincial and central governments with the business climate and welfare of the populations in their districts. So far there is little evidence for this—instead many district governments have decided to create new ways of generating local revenues and this has had adverse effects on the business climate. In particular, the provision of public services has suffered, as documented in a survey of 1,014 businesses in 12 provinces in 2003 (Fauzi 2003) and in new research by Wihana Jaya (2005). There have also been some overlapping and conflicting central government and local government regulations. We remain optimistic, though, that with time regional autonomy will have a significant positive effect on the business climate through lower rates of corruption and increased attention being paid to the needs of the local communities.

Corruption

Corruption in Indonesia continues to be a serious problem. Transparency International publishes a 'Corruption Perceptions Index', which is based on the perceptions of businesses operating in countries around the world. The '2003 Corruption Perceptions Index' ranked Indonesia as 122nd out of 133 countries, with the 133rd country being the most corrupt. This compared with Malaysia at 37th, China at 66th, India at 83rd and Vietnam at 100th. However, on a CPI scale of zero to ten (the least corrupt), the differences were not so striking: Indonesia was rated at 1.9, Malaysia at 5.2, China at 3.4, India at 2.8 and Vietnam at 2.4 (TI 2005). With decentralisation there has been some shift of power from the central government to local governments—especially the district level—and a corresponding shift in corruption. However, on the positive side there are around 435 *kabupaten* and municipalities in Indonesia, with much variation in levels of corruption and attractiveness to investors. The Komisi Pemantauan Pelaksanaan Otonomi Daerah (Commission for Monitoring the Implementation of Regional Autonomy) has published *Pemeringkatan daya tarik investasi 200 kabupaten/Kota di Indonesia, 2003*, which ranks 200 *kabupaten* and cities according to their attractiveness to investors and the 14 factors determining this attractiveness, such as the quality of physical infrastructure, certainty of law, security and labour costs (KPPOD 2004). Therefore, there is a wide variety of business environments in which businesses can choose to operate in Indonesia. A prospective investor also needs to check the local regulations to see if any inhibit local commerce, investment and other economic activities, as sometimes local governments impose these especially in order to increase local government revenues (Ray 2003a).

The World Bank completed a '2003 Country Policy and Institutional Assessment Overall Rating' of low-income countries, which was derived from assessments of economic management, structural policies, policies for social inclusion/equity, public sector management and institutions, and governance. Indonesia is in the second quintile of countries for the first three types of assessment, in the third quintile for public sector management and institutions, and in the fourth quintile for the governance rating (WB 2004a). The first quintile is the best.

Infrastructure

When planning an investment, investors need to carefully check electricity supply because there are problems of both quality and quantity in some areas and the evolving situation is likely to become worse. Before the 1997 Asian financial crisis the Indonesian State Electricity Corporation made contracts in United States dollars with foreign companies to build electricity-generating plants and to supply electricity. With the huge depreciation of the rupiah, the corporation was unable to honour some of these contracts—legal disputes, project delays and electricity shortages followed. A June 2003 World Bank study reports that in Java and Bali, over the short to medium term (as of 2001), the key challenge is that of burgeoning power shortages, and 'already areas outside Java have been experiencing frequent power supply interruptions, and this situation is likely to extend to the crucial Java–Bali power system over the next three years' (WB 2003b:5). The most critical issue currently facing the State Electricity Corporation is the looming shortfall in generation capacity (World Bank 2004b:9). The ASEAN Centre for Energy in 2001 reported that the following areas in Indonesia have deficit power supplies: Bengkulu, Northern Lampung, Dumai-Duri, Tanjung Pandan on Belitung Island, Tanjung Pinang on Bintan Island, Tanjung Balai Karimun on Karimun Island, Lombok Island, West Sumbawa, Kupang, Pontianak, Palangkaraya, Balikpapan, Menado, Ambon, Sorong and Jayapura (ASEAN 2000). However, there are many areas where the supply of electricity is still excellent. The 2002–03 Global Competitiveness Report ranked Indonesia 69th in terms of perceptions of quality of electricity supply, compared with Vietnam at 72nd, China at 54th and Malaysia at 29th, with the first position being the best (WB 2003a:35).

According to a World Bank report, the overall quality of infrastructure in Indonesia has deteriorated since the 1997 Asian financial crisis because public spending had to be reduced sharply in real terms and many committed and planned private infrastructure projects were suspended. The 2002–03 Global Competitiveness Report ranked Indonesia 64th in the world in terms of perceptions of overall infrastructure quality, compared with China at 52nd, Vietnam at 71st and Malaysia at 16th (WB 2003a:35). Indonesia's transportation system has also deteriorated somewhat since the crisis because the huge increase in the government's domestic debt (and consequent large increase in expenditures in the budget on interest payments) resulted in a large decrease in government investment in infrastructure, including in the transportation sector. This in turn proved to be an obstacle to potential economic growth (EIU 2003:29). The author's field research in South Sumatra and West Timor in 2002 found that the quality of provincial roads, especially, had deteriorated, which significantly raised the cost of transportation from different *kabupaten* in West Timor and Kupang and between South Sumatra and Lampung provinces.

The government is encouraging foreign investment in toll roads and railroad infrastructure, as well as increasing its own investment in road infrastructure from Rp3.96 trillion to Rp4.3 trillion from 2003 to 2004 (MIO 2004). The Director General for Prasarana Wilayah (Regional Infrastructure) said that the target was to decrease the percentage of *tingkat kerusakan jalan* (roads damaged) from 15% to 10% by the end of 2004 and that, ideally, Rp9 trillion per year was needed for national roads (MIO 2004). This situation is likely to improve in the future as the percentage of the government budget spent on debt servicing continues to decrease and as there is an increase in the freeing-up of funds for investment and private sector investment in infrastructure and an improvement in the investment climate.

The legal system

It is well known that in spite of new bankruptcy laws and other commercial legislation, the Indonesian legal system functions poorly. Therefore, few businesses rely on the enforceability of contracts via recourse to the legal system as a way of minimising their financial risks. Instead, it is especially important in Indonesia that firms do business with parties that they can trust and with parties that have a track record of honourable behaviour.

Some high-cost inputs

Some inputs, especially those supplied by state enterprises and some strategic industries, are too costly, reflecting in part the restrictions imposed on importing substitutes. This has been a problem with some steel products and some chemicals produced by the plastics and petrochemical industries. This situation has improved with reformation and liberalisation.

Increased regulation of international trade

In recent times there has been an increase in the regulation of international trade, especially in the form of increased protection against imports; quantitative import restrictions are mainly used, but there is some increased regulation of exports as well. Quantitative international trade restrictions usually increase the risk for businesses because their introduction can have a large effect on profitability and, if licensing is involved, usually favours larger businesses over smaller ones (the legal and illegal costs of obtaining licences as a ratio of the size of the transaction decreases with an increase in transaction size). The Ministry of Finance usually favours import duties and export taxes as policy instruments, in contrast with the Ministry of Industry and the Ministry of Agriculture, which favour quantitative restrictions such as quotas and bans on goods that are under their jurisdictions. Ray and Kenward discuss various types of recent protectionism, including a Ministry of Industry and Trade re-imposition of an earlier ban on imports of used clothing, a ruling requiring textile imports to be verified at the port of origin (Ray 2003b:257–8) and a ban on the import of 46 items of used capital goods (Kenward 2004:16).[4] The Ministry of Industry and Trade has also introduced new export-licensing arrangements for wood products and is working on a new presidential decree to re-regulate large-scale modern retailing (Ray 2003b:259). The Ministry of Agriculture proposed increasing the tariff on imported soybeans from 0% to 27%.

The domestic security situation

This chapter concludes with a discussion about how the domestic security situation has impacted on business opportunities in Indonesia. It is also well known that the security situation has deteriorated in the post-Suharto era. This has caused serious problems, especially in the plantation, agriculture and mining sectors. Security is generally good in manufacturing, although in some areas there are problems with local youth gangs extorting levies on trucks passing through 'their territory' and on the loading and unloading of trucks. The seriousness of these difficulties varies substantially from locality to locality.

The deterioriation in the security situation is partly caused by the population's decline in respect for authority of government agencies, including the police and the armed forces. This decline in law and order has been particularly damaging to the agricultural sector. There are widespread reports from North Sumatra to Java of masses of people converging on brackish water-shrimp ponds to steal shrimp just before harvest time (although the main causes of the demise of shrimp aquaculture is a virus and poor water quality) (*Kompas* 2000; 2003a). One Japanese company that cultivates pearls in Sikka Kabupaten in East Nusa Tenggara has been amazed to discover that despite frequent reports of serious thefts of pearls, no robbers have been caught (*Kompas* 2003b). Other forms of theft are also common—for example, the stealing of palm kernel bunches from trees at night-time and of logs in Sumatra and Kalimantan. This has had a strong negative impact on investment in estate crop development, one of the sectors with the greatest potential in Indonesia.

Also in many cities there is a problem with *premanism* (youth gangs), which engage in various forms of extortion that raise the costs of doing business. This problem has been particularly damaging to the reputation of the city of Medan in North Sumatra, where businesses are commonly required to make payments to the local youth gangs to load and unload trucks and to enable trucks to leave the factories to deliver the goods. This has certainly been a significant factor hindering the transplantation of labour-intensive industries in Penang across the Straits of Malacca to Medan. However, in late 2005 the national police, under the newly appointed police chief, General Sutanto, began a crackdown on youth gangs (*Serambi* 2005). This has reportedly reduced youth-gang extortion dramatically in Medan.

In the latter months of 2005 and early months of 2006, the Yudhoyono government's anti-corruption drive picked up steam, with considerable numbers of high-ranking government officials, including the Governor of Aceh, the head of the Election Commission and parliamentarians, being jailed. This anti-corruption campaign has had the effect of making high-ranking officials more cautious in undertaking corrupt practices.

Notes

1 Bank Indonesia provides information about various types of development potential in many districts in Indonesia, although in this author's view it should be used more as a source of ideas about potential, with much further investigation being required before any business plans can be made. Provincial and district investment offices are also a useful source of information about economic opportunities.
2 Point 4 under industrial and trade policies in the Program Matrix of the White Paper.
3 *Propenas* is the national development program.
4 The Ministry of Trade and Industry was divided into two ministries with the inauguration of the Yudhoyono administration.

chapter nine

Malaysia: the contradictions of a remarkable economic transformation

Marika Vicziany

Malaysia's economic response to the Asian financial crisis in 1997–98 was the first occasion on which the international community began to pay serious attention to the question of how Malaysia had reconstructed itself after independence from British rule. Four things in particular characterised Malaysia's unique response to the crisis: first, the speed and decisiveness with which the Malaysian Prime Minister suspended the convertibility of the Malaysian ringgit in order to put an end to currency speculation; second, how Malaysia's response alerted the world to the singular fact that Malaysia was not a country that suffered from the typical indebtedness of other developing nations; third, despite the pain inflicted by the Asian financial crisis, Malaysia bounced back quite rapidly, suggesting that the economy had developed a fundamental resilience; and fourth, and most significantly, in contrast to the social pain experienced in Thailand, Indonesia and South Korea, unemployment in Malaysia was low and never exceeded the 3.9% level of 1998 (WB 2000:i). Low unemployment has emerged as a feature of the Malaysian economy and lies at the root of its successful attack on mass poverty: by 2005 under 0.5% of the Malaysian population lived on less than US$1 per day, compared with 1.7% in Thailand and 8.3% in Vietnam (WB 2005:57–8).

Malaysia's economic resilience is based on the long-term, solid achievements of growth from the 1960s onwards. It needs to be stressed that the socioeconomic transformation described below occurred in the face of a complex social environment in which about 49% of the Malaysian population constituted some kind of minority group.[1] Table 1 summarises what some of those growth thresholds looked like after 1980. However, by 1980 the standard of literacy alone suggested that Malaysia had already achieved significant development in the two decades from 1960 to 1980. By 1980 adult literacy was already at 71% and, even more impressively, female literacy lagged not so far behind at 62%. By regional and global standards, these were important achievements—for example, India, largely acknowledged as an emerging regional and global power, has still not achieved the literacy levels *today* that Malaysia had by 1980.

Malaysian development during the 1960s and 1970s was even more remarkable given the frightening degree of lawlessness and disorder that characterised daily life in Malaysia during the early post-Second World War period. In addition to the work of criminal gangs and opportunists, Malaysia had been racked by a communist insurgency movement and interracial conflict that had escalated as a result of the Japanese occupation, which used racial conflict as a tool for control (Comber 2006:ch 1, 2).

Malaysia's economic transformation after 1980 was even more impressive than the record of the previous two decades. In particular, Malaysia became less and less dependent on agriculture. Throughout the world, the proportion of people living in rural areas is taken as the key indicator of a country's degree of development and diversification. By this measure, Malaysia was an overwhelmingly rural economy in 1980, with about 58% of the population in villages (Table 1). By 1990 the rural and urban populations were of roughly equal importance, and by 2000 only 43% of the population remained in the rural areas, with some 57% being town or city dwellers. How this transition was achieved is the subject of this chapter. The achievements have been considerable; at the same time, serious constraints remain in sustaining the pattern of economic growth into the coming decades. These constraints are very worrying as evidence points to the emergence of a plateau in Malaysia's development trajectory. The lack of innovativeness and a socio-cultural environment in which people are reluctant to openly disagree with any government policies has contributed to this.

Table 1 provides other indicators by which to measure the nature and degree of Malaysia's transformation. After 1980 infant mortality, for example, began to decline rapidly from 31 deaths per 1,000 live births to a quarter of that by 2000. These gains in living standards made palpable differences to Malaysians. For one thing, people were living longer and the population started to increase rapidly. Between 1980 and 2000 the Malaysian population increased by 77% (from 14 million to 23 million). Despite the extra people, the population was becoming wealthier—during the same period the per capita GDP doubled. By the late 1990s economic development in Malaysia was starting to become obvious in more conspicuous forms of consumption—for example, by 2000 one in five people had a mobile telephone.

Table 1: Malaysia's economic growth for the past 20 years [2]

Indicators	1980	1990	1995	2000
Population (total)	13,763,000	18,202,000	20,610,000	23,270,000
Rural population (% of total population)	58	50	46	43
Internet users (per 1,000 people)	na	na	1	214
Mobile telephones (per 1,000 people)	0	5	50	220
Mortality rate, infant (per 1,000 live births)	31	16	11	8
GDP per capita (constant 1995 US$)	2,297	3,104	4,310	4,808
ICT expenditure per capita (US$)	na	na	221	259
Literacy rate, adult total (% of people ages 15 and above)	71	81	84	89
Literacy rate, adult female (% of females ages 15 and above)	62	74	79	85
School enrolment, pre-primary (% gross)	na	35	48	95
School enrolment, primary (% gross)	93	94	103	97
School enrolment, secondary (% gross)	48	56	59	69
School enrolment, tertiary (% of gross)	4	7	12	26

Notes: na = not available; ICT: Information and Communication Technologies
Source: based on data in World Bank (2004c).

Another key measure of a country's economic strength is the nature of its production, in particular the proportion of a nation's wealth that is generated by the different sectors of the economy. Table 2 illustrates the chief contours of this transformation. By 1990 primary industries in Malaysia had already declined as a source of total output to just under a third of GDP (28.5%), dominated by agriculture, forestry, livestock and fishing. The secondary sector was already marginally more important than agriculture, accounting for just under a third of national production (30.5%). Manufacturing was the chief factor in the secondary sector, with total GDP from manufacturing being equal to 26.9% of the total, which was considerably more than the contribution to GDP by agriculture alone (18.7%). Clearly Malaysia was no longer a typically underdeveloped economy.

Table 2: GDP by industry of origin, 1990–2005 (percentages)[3]

Sector	1990	1995	2000	2005
Primary sector				
Agriculture, forestry, livestock and fishing	18.7	10.3	8.7	7.0
Mining and quarrying	9.8	8.2	6.6	5.5
Subtotal	**28.5**	**18.5**	**15.3**	**12.5**
Secondary sector				
Manufacturing	26.9	27.1	33.4	35.8
Construction	3.6	4.4	3.3	3.2
Subtotal	**30.5**	**31.5**	**36.7**	**39.0**
Tertiary sector				
Services				
a. Electricity, gas and water	1.9	3.5	3.4	3.4
b. Transport, storage and communication	6.9	7.4	8.0	8.6
c. Wholesale and retail trade, hotels and restaurants	11.1	15.2	14.9	15.0
d. Finance, insurance, real estate and business services	9.8	10.4	11.8	12.4
e. Government services	10.6	7.1	7.0	5.7
f. Other services	2.1	7.7	7.5	8.0
Subtotal	**42.4**	**51.3**	**52.6**	**53.1**
TOTAL	101.4	101.3	104.6	104.6
Minus imputed bank service charges	5.1	5.3	6.8	6.5
Plus import duties	3.7	4.1	2.3	2.0
GRAND TOTAL	100.0	100.1	100.1	100.1

Source: Government of Malaysia 2001:35.

The most dramatic evidence of economic change before 1990 is provided by the importance of the tertiary or services sector of the Malaysian economy. In 1990 services (at 42.4% of total GDP) were already more important to Malaysia than *either* the primary or secondary sectors. This feature accelerated in the next decade, with the result that the tertiary sector came to dominate the combined primary and secondary production: 53.1% of GDP in 2005 was generated by services, compared with 12.5% by the primary sector and 39% by the secondary sector.

An important qualification needs to be added to this analysis: the growth of the tertiary sector is inconceivable but for the dynamic growth of Malaysian manufacturing—it was the manufacturing sector that acted as the engine of growth by generating the demand for a wide range of services. The nature of that manufacturing sector is the focus of the two case studies that follow, namely the emergence of Malaysia's car industry and the rise of a hard-disk drive industry in Penang. These case studies have been selected because they demonstrate the nature of the inter-relationship between government policy, foreign direct investment, the growing consumer markets in Malaysia and the nature of Malaysia's export-oriented growth. Both case studies also highlight the fragility of the industrialisation process in Malaysia. Economic growth and development was achieved, but can this now be sustained? Has the dependence of the Malaysian economy on government initiatives now become the country's main obstacle to sustained development? The analysis begins with an account of the role of government policies in Malaysia's transition. The chapter then discusses two key industrialisation strategies of the Malaysian government—the creation of an electronics hub in Penang and the national car project.

Government policies in Malaysia's economic transition

The racial conflicts and tensions that appeared to be endemic to Malaysia during the period of Japanese occupation re-emerged with frightening force on 13 May 1969. Riots on this day indicated that a development priority of the government should be not merely economic growth but also greater equity, in particular equity between the different ethnic groups that formed part of the Malaysian nation. The result of this realisation was the introduction of the New Economic Policy (NEP), specifically designed to uplift the social and economic status of the Malay community. By the late 1980s the NEP had achieved some of its key objectives and so a new National Vision Policy was announced for the ten years beginning in 1991.

Despite the racial problems, Malaysian economic growth during the early decades was relatively rapid, largely because Malaysia was beginning from a low base—in particular in the secondary and tertiary sectors. However, every subsequent period of development normally becomes more difficult and requires a developing country to ensure that the foundations for long-term sustainable growth are also being developed. In the Malaysian case, the human resources foundation (namely mass literacy) was built quite rapidly, as noted above. However, the research and capital bases of development also need to be built and these are always more difficult to achieve because they bring a developing country face to face with global competition for scare capital and research and development. The Malaysian Prime Minister's 'Vision 2020' speech recognised this by urging Malaysian industry to focus more sharply on productivity improvements and to move Malaysian industrial production into higher value-added products (Vicziany & Puteh 2004).

The NEP already recognised what the chief economic constraints on Malaysian development were likely to be. At first the NEP focused on the need to create new opportunities for the Malays who had been disadvantaged by previous development strategies. Thus the Malaysian government gave priority to reducing national unemployment and poverty, and this was largely achieved. Industrialisation allowed job diversification to occur. A considerable section of the rural workforce migrated into the new urban centres and took up these new jobs. Particular beneficiaries of this process were the *bumiputeras* ('sons of the soil' or Malays). A key platform in the NEP was the reservation of about 30% of all jobs for the *bumiputeras,* including new public sector positions created by the Malaysian government. In this respect the Malaysian government was following policies of affirmative action introduced in the United States (in the 1960s) and India (from 1950 onwards) (Mendelsohn & Vicziany 1998:ch 10). In the case of Malaysia, however, these policies went well beyond the public sector

Affirmative action policies in developing countries cannot be sustained forever. The fiscal pressures generated by affirmative action can lead to these programs being curtailed. There is also the inevitable backlash from domestic and international communities, which begin to see reservation as a way of promoting people with mediocre skills. This perception can undermine other development policies designed to increase investment in domestic industries. Malaysia's *bumiputera* policies continue, for example, to be a cause for complaint by foreign firms of unfair competition that they must face when doing business in Malaysia. There is also the view that such policies promote other practices that lead to a lack of business transparency, even corruption. This lack of transparency is feared by both domestic and foreign private firms because they think they will be pressured by the government to make economic commitments that are not financially sensible (Vicziany 2001). Most recently Tan Sri Ramon Navarantam (2006a:43, 53–4) has noted how the *bumiputera* policies have contributed to the 'brain drain'. Talented non-Malays who felt that the policies of the NEP were against them voted with their feet by going abroad to seek better opportunities, especially for educational purposes.

In the case of the NEP, by the mid-1980s a contradiction emerged between national concerns with social equality and the need to attract foreign capital in order to promote new industries. As Haggard, Lim and Ong (1998) argue in their study of the hard-disk drive industry in Penang, foreign firms are attracted to locations that minimise the risks of doing business in an overseas environment. Inevitably this means that foreign capital investment flows to the better-off regions of developing countries where all the inputs into the production process are in abundance and of high quality. Karim, Fleming and Doran (2004:3) make the same point. They conclude that foreign direct investment 'inflows are most sensitive to labour productivity but are also quite sensitive to per capital GDP' (Karim, Fleming & Doran 2004:2, 16). The inflow of foreign capital into the better-off regions then reinforces these advantages, exacerbating regional inequalities. This is exactly what happened in the case of Penang, which became a hub for Malaysia's electronics industry. Having recognised the contradictory features of the NEP, it is necessary to stress that, despite the persistent inequality within Malaysia, the socioeconomic status of the indigenous Malays has unquestionably risen during the past half-century largely because of the beneficial aspects of Malaysian economic growth. According to a recent, controversial study by one Malaysian analyst, *bumiputera* ownership of companies in Malaysia has now reached 45%, some 15% beyond the original target of 30% (Ong 2006). This figure alone suggests that the policy may no longer be appropriate to Malaysia's current needs.

Case study of Penang and the hard-disk drive industry

The emergence of Penang as an industrial hub during the 30 years beginning 1970 provides a good illustration of the dramatic transformation that has occurred in Malaysia and also its limitations. From the start Penang was identified as the focus of a high-technology industrial region in which capital-intensive production would dominate. The state government of Penang encouraged those firms that depended on labour-intensive production methods to move out of Penang into other parts of the country. This was in response to the Nathan Report, the work of a United States consultancy company, which mapped out a master plan for Penang (ATIP 1996). The Penang Development Corporation was established and asked to focus on attracting capital-intensive companies to Penang in response to special incentives provided by both the Penang and national government. The end result of these policies was the rise of Penang as a Malaysian city with an international reputation for the manufacture of electronics, in particular hard-disk drives. It was an industrial explosion that depended on foreign capital investment.

By the late 1980s the second generation of investment occurred when significant foreign firms involved in the hard-disk drive industry began to locate themselves in Penang (for example, Maxtor, Conner, Hitachi Metals, Control Data and Applied Magnetics cited in Haggard, Lim & Ong 1998). All of these firms had an established regional presence in Southeast Asia, but came to Malaysia in response to relatively lower labour costs and the better-than-average quality of that labour. Proximity to Singapore was another factor, as senior management in Singapore could keep a sharp eye on operations in Penang (Haggard, Lim & Ong 1998). These second-generation firms built on the industrial heritage created during the 1970s by the first generation of foreign firms that were specialised producers of semiconductors. Much of this initial growth occurred in Bayan Lepas, Penang's first export-processing zone (ATIP 1996). By the 1990s there were 700 factories, 200,000 workers (many from Taiwan) and seven export-processing zones in Penang (ATIP 1996). About 20% of these factories produced electrical or electronic goods (ATIP 1996:Table 1). In 1992, 26% of the electronics producers (some 110 factories) were Taiwanese, 19% were Japanese and 17% were American (ATIP 1996:Table 2). Taiwanese firms controlled 35% of the capital investment but local involvement was much lower—about 19% of firms were Malaysian but they accounted for only 2% of the total capital in Penang. Within the electronics industry, the hard-disk drive sector emerged quickly between 1990 and 1996. By 1996 it accounted for 27% of employment and 16% of output in electronics (Haggard, Lim & Ong 1998: Table 1).

The foreign firms started to generate local demand for inputs, which encouraged local Malaysian firms to start up and supply their needs. Trans Capital, for example, built its business as a direct supplier to the foreign electronics manufacturers; others focused on less-advanced technology. In both cases the relationship with foreign firms enabled local Malaysian companies to move up the technology chain (Haggard, Lim & Ong 1998) via customer–supplier relationships in Penang. For example, Microcut Precision and Newtecho Precision Manufacturing became an adjunct to Seagate, and Jabil Circuit to Maxtor (Haggard, Lim & Ong 1998).

As the Asian Technology Information Program report of 1996 notes, despite this impressive growth in the electronics sector, the majority of firms in Penang were working at lower levels of technology and were vulnerable by their reliance on the demand generated by foreign high-technology companies. The relative cheapness of Penang has also been challenged since the late 1990s—in particular by the Philippines, which has a huge workforce (three times larger than Malaysia) and a per capita income that is a fraction of Penang's (ATIP 1996). Much of Penang's growth depended on government protection which, after 2005, became unsustainable because of pressure on Malaysia to conform to the provisions of the AFTA (see below). The critical question today is whether the domestic firms that grew up on the basis of the characteristics described above are capable of embarking on sustained economic growth. Haggard, Lim and Ong (1998) reported that five of the seven Malaysian-owned firms in the hard-disk drive industry had become export oriented; but what we do not know is how much of this 'success' was based on government support. The ingredients that made for Penang's success in the hard-disk drive industry also contain the seeds that threaten its possible collapse. The hard-disk drive industry first began in the United States and after that migrated to successive low cost production centres;

first to Latin America, then South Korea and Japan, then on to Singapore in the 1980s, and more recently to Malaysia, Thailand, and China.[4]

As new cheaper producers emerge, Malaysia needs to keep moving up the production chain—and this requires the creation of high quality and innovative knowledge workers. Former Prime Minister Mahathir recognised this pressure in his 'Vision 2020' speech. But, again, the performance of the tertiary education sector in Malaysia appears to have fallen short of the need. For example, the most important university in Penang is Universiti Sains Malaysia, but 66% of places are reserved for *bumiputera*. This reservation policy contradicts the composition of Penang's community—the majority is non-Malay (ATIP 1996). On the other hand, Penang has various twinning arrangements with foreign universities, and in 1993 the specialised First Robotics Institute of Science was opened. These two alternative ways of expanding tertiary education in Penang do not, however, address the underlying structural inequalities that define the Malaysian educational system and hold it back. On top of this, in 2001 Penang entered a difficult period when over 16,000 Penang workers were retrenched owing to a global downturn in the IT industry. More than half of the factories that released workers were manufacturing firms, especially in the electronics sector. Seagate Perai, one of Penang's showcase foreign companies, closed down completely. Official data about the kind of workers who lost their jobs in Penang show that Malaysia's transition into a knowledge economy has been very slow: most retrenched workers had few skills, they had low levels of education and were largely rural migrants. Specifically, the Socio-Economic and Environmental Research Institute in Penang has noted that:

- 75% of retrenched workers were 'semi-skilled, unskilled or general workers';
- 12% of retrenched workers were 'professionals and technical personnel';
- About 66% of retrenched workers were women: 'The dominant profile of the retrenched worker is a rural Malay female in the 25–29 age range, previously employed in the production operations of a manufacturing firm';
- 62% of the discharged labourers could no longer be found by the Labour Department when it undertook a survey—presumably because they simply 'melted away' into the countryside from whence they had come; and
- a mere 23% of discharged workers found new employment in Penang (SERI 2002).

In other words, despite the push to make Penang into a capital-intensive industrial cluster of the kind recommended by Porter (see below), labour-intensive processes persisted. Of particular concern is the youthfulness of sacked workers—despite Malaysia's many achievements (including relatively low unemployment), securing full employment for the next generation of Malaysians remains problematic. The Malaysian government has long been aware of these limits to its economic transition. Despite having transformed Malaysia into an export-oriented economy with an export–GDP ratio well over 100 (Arshad 2001:73), those very exports became the core problem when the global Information Technology and Communications (ITC) sector started to contract in the late 1990s. However, Malaysia's industrialisation strategy did not depend exclusively on exports or electronics. The automobile industry, discussed in the following section, constituted another important platform in Malaysia's plans for industrial diversification. Does the record in this industry give us more room for optimism?

Case study of the national car project

Malaysia's development strategy from the 1980s included an old-fashioned approach to modernisation via the development of heavy industry. In particular it was decided that Malaysia needed an automobile industry to generate forward and backward economic linkages and sustainable growth. Without knowing it, Mahathir was adopting the development strategy first used by the Russian Tsars at the end of the 19th century. Many other national governments subsequently imitated the Russian experience by setting up state industries as a way of stimulating national economic growth: first Japan, then South Korea, then India and China .In the case of Malaysia, the national car project was intended to do the same thing. In contrast to the hard-disk drive industry in Penang, where the investments of foreign private firms were paramount, the car industry was to be driven primarily by government investment, which could then be used strategically to involve an advanced foreign partner as a way of accessing foreign technology. Beyond state investment in manufacturing, the government also built up the domestic demand for Malaysian cars through subsidised government purchases by its civil servants and through generous bank interest rates for ordinary consumers (Rashid 2003:1133). From the start of the Proton venture up until 2004, the government of Malaysia invested some Malaysian ringgit (RM) 10 billion in the automobile industry (Mustapa 2004). The result of this effort is summarised in Table 3. By 2001 up to 90% of Proton's sales were local; 10% were exported (the same proportions apply to the Perodua brands) (Arshad 2001:76). On this point alone the nascent car industry was very different from the international orientation of the new Malaysian electronics sector.

Table 3: Returns to investment in Malaysia's automobile industry, 1980 to 2004

Total financial investment by government	RM10 billion
Number of automobile projects	Four: Proton, Perodua, National Truck and Bus, and Modenas motorcycles
Foreign car assembly	Ford, Mercedes, Volvo, Hondo, Toyota, Kia, Hyundai etc
Output in 2004	378,000 passenger cars 103,300 commercial vehicles
Direct employment	100,000 persons (ESCAP figure of 30,000)
Number of component Malaysian car firms	350 firms making 6,000 parts
Contribution to national excise	RM3.3 billion pa = 65% RM2 billion sales tax income pa = 30% of sales tax
Contribution to total government revenue	5% pa
Car exports	To Europe, Middle East and Australia Santan dominates Chinese market
Saving via import substitution effect of protectionist policies	RM2 billion
New joint ventures with foreign firms	Proton and Mitsubishi
Domestic car market	Malaysia is the largest in ASEAN

Sources: Mustapa (2004); ESCAP (2002:8).

By 2000 Malaysia had four automobile producers, 15 assembly companies and three sports car manufacturers, in addition to the 350 local producers of parts (Arshad 2001:74). How was this achieved?

In the first phase, European and Asian firms used Malaysia as an assembly base—Volvo, Peugeot, Mazda and Nissan were all given licences to produce in Malaysia. By the 1980s Malaysia had 15 assembly plants but the backward linkages into component car production had not emerged, largely because the wide variety of brands made it hard to achieve any economies of scale and focus on manufacturing specialised parts. Instead the producers of components found themselves fragmented between 15 different demanding clients (Arshad 2001:71). This historical experience should be remembered by those who are too critical of the degree to which the Malaysian government then insisted that the car industry should focus on a limited number of producers and economies of scale. It is important to remember that government intervention was driven by the perceived need to rationalise car production in the face of mounting competition from large international firms. The strategy made sense at the time; whether it still makes sense today is another matter.

The experience of these early decades gave rise to the national car project or Perusahaan Otomobil Kedua Sdn Bhd (Proton) and the building of a more narrowly focused automobile industry that depended on the Malaysian government's partnership with Mitsubishi Motors Corporation and the Mitsubishi Corporation, both Japanese companies and amongst the largest automobile manufacturers in the world. The Malaysian partner in the joint venture was the Heavy Industries Corporation of Malaysia Berhad (a government-linked company established by the Prime Minister in the early 1980s to encourage heavy industry), which became a major instrument for involving *bumiputera* in Malaysian industrialisation (Fujita 1997/98:156). To deal with the competition of foreign assembly plants, the government adopted tougher measures requiring foreign firms use local content.

Proton was the name given to this 'people's car' and became the focus of Malaysia's strategy of showcasing the development of indigenous heavy industry. Mitsubishi Motors Corporation had 7.9% equity in Proton from the start of the joint venture in 1983 until 2004 (JCN Network 2006).[5] By the early 1990s Malaysia was under pressure from AFTA to introduce an element of competition into its car industry: the Perodua was billed as the small car competitor to the larger more expensive Proton.

Again, state intervention in the form of government-linked companies was essential—they set up a joint venture with Daihatsu and Mitsui (Fujita 1997/98:159). Perodua's reputation eventually overtook Proton's when it became Malaysia's technological showcase in 2001 by winning certification from the International Organization of Standardization (ISO) for ISO 9002 and ISO 9001, which both cover quality management (Arshad 2001:72).

The strategy of setting up state industries as engines of economic growth appeared to be working until the Asian financial crisis. State investment in the national car projects, high tariffs, subsidies and local content laws[6] created demand for a wide range of inputs into car production: glass, engine parts, electrical components, gear shifts and soft furnishings (Arshad 2001:75; Gabilaia

2001). Another achievement of the car industry was its growing capacity to provide substitutes for expensive, high-quality foreign imports. Despite this both car producers have been heavily criticised for, amongst other things, very poor after sales services and the provision of spare parts. The Asian financial crisis also hit the industry and produced a 30% decline in production and sales (Arshad 2001:75-6).

With economic recovery, the Malaysian automobile sector regained its momentum much more quickly than its ASEAN competitors. By 1999 Proton had established a dominant place in the markets of Malaysia and ASEAN: within Malaysia Proton accounted for 70% of all car sales and in ASEAN its market share was 23%, closely followed by Toyota with 22% (Arshad 2001:74, 76). But the speed of recovery was deceptive because the levels of production reached in 1997 were not matched, even in 2001 (Arshad 2001:74). The recovery phase also saw Proton lose market share in the early 2000s. By 2005 Proton was reporting large financial losses and its share of the Malaysian car market was 30%—half of what it had been in 1999. The decline has continued since then with net losses in the year ending March 2007 of some US$174 million.

Rather belatedly, Proton began to design an export strategy to increase shipments from about 17,000 per annum to 100,000 per annum (Malaysiatoday 2005). To assist in this export approach, Proton has been forging collaborations with Citroën, Mitsubishi Motors Corporation, and importers in the Philippines and Vietnam (Fujita 1997/98:160). Unfortunately for Malaysia, Thailand is in a stronger position to access global markets because foreign companies dominate production in Thailand. These recent trends are only the most visible signs of a deep problem with Malaysia's capacity to sustain its automobile industry. The current structural obstacles are many and include the following:

- The international market is flooded with many car manufacturers that have long-term and overwhelming advantages in terms of large-scale production, efficiency and catering to the latest international design preferences, which increasingly stress a combination of efficiency, power and safety.

- The Australian car industry provides a good comparison with the long-term problems of the Malaysian industry, for no loyalty to any national brand can respond to modern consumer preferences in the long run.

- The difficulties of succeeding in the global market cannot be underrated: about five manufacturers account for 80% of the world's car production and the trend towards increasing concentration appears to be unstoppable.

- A persistent problem with Malaysian industry, and one which its showcase car industry has been unable to overcome, is dependency on foreign technology, including design. Between 1995 and 2000 Malaysian car manufacturers signed no less than 98 technical transfer agreements (Arshad 2001:79). This fact, after more than 20 years of automobile production, is not encouraging. The whole rationale of foreign direct investment for a developing country is to bring in overseas capital and designs and then, through a process of imitation and learning, to wean domestic industry off this dependency by developing local research and development and innovation. This has not, however, happened in the Malaysian case. The Malaysian government has also acquired two foreign research and development institutes to help upgrade the quality of Proton production (Lotus Internal and the Michigan Research Institute), but it is too soon to say whether this has made a difference (Arshad 2001:79).

- Despite some attention to research and development, Malaysian cars continue to face declining market presence at home and abroad—they are perceived to be of poor quality and more expensive than small, cheaper South Korean cars. Technical 'tie ups' with foreign car producers are now being explored but again it is too soon to say whether these will produce beneficial results (Arshad 2001:79). Attempts to set up joint ventures with European car manufacturers such as Volkswagen and Peugot-Citroen has floundered for years.

The lack of indigenous innovation in Malaysian industry is especially worrying. One can speculate about the reasons for this weakness. One Australian firm has suggested that social attitudes to manufacturing are a problem.[7] Manual work is typically regarded as degrading and something to be shunned. This particular firm was keen to transfer its research and development functions to Malaysia, but decided against this when it realised how reluctant the Malaysian employees were to leave their computers and desks. Research and development in the manufacturing sector requires the development of industrial prototypes—small-scale models in the form of real materials. These prototypes allow manufacturers to test the product and ensure that the most appropriate raw materials have been used in the right quantities. On the shop floor this requires the 'employee/designer' to test his computer-based patterns by finding and using plastics, metals, woods and other raw material in the construction of prototypes. Putting one's hand to such labour is not highly valued in Malaysia. The Australian firm that reported these difficulties have in the last year, compelled the company to leave Malaysia and relocate to Singapore. Fifteen years ago, this firm built a plant in Malaysia because of the English language abilities of the labour force and the commitment of government to innovation. Malaysia was judged to be superior to Hong Kong, Singapore and Thailand. Now they have abandoned Malaysia, frustrated and disappointed.

One can only hope that the new investment in research and development and prototyping at the Proton plant will be more successful than this example suggests and that it will deliver the innovative competitiveness that the industry needs (Rashid 2003:1137). But even if the new investment works, Malaysia is still confronted with competition from a robust car industry in Thailand—an industry that has been a private sector initiative from the start (Fujita 1997/98:161). By the late 1980s it was clear that the Thai strategy for creating a new automobile industry was gaining ground over the Malaysian one when measured by total car sales (Fujita 1997/98). The Thai industry quickly became export-oriented, which in turn generated more foreign direct investment, which in turn created more local jobs and increased expertise and, finally, increased car exports. In contrast to this, only a fraction of Malaysian cars have been exported, normally to markets where Malaysian imports have been given special privileges (Fujita 1997/98:170).

On top of all these issues is the new competitive pressure that will impact on the Malaysian car industry with the AFTA agreement that seeks to reduce protection and tariff barriers within the ASEAN region. AFTA was established in 1992 and Malaysia agreed to reduce tariffs, subsidies and local content provisions to its car industry in 2005. The Proton car provides a classic case of growth through the protection of infant industries (Gabilaia 2001 provides a detailed list of protectionist measures); a new international environment now challenges the very foundations of Malaysia's development strategy. Thailand may have an easier ride, partly because it has historically had lower protective tarrifs: in 1998, for example, the average tariff on 'completely built up' passenger vehicle imports into Thailand was 80% compared with three or four times that level in Malaysia (Fujita 1997/98:175).

Conclusion

Mahathir's 'Vision 2020' recognised the tough road ahead for the Malaysian economy. To sustain growth, diversify jobs and deliver better living standards to all, Mahathir noted that Malaysia had to move up the value-added chain of production. He also understood that an Information Technology and Communications industry had the capacity to increase Malaysia's ability to achieve sustained economic growth and development. What was not so clear was the way forward. Where does Malaysia's international competitive advantage lie? If China is indeed emerging as the 'workshop of the world', then

Malaysian industrialisation cannot be sustained unless Malaysia develops niche markets and products for which it is famous—palm oil for example—or invents new products around which niche markets can be constructed. This is not an unrealistic scenario: in 2004, for example, Malaysian resource-based exports continued to grow rapidly, while the production and shipment of electronic goods fell (WB 2006:1).

During a seminar held in Kuala Lumpur in 2003, Michael Porter suggested that Malaysia needed to focus on creating dense clusters of companies all located in close proximity to each other—according to his theory, such clusters have the potential to become globally competitive because they feed off each other and develop a strong domestic competitiveness that creates a business culture essential to achieving international competitiveness (Porter 2003:15–16). Local firms also generate local demand for inputs and, because of the competitive atmosphere, they are also very demanding of product quality and price. The problem with this 'solution' is that the Penang electronics/hard-disk drive industry was indeed based on such a cluster. Despite this, the manufacturing base in Penang has not been assured.

The Multimedia Super Corridor is another example of Malaysian thinking in this direction. It certainly has the potential to develop a cluster-based industry, but so far it has not attracted the companies that were originally expected; nor is it clear what industry such a cluster should be focused on. Similarly, Malaysia's attempt to transform itself into a hub for the provision of financial services to the Islamic world, for example, by developing the principles and application of Islamic banking and finance, is not without potential (WB 2006:6), but the relative capital scarcity of Malaysia could be an inhibiting factor. In short, Porter's cluster economics make a lot of sense and he provides many examples of success stories in Europe, the United States and Australia (Porter 2003:17, 32–8). But underlying the success of these clusters is a fierce spirit of competitiveness and private industrial initiative. It is doubtful that this fierce spirit has existed in Malaysia, where government-linked companies are so strong, where *bumiputera* firms are advantaged over others and where the general business world lacks the degree of transparency that makes for a truly open market. Moreover, the Malaysian government continues to believe that planning for change and innovation is possible—yet its own planning mechanisms have suffered the tests of realism that the market imposes. The MSC, for example, was planned without any input from the private sector with the result that few companies have made the MSC their home. Porter stressed the contrast between a genuine cluster-based strategy and an 'industrial policy' designed by the state (Porter 2003:38); the former promoted competition while the latter did not. The cluster strategy requires collaboration between all the relevant stakeholders, not only the government and its favoured companies (Porter 2003:46). In the Malaysian case, a commitment to competition would require the state to dismantle the *bumiputera* policies, increase transparency, reduce the influence of government-linked companies and provide a conducive environment to all Malaysian businesses including those run by non-Malays.

Another option is to develop a special economic relationship with China, perhaps based on sharing relative strengths—for example, Malaysia might provide educational, tourist and halal exports to China, and China might consider using Malaysia as a base for furthering relations with the Islamic world in general (Badawi 2005). In the meantime, Malaysian exports to China have been growing at about 27% per annum in recent years (WB 2006:10). A related option that is absorbing a lot of diplomatic time is reforming ASEAN to encourage intra-regional economic co-operation and development. The hope is that Malaysia might find the niche markets it needs at its doorstep. However, trade trends are not encouraging on this account, with the share of Malaysian shipments to ASEAN in decline (WB 2006:10). Moreover, relations within ASEAN remain strained over many issues such as the conflict between Indonesia and Singapore over the latter's dredging of sand, Indonesian labourers working in Malaysia and the volatility of Pattani Muslims on the Thai-Malaysian border.

The reform of ASEAN increasingly includes the idea of bringing the Australian economy in from the cold. Under Mahathir's leadership, the relationship between Australia and Malaysia was acrimonious, at least at the prime ministerial levels. But today Malaysia and ASEAN more generally cannot afford to ignore the potential of closer economic relationships with Australia, which has a significant and prosperous domestic market of over 20 million people. Ongoing negotiations between Australia and Malaysia for a Free Trade Agreement also recognise the potential for such regionalism. Australian–Malaysian trade is worth about AU$10 billion a year and Malaysia is Australia's ninth largest trading partner (DFAT 2006). Porter also noted the potential of cross-border and regional initiatives as a way of building Malaysian competitiveness (Porter 2003:39-44).

Whichever options Malaysia decides to focus on, one factor common to all forward-moving strategies will be the need to increase the number and proportion of students with tertiary education. In the late 1990s Malaysia was different from other East Asian success stories in this respect. As one World Bank report notes, 'Malaysia's university enrolment (for age groups 19 to 24) at 11% falls behind...[the rate is] 60% in Korea and 35% in the Philippines' (WB 2000:ii, 55). Malaysia also has a long history of subsidising the tertiary education of the wealthier sections of the population at the expense of the poorer—this acts as one of the most significant constraints on converting tertiary education into an opportunity for all (WB 2000:57). Merely increasing expenditure at the tertiary level will not remedy this problem—Malaysia needs to focus on a more equitable distribution of advanced educational opportunities, including a more equitable treatment of ethnic groups. Urgent reform is also needed of the intellectual climate in Malaysian universities. After the trial of Anwar Ibrahim, the Malaysian government required all Malaysian university staff to take an 'Oath of Good Conduct'. In effect, this makes it virtually impossible for an academic to write critically about government policies in Malaysia—this in turn has not only stifled academic debate but also produced a generation of graduates who are not trained or committed to critical analysis. Producing a pliant labour force hardly matches the urgent need for innovative thinking in Malaysia today.

Another worrying factor in establishing a growing tertiary sector is the downward trend in domestic investment since the Asian financial crisis— between 1991 and 2004 private domestic investment as a share of GDP fell from about 29% to 12%. This downward trend makes it difficult to see how the privatisation of education, especially tertiary education, can continue at a level that meets the needs of educational infrastructure inside Malaysia (WB 2006:9). The arrival of foreign colleges and universities bringing in investment for tertiary education is one way around this problem.

There is certainly urgency about the need to address Malaysia's long-term development strategy. Malaysia's most outspoken politician, the Democratic Action Party's National Chairman, Lim Kit Siang, noted in 2002 how Malaysia's international competitiveness was declining 'as reflected by the 14-place plunge in three years in Malaysia's ranking in the Global Competitiveness Report 2001' (Lim 2002).[8] In 1997 Malaysia was ranked 17th; by 2000 it was 29th. In 2001 it slipped to 37th (WEF 2002:2). The ranking remained low in 2004, at the 31st position, and then improved slightly in 2005 to 24th position (WEF 2006a). This low ranking is more disappointing when one remembers that Malaysia, unlike Vietnam and Thailand, has not had to struggle with the rising costs of oil imports (Malaysia is a net exporter of oil), the loss of poultry owing to Avian Influenza or high inflation (WB 2005:12–13, 21–3, 29).

In summary, Malaysia has certainly experienced a remarkable economic transformation since independence, but at the turn of the 21st century serious questions have emerged about the future. The uncertainties are taking their toll by inducing high levels of stress and social disharmony within families and, in particular, between the generations, and between Malaysia's diverse economic regions. The way forward requires Malaysia to find economic niches that cannot be displaced by the next serious erosion of Asian wages. To this extent, Mahathir's 'Vision 2020' was focused in the right direction—moving up the technology and skills scale. Exactly how this can be achieved, however, is unclear.

Government intervention is unlikely to provide major solutions, mainly because the overriding social concerns of government continue to place a priority on pro-*bumiputera* policies. It is salutary to remind ourselves that the Malay or *bumiputera* community of Malaysia constitutes only 51% of the total population and that there are sizeable 'minorities' of Chinese and Indians—24% and 7% of the population respectively. Instead of old approaches that did work in the past, the government needs fresh ideas, including a stronger commitment to an open civil society that encourages political, social and intellectual debate—these are the preconditions for creativity, innovation and the competitive spirit. The old authoritarianism is no longer relevant. The call for better labour planning in order to match new educational strategies with job opportunities smacks of the old authoritarianism and ignores the lessons of the socialist economies (on Malaysia's policy of 'picking winners', see MiGHT 2004:41–72). In the Soviet Union, and even more so in the People's Republic of China, labour planning was pushed to its limits but still failed to deliver the needed results.

Instead of failed state projects, Malaysia needs to produce an educational system that is more open, creative and better able to produce individuals with high levels of competency so that they are flexible in the workplace. On-the-job and life-long training and learning are key characteristics of most successful companies, but they also need to recruit good quality raw material. A more open civil society with a more transparent business sector has a better chance of providing the necessary preconditions for sustained economic growth than authoritarianism, state control and social engineering.

A new openness is already manifesting itself in Malaysia, where a vigorous public debate has at last emerged about the direction that the economy should take and whether the government is moving fast enough to give encouragement to the most competitive elements (Navaratnam 2006a; Shamsul 2006). This debate has not come a moment too soon—as Navaratnam notes, the *bumiputera* policies of the NEP period have persisted so long, failed to deliver their promises and have simultaneously alienated the non-Malays. Instead of promoting national unity, Malaysia now faces the risk of disillusionment being converted into discord (Navaratnam 2006b). This risk will compel a major reassessment of national policy.

Notes

1. Malays account for 51% of the population, Chinese for 24%, indigenous people for 11%, Indians for 7% and non-Malaysian citizens for 6.8% (State Department 2006). The non-Malaysian citizens account for about one-fifth of the Malaysian workforce and are largely short-term, contract labourers from the region.
2. This table is extracted from Vicziany and Puteh (2004).
3. This table is extracted, with the permission of the author, from Puteh (2006).
4. India is unlikely to emerge as a competitor in this area, as its specialty is the production of customised software; hardware production, by contrast, remains problematic (see Vicziany 2001).
5. In February 2006 the two companies again saw the benefits of closer collaboration, and a new agreement was signed; but there are no intentions of either side seeking to form a joint venture for the purposes of production (JCN Network 2006; Malaysiatoday 2006).
6. In late 2005 Malaysia started conforming to the Trade Related Investment Measures agreement, including a pull back from its policy on local content for Malaysian industries. Until then, car makers had to comply with various versions of the original 1979 Mandatory Deletion Program (Fujita 1997/98:156).
7. Based on in-depth fieldwork and interviews by the author in Australia in 2000 and 2006. The firm has requested that its interviews remain anonymous.
8. The 2001 Global Competitiveness Report was a threshold exercise because Jeffrey Sachs and John McArthur calculated a new index called the Growth Competitiveness Index. In 2006 the report included 117 countries, up from 104 countries previously. The executive summary explains the variables used to calculate the index as including: 'the quality of the macroeconomic environment, the state of the country's public institutions, and...the level of its technological readiness' (WEF 2006b:xiv). The innovation indicators are of two kinds: core and non-core—a division used to record the difference in technology in countries at various stages of economic development.

chapter ten

Singapore: economic success and resilient authoritarianism

Lesley McKaig

Since becoming a self-governing island state in 1959, Singapore has rapidly achieved an outstanding economic transformation. From the outset Singapore was open and hospitable to the international economy. It became a regional hub, reaching out to international markets and luring foreign capital and foreign corporations. This outward approach underscored all stages of Singapore's economic history for a number of historic, economic and political reasons. The need to be linked to the international economy became more pressing with Singapore's sudden expulsion from the Federation of Malaya in 1965, after only two years of membership. This alliance would have provided Singapore with a resource-rich hinterland, as well as a large and proximate regional market. The industrialisation policy of import substitution in the early 1960s, designed to protect Singapore's infant local industries, was no longer feasible once Singapore was forced to go it alone. Singapore's lack of natural resources led it into a vigorous trade policy almost from the beginning. Its limited market size allowed firms no prospect of economies of scale, while industrial production necessarily meant importing most inputs. Embracing the world's markets was Singapore's only hope.

But the island itself was not without some initial advantages: it had an energetic, hardworking and literate labour force, high rates of employment, a high savings rate, and a strategic location on important transport routes—initially shipping and later aviation. Moreover, since the island of Singapore is geographically compact, the Singaporean government would find it easy to communicate with the people and implement its policies. This proved to be important for Singapore, as success depended on rapidly building an infrastructure and business environment that could meet the needs of international commerce.

A further advantage was that Singapore's British colonial heritage provided a historical basis for free trade. Britain's laissez-faire economic policy had allowed Singapore's entrepot functions to flourish. Colonial Singapore collected and processed the raw materials, such as rubber, timber and tin, from the Southeast

Asian region, before their on-shipment to Europe. As a free port, Singapore also distributed imported manufactured goods from the United States and Europe throughout the region. In the late 1950s, prior to its economic growth, Singapore had little agriculture and featured swampy mangroves, but it already possessed a rail and road network and a deep port. In the year 1960 more than 10,000 foreign ocean-going vessels and 8,000 coastal and native craft used Singapore's harbour (Dobby 1961:145). This aspect of its entrepot role remained successful throughout the following decades. Singapore's colonial legacy was also more benign than in some nations, such as South Korea, where imperialism had generated a view that working closely with foreign powers risked economic exploitation. In post-colonial South Korea (and also in India), the history of imperialism gave rise to autarkic policies designed to defend domestic economies even if this meant that foreign direct investment was shunned. Singapore was very different in this regard.

Singapore's economic development has been marked by relatively clear-cut phases of economic and business growth. Its growth record, while not even over time, has been outstanding, especially in the 1970s and 1980s (see Table 1), even when compared to its contemporaries, the other fast-growing economies of South Korea, Taiwan and Hong Kong.

Table 1: GDP growth, 1961–2002* (% change per annum)

Year	GDP growth	Year	GDP growth	Year	GDP growth	Year	GDP growth
1961	8.5	1972	13.3	1983	8.2	1994	10.1
1962	7.1	1973	11.3	1984	8.3	1995	8.7
1963	10.5	1974	6.8	1985	−1.6	1996	7.5
1964	−4.3	1975	4.0	1986	1.9	1997	8.4
1965	6.6	1976	7.2	1987	9.4	1998	0.4
1966	10.6	1977	7.8	1988	11.3	1999	5.4
1967	13.0	1978	8.6	1989	9.4	2000	9.9
1968	14.3	1979	9.3	1990	8.8	2001	−2.4
1969	13.4	1980	9.7	1991	6.7	2002	2.2
1970	13.4	1981	9.6	1992	6.0		
1971	12.5	1982	6.9	1993	10.1		

* 1961–94 at 1985 market prices.

Sources: Rodan 2001: Table 5.1, p 147; Table 5.2, p 149; Table 5.4, p 155; and *Singapore Fact Sheet*, Australian Department of Foreign Affairs and Trade September 2003.

The process behind Singapore's economic development has been widely discussed. Two interconnected debates have emerged. One, the debate about the role of the state versus market forces, asks whether the state has been too interventionist or whether it has promoted the free market economy—as claimed by the People's Action Party (PAP), the governing party—rather than authoritarianism. The second debate concerns the relative importance and interaction of three groups of entrepreneurs: the local private business sector, the international corporations and the state.

The PAP[1] has held political power since the August 1965 inception of the Republic of Singapore, which has been labelled by some as a paternalistic state. PAP has played a prominent role in Singapore's economic and social development. It has planned, motivated and implemented economic policies, but it has been flexible in redirecting changes when needed. Above all, the state has tended to develop policies in anticipation of change. This is perhaps best demonstrated by the different policies and development phases that define the history of Singapore: import substitution in the early 1960s; export orientation from 1965; the so-called second industrial revolution into higher value-added production in 1979; and today's promotion of outward foreign direct investment.

Lim Chong Yah's argument is central to the debate about state versus market. According to Lim, the PAP chose 'democratic socialism' because it balanced a moderate degree of national planning and government ownership of economic assets with a major role for the private sector (Lim 1988:61). Is Lim right? To what extent has Singapore's economic development been market conforming or has government policy successfully altered market signals in order to achieve other national goals? Krause gives two ways of measuring the extent of government intervention (Krause 1987:4). The first is whether or not the state distorted relative prices (for example, through import protection, price control and cross-subsidisation). The second is the extent to which the state intruded in the economy through the regulation of businesses and the involvement of public sector enterprises. Krause argues that Singapore's experience is complex—while it has seen relatively little price distortion, it has still been essentially interventionist. Singapore's government largely allows the market to determine prices and generally allows decision making at the firm level to proceed with little interference. However, by using its regulations and institutions, the government structures the economic incentives in order to achieve its desired outcomes. To Krause, the Singaporean experience is therefore a complex blend of interventionism and free trade.

It is likely that this duality occurs because of the great influence of the large foreign corporations on Singapore's economy. Indeed Huff maintains that despite the PAP's subsidies to the private sector (such as investment incentives, provision of infrastructure, and labour education and training), there was no need for the state to monitor how the firms used such subsidies (Huff 1999:5). According to Huff, the important reason was that because the firms were mainly multinational corporations, they aimed for international competitiveness and were export oriented. They were, in other words, market driven from the start—largely because the domestic Singaporean market itself was too small. In this way the Singaporean government had confidence in the motives and anticipated behaviour of its foreign capitalists.

Ow Chin-Hock (1986) argues similarly that the Singaporean government 'adopted basically the free enterprise system, but with extensive government intervention'. According to him, two ingredients fomented this unusual mix—the pragmatism of the state and Singapore's disciplined, hardworking, harmonious and cohesive society (Ow 1986:234, 240, 249). The government's economic prowess and the spirit of free enterprise would not have constituted sufficient preconditions without the incorporation of social policies designed 'to ensure more equitable economic opportunity' and 'to create a disciplined and achievement-oriented society' (Ow 1986:234). These social policies included population control, the provision of housing, education, medical and health services, compulsory savings, a closely guarded industrial relations policy, a wages policy and numerous behavioural campaigns to ensure that the government was communicating with the Singaporean people and getting their backing.

Singapore's social policy harnessed the people to the economic development drive and thereby ensured a stable and compliant social backdrop for foreign investors. This was not with any explicit, authoritarian brutality, as had occurred in South Korea, but rested on an implicit, even subtle, fashioning of attitudes by the PAP of its people. The government distributed wealth to ensure that all classes received the basic necessities. It was not intended to achieve an egalitarian society (and so dull the drive for hard work) but to create a meritocracy, where rewards and prestige went to those most able, enterprising and dynamic (Ow 1986:235). Complacency was not seen as a generator of economic success. The chief exception to this process of peaceful social engineering was the draconian action taken against Singapore's communist parties.

Galvanising social support for the economic development strategies of Singapore was also driven by pragmatic economic considerations. Ramesh (1992) argues that the Singaporean government's main strategy has been to promote the family, community and employers and in this way to minimise its social security role. Market liberalisation could be at odds with an overly generous social welfare system. By delivering just enough social welfare, the Singaporean state created a population that it considered integral to the economy—one that sought progress and was disciplined but, perhaps even more importantly, which also ensured the creation of social and political stability without which foreign investment would not be attracted. Indeed, the most important factor cited by foreign investors in establishing manufacturing facilities in Singapore was political stability (Chng et al 1986:68). This achievement falls to the credit of the PAP's policies.

Where the Singaporean government has failed miserably is in the promotion of a civil society that is relatively open to new intellectual ideas, debate and political pluralism. Political dissension has not been tolerated and any lack of enthusiastic co-operation with state priorities still provokes government threats. The least draconian of these threats are publicity campaigns stating that unless Singaporeans conform they risk losing everything, especially their prosperity. At a more sinister level, Singapore is defined by a policy of political repression that involves controls over media, freedom of assembly and political activities in general (Gomez 2005). It is this climate of fear and authoritarianism that has allowed the PAP to claim that it has the support of the people. At the same time, there is plenty of evidence to show that probably the majority of Singapore's citizens have been willing to trade their political and intellectual freedom for prosperity. That prosperity has depended on attracting foreign conglomerates, which have spearheaded economic growth since 1965. Yet the high dependence on international capital and markets has also given rise to local discontent—especially amongst home-grown Singaporean entrepreneurs who feel they have been usurped not only by multinational corporations (MNCs), but also by public sector enterprises.

The role of multinationals in Singapore's development

From the beginning the PAP set out to attract large-scale firms with world-class standards, which would manufacture for a world market. Singapore's existing indigenous entrepreneurs were not considered appropriate for pioneering the transformation of their nation's economy by way of export-led manufacturing. Singapore's entrepreneurs were experienced in trade and commerce but not in manufacturing. The PAP also regarded the scope of the business networks developed by the Chinese entrepreneurs as inadequate for the proposed attack on world markets. The Chinese traditionally based their business prowess on networks through clans, common dialect groups and ancestral origins. These would have been suitable for a regional push but Singapore's government was more ambitious than this. Hence, local business networks were essentially bypassed. This contrasts with the contribution of the overseas Chinese to the economic growth of other Asian countries, where informality and opportunism, and networks that span many borders, were used to good effect. According to one of the key findings in a study of Southeast Asian nations, the overseas Chinese enterprise groups throughout East Asia have grown into a significant economic driving force (Ch'ng 1993:8). Though the overseas Chinese constitute a minority in other Southeast Asian nations, they have accounted for an astonishing share of the economic successes in the region, even without much formal political power. In contrast, the Singaporean Chinese comprise approximately 77% of the population of 4.6 million, yet the PAP chose not to utilise local Chinese entrepreneurs to ignite the new nation's growth. Significantly, there is no major discussion on Singapore in Ch'ng's book.

So the large foreign MNCs dominated the manufacturing sector and essentially fuelled Singapore's economic development almost from the beginning. Singapore thus contrasted dramatically with the other Asian newly industrialised economies (Taiwan, South Korea, Hong Kong) and Japan in the high share of foreign direct investment in its GDP. Between 1985 and 1988, formative years for value-added production in many of these economies, the share of foreign direct investment in GDP was a mere 2% in South Korea and 8% in Taiwan, but 54% in Singapore. Even Hong Kong, with an inward foreign direct investment flow of 20–26%, greatly relied on local entrepreneurs for its manufacturing (Lall 1991:147 cited in Chowdhury & Islam 1993:108).

In addition to providing economic incentives, an efficient infrastructure and a compliant labour force, the Singaporean state assisted the MNCs directly through its Economic Development Board, which focused on large projects dominated by foreign firms. As Low (1993) points out, it relayed useful and timely information to overseas investors but, more importantly, it made them feel wanted and welcomed. Hughes (1993a), however, goes further than this in suggesting that the Economic Development Board tactics were to 'cajole, nurse and sometimes even bully' the MNCs. Not everyone agrees with this assessment. Huff (1999), for example, insists that the closeness of the relationship between the state and foreign corporations should not be exaggerated and that at times the relationships were tense and frosty.

Despite some inevitable tension, the relationship between the Singaporean government and the MNCs proved to be mutually beneficial. The MNCs at first changed the structure of production in Singapore from labour-intensive to capital-intensive production and then moved the economy into becoming a specialist provider of international services. The MNCs also specialised amongst themselves. For example, the Japanese MNCs tended to concentrate on manufacturing, later moving to more skill-intensive production, whereas the United States companies were concentrated more on finance and banking.

The role of the MNCs in Singapore's development was not confined to internationally competitive production and exports. They also became the agents of Singapore's technology policy. It was assumed that the MNCs would upgrade their technology, oversee product innovation, import or invent new techniques and augment the supply of technologically competent personnel. Beyond this they also provided crucial foreign-exchange income, contributing an impressive 82% of Singapore's direct exports and 70% of the gross output in the manufacturing sector (Lim 1988:255). The MNCs brought in capital funds and employed more than half of the island's labour (Lim 1988:255). Thus from the mid-1960s the MNCs provided the key ingredients for growth: access to capital funds, managerial skills and experience, technological innovation, professional personnel, and linkages to markets and suppliers. In providing all this they enabled Singapore to participate in the global networks of production and marketing and, from this, to take advantage of the many benefits of economies of scale.

Much has been written about the costs, as well as the benefits, of relying on inward foreign direct investment, and the true extent of the MNC contribution to Singapore's development needs to be examined closely. Were the advantages to Singapore perhaps more apparent in the earlier stages of economic growth than in the later, higher technological and more sophisticated innovative stages? To consider this we need to ask to what extent MNCs stimulated local, indigenous innovation. To what extent did they readily transfer the desired technology? Is there evidence of technological deepening within Singapore?

The disadvantages of depending on multinationals

Technology transfer is influenced by many factors, such as the stage of economic production and nature of corporate ownership. In the early phase of industrialisation, simple manufacturing techniques may be embedded in the industrial machinery itself, and outdated processes may more readily be transferred than during the later phases, which involve more advanced and often highly complex types of technology. Ownership structures can also influence the effectiveness of the technology acquired; wholly owned foreign companies tend to control their proprietary technology (especially the most advanced and sophisticated technology) more tightly than joint ventures, where such information is often less jealously guarded and can be traded within the business relationship. Most of Singapore's MNCs do not, in fact, carry out research and development projects within Singapore, despite attempts by the PAP to encourage this. According to one Japanese analyst, Kunio Yoshihara (cited in Chee 2001:46), technology transfer was so weak that Singapore represented a 'technologyless industrialisation', becoming just an 'offshore centre for foreign capital'.

MNCs also adversely affected the structure of Singapore's industry: national assets were concentrated in the hands of foreign firms, which tended to dominate the economy because they were primarily so large. These characteristics tended to further entrench the market power of MNCs relative to the small and medium-sized enterprises (SMEs), which were mainly local firms.

MNCs have also been a determining factor in the distribution of income in Singapore. The PAP redressed this issue in its social development policy by partially redistributing wealth amongst the population through, for example, providing subsidised housing. But the story of income re-distribution is more complex than this. The PAP used income policy to lower costs to industry. Before 1979 incomes were capped—a policy that was designed to encourage labour-intensive production. In 1979, however, the state decided to increase the role of value-added production in the national economy and also to raise the level of technological sophistication, and boost the contribution of manufacturing to economic growth (Rodan 2001:146). It did this by trying to remove the existing comparative advantages in labour-intensive production by 'correcting' the capped wages level and allowing it to rise to the market level. Virtually overnight labour costs escalated dramatically, leaving foreign investors largely unimpressed with such a manipulation of 'their' marketplace. While workers were delighted, the government soon realised that labour productivity was not rising in line with labour costs. Workers were berated for their poor work attitude, and the government, fearing that workers were not sufficiently appreciative of the state's welfare, introduced a partial system of company welfarism, whereby the workers' 'well-being' was tied more overtly to the success of its private sector employer (Rodan 1985:35).

The high reliance on foreign investment also meant that the potential linkages amongst the local business community, within Singapore and the region more generally, were not realised. MNCs, it appears, crowded out indigenous Singaporean entrepreneurs rather than boosting their activities (for example, by providing inputs into the activities of MNCs). The PAP actively pursued foreign direct investment with financial incentives such as generous tax breaks that were not granted to local entrepreneurs. Such fiscal generosity was afforded because of the compulsory employer–employee-funded Central Provident Fund, a huge financial reserve used at the government's discretion. The fund provides the government with funds at below-market prices to finance both its development and social policies (Huff 1999:6). This access to lucrative funds allows the PAP to keep taxes low.

Despite the well-known authoritarianism of the Singaporean state, the daily business of foreign companies was largely left to operate unencumbered by state directives. There were no requirements to form joint ventures with locals as a prerequisite for entering Singapore; no requirement that they employ a certain proportion of locals in management positions or the more technical and skilled jobs; no requirement to use a certain percentage of locally produced components in production. Often the PAP liaised with the MNCs to determine what infrastructure and investments might be advantageous to Singapore's economic development, but typically this was driven by the Singaporean government's determination to please foreign capital.

The local entrepreneurs, who had few such incentives, resented the PAP's attitude towards them. Bureaucrats were in the habit of suggesting that home-grown business people suffered from a *kia su* mentality—they were averse to risk and afraid to lose. This resentment is easy to understand given the innovative attitudes and capital-investment characteristic of the overseas Chinese throughout Southeast Asia. Yet Lee and Low (1990) argue that Chinese Singaporeans prefer to pursue a career with large corporations, either in an MNC or the public sector, rather than set up their own businesses. This mentality, where failure is perceived to be a disgrace and a 'loss of face', means that the prospect of failure (and therefore risk taking) is avoided at all costs.

But if there is a *kia su* mentality, does this simply reflect traditional Chinese Singaporean attitudes or is it encouraged by other factors? If it can be altered by appropriate government policy, then the local business community should not be condemned for being the victim of cultural stereotypes that are yet to be proven as acting as constraints on entrepreneurship. Indeed, it might be argued that the PAP itself has contributed to this risk-averse attitude with its social policy, which is designed to create stable and compliant Singaporeans. It could also be that the authoritarianism of the Singaporean state has scared off innovators and innovation. Whatever the case may be, the lack of local entrepreneurial dynamism is not irreversible. Some recognition of this may be seen in the introduction of the SME Master Plan in 1989, by which the PAP seeks to redress the relative weaknesses of local business culture by providing training and assistance to local companies with new projects.

The role of public sector companies

The second stream to the entrepreneurial debate in Singapore raises questions about state entrepreneurship. The government uses holding companies, through which it conducts the business of its government-linked companies. The PAP's entry into business started with the establishment of the Economic Development Board in 1961, which not only made loans and assisted private businesses but also took an equity position in business projects. The original pattern was for the government to move into high-risk sectors, including major industrial projects such as steel production, ship repair and petrochemicals. These were areas in which businesses were reluctant to venture or did not want to assume all the risk. This high degree of government entrepreneurship makes it less easy to accept the market-conforming viewpoint of the PAP on Singapore's economic success.

The structure of the government's holding companies is complex, involving a variety of institutions and spanning both domestic and international spheres. One company, the Government Investment Corporation (a private corporation wholly owned by a subsidiary of the government), is a major global investor in equities. Established in 1981 as an offshoot of the Central Bank of Singapore, by 2004 it was managing assets worth US$100 billion. It was created when the Central Bank had begun to accumulate massive reserves from a mixture of the state's prudent fiscal policies, the Singaporeans' high rate of savings (53%) in the Central Provident Fund and the growing balance of trade surpluses. This was a bold strategy in which the aim of the Government Investment Corporation was and has been to actively manage the nation's reserves—it is an investor in areas such as public equities and real estate, and grasps any other special opportunities that might arise (Borrell 2003).

Many other government enterprises are centrally owned by another giant corporation, Temasek Holdings Ltd. This investment arm of the government was incorporated in 1974 to take over 36 enterprises in which the government had taken equity during Singapore's early drive to industrialise. Its massive assets were estimated (by Temasek itself) to be valued at Singaporean dollar (S$) 90 billion in 2004 (Temasek 2004). These investments are of enormous national significance. Temasek's major listed companies account for 27% capitalisation of the local stock exchange and, according to government statistics, Temasek generates 12.9% of Singapore's GDP. Overall, informal estimates suggest that state enterprises generate perhaps as much as 60% of GDP (Dodd 2001:64). An analysis of the top-500 Singapore-based companies in 1988 depicted government-linked companies as being responsible for 60.5% of total realised profits in Singapore (Rodan 2001:167). Although Temasek is arguably the most important holding company for investments by the PAP and is a registered company, it and many of its subsidiaries are exempt from the requirement to file financial accounts. According to Low (cited in Dodd 2001:64), the 'Government may be honest, accountable and efficient. But transparency is not its strong suit.'[2]

In 2004 Temasek invested in a wide range of industries: telecommunications and media, financial services, property, transportation and logistics, energy and resources, infrastructure, engineering and technology, pharmaceuticals and biosciences. Its Singapore-based companies included Singapore Airlines, SingTel, DBS Bank, SMRT Corporation, Neptune Orient Lines and Keppel Corporation, among others (Temasek 2004). It was also a major overseas investor—in India, China, Vietnam, Indonesia, Australia, the United States, Europe, Japan, South Korea, Taiwan and elsewhere.

In 1983 another major state company, Singapore Technologies, was formed in keeping with state policy to promote higher value-added production (Rodan 2001:148). The government also expanded its overseas investments using joint ventures under this company's auspices (Rodan 2001:148).

The government's influence extends beyond the companies in which it has equity because the same elite government personnel are often recycled across the boards of directors of the Government Linked Companies (GLCs). This may not be so unusual, for in Australia many of the same senior personnel appear on the boards of major companies, and in the Japanese *keiretsu* and the South Korean *chaebol* board members have been cross-linked within their own conglomerate subsidiaries. What is unusual, however, is that members of this group of GLC appointees are elite public servants who also constitute Singapore's business elite. There is no major group of influential private sector entrepreneurs in Singapore. These connections between civil servants and state-owned enterprises support not merely a culture in which business accountability and transparency is lacking, but also provide the underpinnings of authoritarian state power.

The structure and influence of these government companies and investments may not be under challenge from within Singapore, but internationally they are. As the PAP seeks to compete and invest in the international market—and in the process to create Singapore's new MNCs—the international community is asking questions about the competency and business acumen of these special state servants. International opinion does not share the view of the PAP that these companies are regular commercial entities; rather, they are seen for what they are—government companies. This extensive state role is clouding the claim that Singapore is a free market economy; it also provides yet one more factor that is perceived as crowding out local, private business initiative in Singapore.

But how can one assess the overall efficacy of the government in its role as manager of the Singaporean economy? Since the 1990s Singapore's economic growth rates have been slower and have fluctuated. Certainly the 1997 Asian financial crisis dealt a blow when GDP growth fell to 0.4% in 1998 (Rodan 2001:154) and the economy seemed to be in a shallow recession. Singapore's stock market lost 47% of its value between July 1997 and August 1998 (Tan 2001:26). Depreciations in the region's currencies, equity and property markets all affected Singapore's banking sector, and non-performing loans increased. Singapore's wealth fell as consumption and investment faltered, and business confidence waned (Tan 2001:26). Redundancies increased and the official unemployment rate rose from its usual 2% to 4.4% in December 1998 and remained at 4.6% as late as 2003. Even the GLCs, once the haven for security of tenure, eventually retrenched labour. In 2003 the PAP warned that until companies downsized even further, economic revival could not occur (Cheesman 2003). Singapore's exports lost competitiveness in the face of the massive currency depreciations of Asian neighbours. These were difficult years for an economy that was so exceptionally dependent on foreign trade. Singapore's total exports, about twice the value of GDP (*BT* 2001), included a large volume of re-exports (imports re-exported without processing) and were indicative of Singapore's enduring entrepot role.

The Asian financial crisis did not hit Singapore directly, but it did hit indirectly through its regional neighbours and for this reason and others it recovered quickly from the slump. Rapid recovery was largely due to Singapore's strong economy and stable economic institutions. The PAP's macro-economic management had always been sound. Singapore's dollar had steadily appreciated over the growth decades, and had been managed against a basket of currencies of its major trading partners. Unlike some of its neighbours, this meant Singapore had little United States dollar debt (since the Singaporean dollar interest rates were lower than the United States dollar rates of interest, making it unattractive for Singapore's companies to borrow in United States dollars). Corporations and financial institutions in Singapore were therefore not exposed to the massive short-term foreign debts, which contributed to the economic collapses in South Korea, Thailand and Indonesia. The PAP's caution with regard to its banking and financial services, its effective bank regulation and conservative bank behaviour meant that the financial sector avoided many of the problems of other Asian banking systems. Inflation had remained low over the years, interest rates were historically low and the high standard of corporate governance attested to the effectiveness of close government scrutiny.

The solidity of Singapore's economy was reflected in its attitudes towards economic recovery after the Asian financial crisis. The PAP vigorously endorsed the message of the rational economists of the West, most notably in the policies of the IMF. In October 1997, when addressing the Fortune 500 Forum in Boston in the United States, Singapore's Senior Minister, Lee Kuan Yew, stated that 'in nearly every economic crisis the root cause is political, not economic' and that policy mistakes are costly in global markets where communications are so instant: he added that governments must therefore reform quickly to win back foreign-investor confidence (Richardson 1997:2). In an economy as open as Singapore's to trade, investment and MNC involvement, this seemed especially true.

But this is a paradoxical statement from Lee Kuan Yew, for while he promoted Singapore's free and open economy, the GLCs continued to monopolise some sectors of the economy. This raises the legitimate question of whether the PAP actually understands the meaning of 'market rules'. This is an issue that the Singaporean government has avoided altogether. The state has always maintained that the economic fluctuations of the 1990s, including the 1997 Asian financial crisis, were cyclical in nature and that Singapore was a victim of its links with the global and regional economies. Alternatively, could these problems have been structural—namely, a direct consequence of Singapore's process of economic development? Could it be that the economic crisis of the late 1990s merely served to expose Singapore's existing vulnerabilities?

The significance of the Asian financial crisis in Singapore

Few other nations were so dependent on the rest of the world for trade and investment as Singapore. It is hardly surprising that Singapore was vulnerable to the 1997 Asian economic crisis and the 2001 recession, when the United States-led global technology resources bust caused Singapore's GDP growth rate to slump to –2.4%. According to the PAP, global economic crises have a contagious impact on Singapore and the nature of its open economy means that economic downturns in Singapore are cyclical, not structural. Thus, when delivering the 2003 Budget, the Deputy Prime Minister and Finance Minister, Lee Hsien Loong, warned of harder times ahead and of expected slower growth, not only because of Singapore's higher level of development, but also because of the difficult external conditions (*ATI* 2003:9–10). The 2003 Budget was in deficit, aggregate demand had been low (to the point that economists feared deflation), the export market was increasingly competitive, and neighbouring economies were successfully luring the prized foreign direct investment funds away from Singapore. Singapore's cost structure was higher than its less economically developed neighbours and the PAP had at times admonished its people about this.

The weaknesses of Singapore's development strategy

Despite its strong macro-economic policy, its well-managed financial sector and good corporate governance, was the Singaporean government blameless? Could it be that the structural problems emerging in Singapore pointed to a weakness in the nation's basic model of economic development? Certainly, Singapore's structural problems contributed to its vulnerability. In particular, the following four structural difficulties can be identified: high dependence on a limited range of industries, dependence on MNCs, the underdeveloped nature of the local entrepreneurial sector and rising regional competition.

Singapore has been particularly vulnerable to slumps in external demand because of its high dependence on a small range of industries, such as electronics, chemicals and engineering manufacturing. In 2004 electronic products accounted for over 40% of total industrial output (Global Edge 2005). Singapore is the world's leading producer of disk drives, and there have been significant investments in wafer-fabrication plants. True, Singapore invested heavily in crude petroleum refining and petrochemicals, but this was not enough to buffer the slump in demand for electronics. Singapore has since become more aware of this and has sought to diversify its industries by promoting the service sector in particular—telecommunications, financial services and aviation—and by developing a knowledge-based economy in biomedical sciences, pharmaceutics, biotechnological, medical services and healthcare services. It has a strategy to promote companies engaged in knowledge-intensive activities such as discovery research, product development, clinical research and high-technological manufacturing.

Despite this, much appears not to have changed. These new industries are being created less with local talent and more by way of foreign expertise. Moreover, Singapore's dependence on foreign corporations for its economic development still does not seem to be acknowledged by the government as a problem. Even when the state seeks to restructure the economy, as in the above examples, it has sought to do so by attracting large foreign corporations into new industries. There does not seem to be an effective promotion of local entrepreneurs or foreign SMEs despite the business master plan, 'SME 21' (Chee 2001:68). Identifying a future for foreign SMEs is, moreover, unlikely to help build a new development strategy. Rather, it suggests an inability to get beyond a dependency on foreign investment and foreign innovation. The 2003 Budget is especially revealing: employers were offered higher tax concessions to import foreign talent. Local firms were also encouraged to contact foreign experts via the 150,000 strong Singaporean diaspora (*ATI* 2003:10).

A persistent problem for decades has been the lack of a thriving local entrepreneurial sector. State policy to invigorate this sector seems to have been piecemeal and sparse. The PAP resolved to promote local business—for example, its National Day message in August 2000 encouraged Singaporeans to be more entrepreneurial, to take risks, to be nimble-footed in business and to confront the global economy. Singapore has also been following a policy of privatisation. This is supposed to include the PAP reducing its stake in Temasek Holdings. But according to the paradoxical Temasek Charter released in July 2002, the PAP intended to be 'more active and demanding as a shareholder than it was before': Temasek 'will exercise its shareholder rights to influence the strategic directions of its companies' (Khanna 2002:4; Temasek 2004). This implies a tightening of the already firm grip of the government over its multitude of companies under the Temasek Group. It does not indicate a selling-off of government-owned firms, which might provide a chance to strengthen the local private business sector through increased competition.

Despite some talk of privatisation, no concerted attempt has been made to dilute government-controlled and government-owned enterprises. If anything, a more obvious intention seems to be to entrench state power even more firmly. In line with the government's stated aim to increase competition, it has been considering developing a 'competition policy', similar to the one that operates in Australia. This, however, would have implications for foreign MNCs hoping to compete in sectors dominated by the GLCs (for example, electronics manufacturing, media, engineering, aviation and telecommunications) (Ferguson 2001:14). But would the GLCs really welcome this competition?

How willing is the Singaporean government to contemplate exposing state-owned enterprises to the competition of MNCs? More fundamentally, exactly how can a new competition policy assist the emergence of a stronger local, private business sector? If state companies are to be exposed to the competition of MNCs, can that atmosphere really help the more vulnerable Singaporean SMEs? As yet, these issues have not been resolved. In the meantime, despite the rhetoric of privatisation, state ownership and management of public sector companies has not been achieved.

The fourth, much larger, problem facing Singapore today is the increasing competition within the Southeast Asian region, especially from China. The policy response for some years has been to make Singapore the regional and international hub for service sector expertise and business. Indeed, the service sector has been important to Singapore since its entrepot role under British colonialism; even though for some years it was subsumed by the drive for export-led manufacturing, this sector endured. Given Singapore's strategic location, with its competitive port and aviation facilities, pliant labour force and welcoming policies for foreign capital, Singapore seems to have a comparative advantage in this area. This is acknowledged by the current policies promoting service exports. At the same time, Thailand has also identified a role similar to Singapore's—so regional competition is also growing (see Treisman's chapter in this book).

The government's solution to regional competition has also involved linking with other fast-growing regions and the expansion of outward foreign direct investment. First, bilateral trade agreements both within and outside the Asian region have been actively pursued. In 2004 Singapore signed bilateral agreements with Australia, Canada, Mexico, India and South Korea. These relationships should maintain the strong trade and investment levels crucial to Singapore and can be seen as a means of countering the importance of China as a destination for international investment. As ASEAN expands its membership, frees trade restrictions and becomes a stronger regional organisation, Singapore is likely to benefit from the access this provides to a regional hinterland rich in resources and markets.

The second policy to mitigate the international competition involves overseas acquisition, or outward foreign direct investment, by Singapore. This is envisaged as the next stage in Singapore's economic development. But who would be Singapore's foreign investors abroad? Certainly there are now some successful local entrepreneurs investing overseas, but the PAP plans that overseas investment will mainly come from the GLCs who have already so vigorously embraced this form of globalisation.

Singapore today

In conclusion, the current problems in Singapore's economy appear to reflect deeper, structural weaknesses in its basic model of economic development. Singapore's problems cannot be explained away as the incidental results of cyclical change. At the core of the problem lies the refusal of the government to abandon its historical role as the country's leading local entrepreneur. There can be no doubt that state economic control is linked to the political authoritarianism for which Singapore has become well known. Building local entrepreneurial talent also contains the seeds of political risks—the risk being that the drive of the entrepreneurs will overshadow the capacities and powers of the country's elite civil servants. Given state hesitancy, the policies that appear to promote new foreign and local companies need to be studied carefully and understood in a wider political context. In particular, questions need to be asked about the

PAP's new economic strategy to create its own MNCs by expanding the role of the GLCs. Will this strategy really free up the private sector?

This chapter concludes with a case study, which has been selected to demonstrate that the capacities of indigenous, local Chinese entrepreneurship are not as feeble as government policy announcements may suggest.

A case study of Pacific International Lines

While local entrepreneurs may not have been the main thrust behind Singapore's economic development, enough successes exist to testify to the business acumen of the Chinese and thus, in Singapore's case, to the strong potential for the development of a solid domestic private business sector.

The founder of Pacific International Lines (PIL), YC Chang, left Fujian province, China, in 1937 to join his father in Singapore in search of business opportunities just after the outbreak of the Sino–Japanese War. He worked in Malacca for his uncle in shipping, then for a trading firm dealing with Indonesia and Australia. The trading firm subsequently floundered, only to be revived when Chang convinced his boss to expand into ship owning. So for 18 years he worked as general manager in this company, which had begun with small coastal ships and expanded to ocean-going ships.

In 1967 Chang and some trusted and experienced friends established PIL, a Singapore-registered company, which also began as a coastal ship-owner/operator and became one of Asia's largest ship owners and, through its listed subsidiary, the world's second-largest maker of containers. Chang contributed approximately S$3 million of his own money, with S$250,000 from each of his ten partners. At that time Chang took advantage of the PAP's provision of financial incentives for companies to register their vessels in Singapore as part of its export-led growth policy.

PIL is a privately owned business, with Chang's family controlling 85% of the stock; despite many approaches from banks for it to be listed publicly, Chang has no plans to do so. PIL owns and operates 100 fully containerised ships, which operate out of 120 ports. Its container volume continues to grow—on 31 December 2004 it had 12 container vessels on order and due for delivery in November 2006. Over time the business has diversified into the related fields of logistics, such as supply-chain management, consolidation and distribution facilities, warehousing, container depot operations, trucking, global ship agencies, container manufacturing, marine engineering and real estate.

From the beginning Chang saw the potential that the People's Republic of China had to offer in transporting Chinese goods to international markets, and in 1967, the same year he set up PIL, he started a service from China to the Middle East. Chang acknowledged that his affinity with the Chinese mentality made it easy to negotiate with the Chinese state. Chang was typical of many overseas Chinese living in Southeast Asia whose connections with their homeland, mainland China, subsequently attracted them back as foreign investors, so gaining business advantages well before the liberalisation of China's economy. As a result PIL still maintains strong relations with its longstanding Chinese customers, essentially the big national, state-run companies. PIL covers the long coast of China from north to south with its branch network. Its ships travel from China to Africa, the Red Sea and the Persian Gulf, and PIL uses Singapore as its main transhipment hub for Southeast Asia.

Chang typified the business methods of overseas Chinese entrepreneurs by building his empire gradually to ensure consolidation at each stage. As he put it, 'there is always somebody who is bigger and stronger than you. That has always been my motto' (Fang 2005).

For this reason the small and still-untested PIL had chosen to invest in China, rather than the United States or Europe where competition was already established and ferocious. Gradually, as PIL has gathered economic strength and capital, it has grown in scope. The company employs approximately 600 workers at its headquarters in Singapore and another 1,000 overseas.

Hard work and trust were crucial to Chang's success, and he often cites his commitment to his Middle Eastern customers when he persevered and delivered cargo to them during the 1990 Gulf War. The structure of his family empire has allowed his quick decision making to exploit opportunities and to avoid disasters. For example, when PIL ships delivering cement to Saudi Arabia became blocked by traffic in the port of Jeddah, the heat threatened to set the cement into hard concrete blocks; Chang, acting quickly, chartered smaller feeder vessels to unload the cargo from his ships to port, thus meeting his promise to the customer and saving his cargo.

Today Chang is Executive Chairman and controls finance, ship purchasing and building, and the detailed reports. He leaves the rest of the business to his sons and a team of professionals. Chang's fifth son, SS Teo, is Managing Director and echoes his father's tradition and mentality in keeping a low profile. When asked why the fifth son took the helm, Chang responded that he was the hardest worker. His family still firmly controls the conglomerate's business, as well as its succession.

At a gala dinner held in February 2005, the inaugural Singapore International 100 Ranking was announced. This was organised by the republic's trade and enterprise promotion agency, the International Enterprise Forum. PIL was not only ranked number one amongst the privately owned companies in Singapore in terms of revenue from overseas markets, but was also first for the North Asia markets and second for China, India and the Middle East in terms of revenue from overseas markets. Of the top-100 ranked companies in Singapore overall, the first five leaders were Singapore Airlines, Neptune Orient Lines, Singapore Telecommunications Ltd, Keppel Corporation and CapitaLand Ltd—all state enterprises. PIL rated sixth in this list.

Notes

1 The 2001 election returned 82 of the 84 seats in parliament to the PAP. There were no opposition members in parliament between the years 1968 to 1981 (DFAT 2004).
2 Note, however, that the government website for Temasek is detailed.

Bibliography

AFX Asia 2003a, 'China's D'Long Group fails to buy stake in Shenyin & Wanguo Securities', 30 July.

—— 2003b, 'China's Torch Investments to expand auto portfolio, but analysts doubtful', 1 September.

AFX News 2004, 'Beijing Hyundai produces 100,000th car, to introduce Tucson SUV this year', 27 May, www.afxnews.com, viewed 14 June 2004.

Agence France-Presse 1997, 'Thai bank in talks with Citibank and other potential foreign partners', 20 November, http://global.factiva.com, viewed 1 April 2006.

Alatas, Hussein 1977, *The myth of the lazy native*, Frank Cass, London.

Alpert, WT and S Sanders 2005, 'Recent economic history' in Alpert, WT and S Sanders (eds), *The Vietnamese economy and its transformation to an open market system*, ME Sharpe, Armonk.

AMC Regulations 2000, 'Regulations governing asset management companies', People's Republic of China State Council Document No 297, 10 November, www.jscq.com.cn/next/zcfg/zhongjin/007.htm, viewed November 2004.

Amsden, A 1989, *Asia's next giant: late industrialization in Korea*, Oxford University Press, New York.

—— 1992, 'A theory of government intervention in late industrialization' in Putterman, L and D Rueschmeyer (eds), *State and market in development: synergy or rivalry?*, Lynne Rienner, Boulder.

Amsden, A and T Hikino 1994, 'Staying behind, stumbling back, sneaking up, soaring ahead: late industrialization in historical perspective' in Baumol, W, R Nelson and E Wolf (eds), *Convergence of productivity*, Oxford University Press, New York.

Appleton, S, J Knight, L Song and Q Xia 2002, 'Labor retrenchment in China: determinants and consequences', *China Economic Review* 13.

Ariyadasa, C 2003, 'India opens first petrol station in Sri Lanka', *rediff.com*, 28 May, www.rediff.com/money/2003/may/28lanka1.htm, viewed February 2005.

Armitage, C 2003, 'China's "Iron Rice Bowl" gets the chop', *Australian,* 13 January.

Arshad, Siti Iswalah 2002, 'Malaysia', *Development of the automotive sector in selected countries of the ESCAP region: proceedings and country papers at the regional consultative meeting on the Promotion of Intraregional Trade and Economic Cooperation in the Automotive Sector*, United Nations, New York www.unescap.org/tid/publication/indpub2223.pdf viewed March 2005.

ASEAN Centre for Energy 2000, 'Indonesia: areas with deficit power supply', www.aseanenergy.org/energy_sector/electricity/indonesia/deficit_areas.htm, viewed 11 August 2004.

ASEAN Secretariat 2005, *Member countries*, ASEAN Secretariat, www.aseansec.org/74.htm, viewed 28 May 2005.

Asia Pulse 2004a, 'Key events in Hyundai–Daimler–Chrysler relationship', 12 May, http://web.lexis-nexis.com/universe, viewed 14 June 2004.

—— 2004b, 'Hyundai, Kia blamed for discriminating against local customers', 8 June, http://web.lexis-nexis.com/universe/, viewed 14 June 2004.

Aswicahyono, Haryo R Atje and Thee KW 2004, *Indonesia's industrial competitiveness: study of the garments, auto parts, and electronic components industries*, report for the Development Economics Research Group, World Bank, Jakarta.

ATI (*Asia Today International*) 2003, 'Tougher times ahead...', April–May, 21(2).

ATIP (Asian Technology Information Program) 1996, 'Technology and industry in Penang, Malaysia', ATIP96.107, Washington, www.atip.org/ATIP/public/atip.reports.96/atip96.107.html, viewed February 2005.

Badawi, YAB Dato' Seri Abdullah Bin Haji Ahmad 2005, opening address, Malaysia–China Business Forum 2005, Seri Kembangan, 12 August, www.pmo.gov.my/WebNotesApp/PMMain.nsf/314edc1f96172e0a48256f240017b913/f083aa97a9b018ad4825705e0006abec?OpenDocument, viewed March 2006.

Bagchi, AK 1972, *Private investment in India 1900–1939*, Cambridge University Press, Cambridge.

Balse, H 2002, 'Reliance gas find 40 times bigger than Bombay High', *rediff.com*, 31 October, www.rediff.com/money/2002/oct/31ril.htm, viewed February 2005.

BI (Bank of Indonesia) 2006, www.bi.go.id, accessed 23 August.

BT (Bank of Thailand) 2005, *Economic Data*, Bank of Thailand, www.bot.or.th/bothomepage/databank/EconData/EconData_e.htm, viewed 2 July 2005.

Basri, M Chatib 2004, 'Economic update 2003: after five years of *reformasi ekonomi*, what next?' in Basri, M Chatib and P van der Eng (eds), *Business in Indonesia: new challenges, old problems*, Institute of Southeast Asian Studies, Singapore.

BDU (*Business Daily Update*) 2004, 'Private enterprises doing it tough', 15 March.

BI (Bank Indonesia) 1997, *Report for the Financial Year 1996/97*, Bank Indonesia, Jakarta.

—— 2004, *Annual Report 2003*, Bank Indonesia, Jakarta.

Bird, K 2004, 'Recent trends in foreign direct investment' in Basri, M Chatib and P van der Eng (eds), *Business in Indonesia: new challenges, old problems*, Institute of Southeast Asian Studies, Singapore.

BizAsia 2003, 'Hyundai on export drive', 16 April, www.bizasia.com, viewed 2 December 2003.

BKPM (Badan Koordinasi Penanaman Modal)) 2000, 'Negative list based on presidential decree 96/2000jo.118/2000', www.bkpm.go.id/en/dni.php, viewed 2 August 2004.

BL (Business Line) 2002, 'Reliance, 3 others allowed to sell petrol, diesel', 25 May http://www.thehindubusinessline.com/2002/05/25/stories/2002052502680100.htm viewed February 2005.

Blakely, R 2005, 'India eyes Yukos's former star asset', *Timesonline*, 7 January, http://business.timesonline.co.uk/article/0,,16614-1429793,00.html, viewed February 2005.

Bobb, D and M Bhupta 2004, 'Ambani vs Ambani', *India Today*, 6 December.

Bonin, J and Y Huang 2001, 'Dealing with the bad loans of the Chinese banks', *Journal of Asian Economics*, 12.

Borrell, J 2003, 'Profile: Singapore', *Venture Capital Journal*, www.ventureeconomics.com/vcj/protected/1047652058544.html, viewed 27 April 2006.

BPS (Biro Pusat Statistik) 1988, *Statistik Indonesia*, Biro Pusat Statistik, Jakarta.

—— 1998, *Statistik Indonesia*, Biro Pusat Statistik, Jakarta.

Breslin, S 1996, 'China: developmental state or dysfunctional state?', *Third World Quarterly* 17(4).

BT (Business Times) 2001, 'Singapore economy is not primarily export driven, says Morgan Stanley', Singapore, 5 February.

Burgess, C 2003, 'The challenge of globalization and international migration for the new Japan', *(Re)constructing identities: international marriage migrants as potential agents of change in a globalising Japan*, draft PhD thesis, Monash University.

Bush, GW 2002, 'State of the Union address', 29 January, Washington.

CAGI (Comptroller and Auditor General of India) 2003, *Report No 1 of 2003 (PSUs), Overview*, www.cag.nic.in, viewed February 2005.

Cao Y, Qian Y and B Weingast 1999, 'From federalism, Chinese style to privatization, Chinese style', *Economics of Transition* 7(1).

Castle, J 2004, 'Investment projects: a view from the private sector' in Basri, M Chatib and P van der Eng (eds), *Business in Indonesia: new challenges, old problems*, Institute of Southeast Asian Studies, Singapore.

Chandler, C 2002, 'Trying to make sense of bad debt reform: China selling bank assets to solve the problem', *Washington Post*, 15 January.

Chang C and Wang Y 1994, 'The nature of the township and village enterprise', *Journal of Comparative Economics* 19(3).

Chang, Ha-Joon 1993, 'The political economy of industry policy in Korea', *Cambridge Journal of Economics* 17(2).

Chang, L 1992, 'Financial mobilization and allocation: the South Korean case, *Studies in Comparative International Development* 27(4).

Chan-Tiberghien, J 2004, *Gender and human rights politics in Japan: global norms and domestic networks*, Stanford University Press, Stanford.

Chee SJ 2001, *Your future my faith our freedom*, Open Singapore Centre, Singapore.

Cheesman, B 2003, 'Singapore faces more job pain', *Australian Financial Review*, 27 July.

China-Asean.net 2001, *The national economy of Thailand*, China–ASEAN Business Network, www.china-asean.net/asean_biz/thailand/country_econ/Asean_th_econ_brief.html, viewed 26 May 2005,

Ch'ng DCL 1993, *The overseas Chinese entrepreneurs in East Asia. Background, business practices and international networks*, Committee for Economic Development of Australia.

Chng MK, Low, L, Tay BN and A Tyabji 1986, *Technology and skills in Singapore*, Institute of Southeast Asian Studies, Singapore.

Cho Soon 1994, *The dynamics of Korean economic development*, Institute for International Economics, Washington.

Cho, YJ 2001, 'The international environment and Korea's economic development during 1950s–1970s', *Economic Papers* 4(2).

Choe C and Yin X 2000, 'Contract management responsibility system and profit incentives in Chinese state-owned enterprises', *China Economic Review* 11.

Chowdhury, A and Islam, I 1995, *The newly industrialising economies of East Asia*, Routledge, New York and London.

Chung, Jin-Young 1990, 'South Korean strategies for dynamic transformation: 1961–1988' in Lim, G-C and Wook Chang (eds), *Dynamic transformation: Korea, NICs and beyond*, Consortium on Development Studies, Urbana and Seoul.

CICT (China Industry and Commerce Times) 1997, 19 March.

Citibank 2005, *About us*, Citibank Thailand, www.citibank.co.th/portal/iptLightPage.jsp?bus=thgcb&path=/thgcb/english/global_htm/CBThailand.htm&lang=ENG&beanID=476&viewID=MY_PORTAL_VIEW, viewed 25 May 2005.

Clifford, ML 1994 *Troubled tiger. Businessmen, bureaucrats, and generals in South Korea*, ME Sharpe, Armonk.

Cohen, S 2001, *Emerging power India*, Brookings Institution Press, Washington.

Colebatch, T 2001, 'Korea battles the debt devil', *Age* 16 June.

Comber, L 2006, 'Malaya's secret police 1945–60: the role of the Special Branch in the Malayan Emergency', PhD thesis, Monash University.

Cummings, B 1984, 'Legacy of Japanese colonialism in Korea' in Myers, RH and MR Peattie (eds), *The Japanese colonial empire, 1985–1945*, Princeton University Press, Princeton.

Das, DK 2006, 'The Chinese and Indian economies: comparing the comparables', *Journal of Chinese Economic and Business Studies* 4(1).

Dawn 2005, 'India to buy Iranian gas', 8 January, http://www.dawn.com/2005/01/08/ebr10.htm, viewed February 2005.

Deyo, F (ed) 1987, *The political economy of the new Asian industrialism*, Cornell University Press, Ithaca.

DFAT (Department of Foreign Affairs and Trade) 2004, 'Country information, Singapore', Commonwealth of Australia, Canberra, www.dfat.gov.au, viewed 8 September 2004.

—— 2006, 'Australia–Malaysia free trade agreement negotiations', www.dfat.gov.au/geo/malaysia/fta/index.html, viewed March 2006.

Dhawade, S 2001, 'Ambanis rank third among world's richest Indians', 28 March, www.rediff.com/money/2001/mar/28ambani.htm, viewed February 2005.

DM (Department of Manpower) 2003, *President of Republic of Indonesia Act Number 13 Year 2003 Concerning Manpower*, Republic of Indonesia.

—— 2005, Ditjen Pembinaan Hubungan Industrial [Directorate General for Overseeing Industrial Relations], Republic of Indonesia.

Dobby, EHG 1961, *Southeast Asia*, University of London, London.

Dodd, T 2001, 'Singapore Inc', *Australian Financial Review*, 24 April.

Dollar, D 2004, 'Reform, growth and poverty' in Glewwe, P, N Agrawal and D Dollar (eds), *Economic growth, poverty and household welfare in Vietnam*, World Bank, Washington.

Domain-b.com 2004, 'Oil import bill up 56 % till October', 2 December, www.domain-b.com/industry/oil_gas/20041202_oil_import.htmlomain-b.com, viewed February 2005.

—— 2005a, 'Government approves panel for oil PSUs revamp', 17 January, www.domain-b.com/industry/oil_gas/20050117_revamp.html, viewed February 2005.

—— 2005b, 'Restructure oil PSUs, says PM', 17 January, www.domain-b.com/economy/governance/20050117_oil.html, viewed February 2005.

—— 2005c, 'India signs to import LNG from Iran', 8 January, www.domain-b.com/economy/governance/20050108_import.html, viewed February 2005.

du Mars, R 2004, 'Hynix suspends talks with Citigroup', 14 April, www.TheDeal.com, viewed 14 July 2004.

EAAU (East Asia Analytical Unit) 2000, *Indonesia: facing the challenge*, Department of Foreign Affairs and Trade, Commonwealth of Australia.

Eckert, CJ 1991, *Offspring of empire: the Koch'ang Kims and the colonial origins of Korean capitalism, 1876–1945*, University of Washington Press, Seattle and London.

—— 1993, 'The South Korean bourgeoisie: a class in search of hegemony' in Koo, H (ed), *State and society in contemporary Korea*, Cornell University Press, Ithaca and London.

Economist 2003, 'Chinese firms expand overseas', 4 September.

EII (Euromoney Institutional Investor PLC) 2002, 'Citi Thailand office seeks better CSD links', 26 August, http://global.factiva.com, viewed 1 April 2006.

EIU (Economist Intelligence Unit) 2000 *Vietnam: country profile*, London

—— 2002a, *Country report. South Korea*, EIU, London.

—— 2002b, 'Magnet or morass? South Korea's prospects for foreign investment', report commissioned by the Korean Ministry of Commerce, Industry and Energy and the Korean Trade-Investment Promotion Agency.

—— 2003, *Indonesia country profile 2003*, New York.

Equityequation 2002, 'Dhirajlal Hirachand Ambandi: 1932–2002', www.equityequation.com/dhirajlal_hirachand_ambani.htm, viewed February 2006.

ESCAP 2002, *Development of the automotive sector in selected countries of the ESCAP region: proceedings and country papers at the regional consultative meeting on the promotion of intraregional trade and economic cooperation in the automotive sector*, United Nations, New York www.unescap.org/tid/publication/indpub2223.pdf, viewed January 2006.

Eslake, S 2006, 'Catch me if you can: India and China', *Monash Business Review* 2(1).

ET (*Economic Times*) 2005, 'Split infinitive: here's why Ambanis should stay together', 31 January, http://economictimes.com, viewed February 2005.

Evans, PB 1989, 'Predatory, developmental and other apparatuses: a comparative political economy perspective on the Third World state', *Sociological Forum* 4(4).

Ewing, RD 2006, 'The new multinational: Lilliputian not leviathan', www.atimes.com/atimes/Global_Economy/HD05Dj01.html, viewed August 2006.

Fang, N 2005 'SS Teo, Managing Director, PIL interview with Nicholas Fang', *Singapore Sunday Times*, 6 February.

Fauzi, Indra N 2003, 'Persepsi Pelaku Usaha Terhadap Iklim Usaha di Era Otonomi Daerah', Partnership for Economic Growth Publication No 132, August, www.pegasus.or.id/publication.html, viewed 14 August 2004.

Ferguson, I 2001, 'Island nation undergoes a restructure', *Australian Financial Review*, 20 June.

FIT (Financial Times Information) 2004, 'Win some lose some', 24 April, http://web.lexis-nexis.com/universe/doc, viewed 14 June 2004.

Forbes.com (2005), 'India Reliance group's Ambani brothers reach deal on dividing business empire', 19 June http://www.forbes.com/finance/feeds/afx/2005/06/19/afx2099903.html

Frank, AG 2003, *ReOrient: global economy in the Asian age*, Yesan Publishing Co, Seoul.

Freehill, Hollingdale and Page 2002, *Vietnam: legal and regulatory framework*, Freehill, Hollingdale and Page, Hanoi.

Fujita, M 1997/1998, 'Industrial policies and trade liberalisation – the automotive industry in Thailand and Malaysia' in Omura, Keiji (ed), *The deepening economic interdependence in the APEC region*, APEC Study Centre and Institute of Developing Economies, Japan External Trade Organisation.

Fukuoka, Y 1996, *Zai-nichi Kankokujin/Chosenjin* [Koreans resident in Japan], Chuo Koronsha, Tokyo.

Funabashi, Y 2000, *Aete Eigo Koyogo Ron* [A humble proposal to have English as one of the official languages], Bungei Shunju, Tokyo.

Furnivall, JS 1939, *Netherlands India: a study of plural economy*, Cambridge University Press, Cambridge.

Furuzawa, H 2005, 'The impact of industrialization on food-processing' in Nakayama, S and K Goto (eds), *A social history of science and technology in contemporary Japan*, volume 3, Trans Pacific Press, Rosanna.

Gabilaia, T 2001, 'Malaysian proton and AFTA: a threat or advantage?', TED Case Studies, June, www.american.edu/TED/proton.htm, viewed March 2006.

GAIL 2005a, 'Indian Energy Industry', in *Energy Zone*, www.gailonline.com/energyzone/energy.html, viewed February 2005.

—— 2005b, 'Statistics', www.gail.com, viewed February 2005.

Gazette 2003, 'China buys RJ project', 25 June.

GI (Government of India) 2005, *Annual economic survey 2003–2004*, New Delhi, http://indiabudget.nic.in/es2003-04/esmain.htm, viewed February 2005.

Global Edge 2005, 'Singapore economy', US Dept of State country background notes, http://globaledge.msu.edu, viewed 13 April 2006.

Gomez, J 2005, 'International NGOs: filling the gap in Singapore's civil society', *SOJOURN: Journal of Social Issues in Southeast Asia* 20(2).

Goswami, O 1991, *Industry, trade and peasant society: the jute economy of eastern India 1900–1947*, Oxford University Press, Delhi.

—— 2003, 'India 2003–2010: economic and political scenarios', presentation to Confederation of Indian Industries, India Brand Equity Foundation, www.ibef.org/artdisplay.aspx?cat_id=84&art_id=2160, viewed February 2005.

Haggard, S 1990, *Pathways from the periphery: the politics of growth in the newly industrializing countries*, Cornell University Press, Ithaca.

—— 2000, *The political economy of the Asian financial crisis*, Institute for International Economics, Washington.

Haggard, S, Lim PL and A Ong 1998, 'The hard disk drive industry in the northern region of Malaysia: report 98–04', Information Storage Industry Center, University of California, San Diego, December http://isic.ucsd.edu/papers/malaysiahdd.shtml, viewed December 2005.

Hamilton, C 1983, 'Capitalist industrialisation in East Asia's four little tigers', *Journal of Contemporary Asia* 13(1).

Hampden-Turner, C and F Trompenaars 1994, *The seven cultures of capitalism: systems for creating wealth in the United States, Britain, Japan, Germany, France, Sweden and the Netherlands*, Judy Piatkus, London.

Hanfley, P 1992, 'Banking on Bangkok', *Far Eastern Economic Review*, 16 January.

Harris, F 1958, *Jamsetjee Nusserwanjee Tata*, Blackie, London.

Harsch, E 2004, 'Africa and Asia forge stronger alliances', *Africa Recovery*, 18(1).

Hay, D, D Morris, G Liu and S Yao 1994, *Economic reform and state-owned enterprises in China, 1979–1987*, Clarendon Press, Oxford.

Hill, H 1997, 'Towards a political economy explanation of rapid growth in ASEAN', *ASEAN Economic Bulletin* 14(2).

Hirson, M 2005, 'The rise and fall of D'Long: China's private conglomerates and the quest for capital', *Perspectives* 6(4).

Ho, S 1994, *Rural China in transition: non-agricultural development in rural Jiangsu, 1978–1990*, Clarendon Press, Oxford.

HRW (Human Rights Watch) 2003, *Sudan, oil and human rights*, New York, http://www.hrw.org/reports/2003/sudan1103, viewed February 2005.

Huang G 2001, 'Do a good job on the debt–equity swap', speech to the third session of the Ninth Political Consultancy Bureau of China', http://www.beinet.net.cn/macro-econ/qg313.html, viewed November, 2004.

Huang Y, Woo WT and R Duncan 1999, 'Understanding the decline of China's state sector', *MOCT-MOST: Economic Policy in Transitional Economies* 9(1).

Huff, WG 1999, 'Turning the corner in Singapore's development state?', *Asian Survey*, 39(2):214-242.

Hughes, H 1993a 'An external view' in Low, L, MH Toh, TW Soon, KY Tan, H Hughes and KS Goh (eds), *Challenge and response: 30 years of the economic development board*, Times Academic Press, Singapore.

—— 1993b, 'East Asia. Is there an East Asia model?', Economics Division Working Papers, Research School of Pacific Studies, Australian National University, Canberra.

ICG (Indonesia Country Gateway) 2004, www.indonesia-gateway.web.id/content.php ?id=eco&sid=investment&pid=environment, viewed 15 August 2004.

II (India Infoline) 2004, 'Annual report analysis: Reliance Industries Ltd, juggernaut on the roll', 4 August, www.indiainfoline.com/sect/rein.pdf, viewed February 2005.

ILO (International Labor Organization) 2000, *World labor report 2000: income security and social protection in a changing world*, ILO, Geneva.

IMF (International Monetary Fund) 2000, 'Thailand: selected issues', prepared by Endo, T, M Griffiths, V Haksar, S Schwartz, S Barnett and I Lee, *IMF Staff Country Report*, No 00/21.

—— 2001, *Social dimensions of the IMF's policy dialogue*, International Monetary Fund, Washington.

—— 2004, 'Thailand: selected issues', prepared by Barnett, S, R Baqir, T Becker, A Schaechter and C Daseking, *IMF Staff Country Report*, No 04/1.

Ito, T 1997, 'Japan's economy needs structural change', *Finance and Development*, June.

Jaya, Wihana Kirana 2005, discussions with the author, Monash University.

JCN Network 2006, 'Mitsubishi Motors and Proton sign memorandum on new cooperation agreement', 3 February, www.japancorp.net/Article.Asp?Art_ ID=11827, viewed March 2006.

Jha, S 2005, 'Planning ahead for energy', 18 Jan 2005, www.domain-b.com/economy/ governance/20050118_energy.html, viewed February 2005.

Johnson, C 1982, *MITI and the Japanese miracle: the growth of industrial policy, 1925–1975*, Stanford University Press, Stanford.

Joint Statement between President George W Bush and Prime Minister Manmohan Singh 2000, White House, Washington, July, http://www.whitehouse.gov/news/ releases/2005/07/20050718-6.html, viewed February 2005.

JoongAng Daily 2004, 'Power of research cited in Shanghai firm's growth', 24 March.

Karim, Noor Al-Huda A, Euan Fleming and Howard Doran 2004, *An analysis of the regional distribution of foreign investment inflows in the manufacturing sector in Malaysia*, Working Paper Series in Economics, No. 2004-22, University of New England, Armidale.

Kazakevitch, G and R Smyth 2005, 'Gradualism versus shock therapy: (re) interpreting the Chinese and Russian experiences', *Asia Pacific Business Review* 11(1).

Kenward, LR 2004, 'Survey of recent developments', *Bulletin of Indonesian Economic Studies* 40(1).

Khanna, S 1987, 'The new business class, ideology and state: the making of a 'new consensus', *South Asia* 10(2).

Khanna T and K Palepu 1997, 'Why focused strategies might be wrong for emerging markets', *Harvard Business Review* 75(4).

Khanna, Vikram 2002, 'Progressive journey', *Business Times*, 9 August, Singapore.

Kim, Min-Koo 2004, 'Korean shipbuilders vying to develop new technologies', *Business Korea*, 3 May, www.mk.co.kr.

KKC (Keizai Kikaku Cho, Economic Planning Agency) 2000, *Heisei juni-nenpan kokumin seikatsu hakusho* [*The 2000 white paper on lifestyles of the populace*], Okura Sho Insatsu Kyoku, Tokyo.

KMKBPRI (Kantor Menteri Koordinator Bidang Perekonomian Republik Indonesia) 2004, white paper report, www.ekon.go.id/berita/20040810/20040810_2.shtml, viewed 14 August 2004.

Koike, K 1988, *Understanding industrial relations in modern Japan*, translated by Saso, M, Macmillan Press, London.

— 1995, *The economics of work in Japan*, Toyo Keizai Shinposha, Tokyo.

Komai, H 2001, *Foreign migrants in contemporary Japan*, translated from Japanese by Wilkinson, J, Trans Pacific Press, Melbourne.

Kompas 2000, 'Oknun TNI Jarah Udang', 12 February.

Kompas 2003a, 'Belum Pulih Budidaya Udang di Jateng', 9 June.

Kompas 2003b, 'Pencurian Mutiara di Sikka, Merugikan Investor PMA', 11 August.

Kosei Rodo Daijin Kanbo Tokei Joho Bu (Statistics and Information Department, Minister's Secretariat, Ministry of Health, Labour and Welfare, Japan) 2002, *Rodo Tokei Yoran Heisei Jusan Nendo* [Handbook of Labour Statistics 2001], Zaimu Sho Insatsu Kyoku, Tokyo.

Koshiro, K 1982, 'Ryoko na Koyo Kikai no Kishosei to Nihonteki Roshi Kankei' [The Scarcity of Good Jobs and Japanese Industrial Relations], *Nihon Rodo Kyokai Zasshi* 24(1).

KPPOD (Komisi Pemantauan Pelaksanaan Otonomi Daerah) 2004, www.kppod.org/region/lampiran%201.pdf, viewed 11 August 2004.

Krause, LB 1987, 'Thinking about Singapore' in Krause, L (ed), *The Singapore economy reconsidered*, Institute of Southeast Asian Studies, Singapore

Krugman, P 1994, 'The myth of the Asian miracle', *Foreign Affairs* 74(6).

—— 1999, *The return of depression economics*, WW Norton, New York.

Kunio Yoshihara 1988, *The rise of ersatz capitalism in Southeast Asia*, Oxford University Press, Singapore.

Kuznets, PW 1994, *Korean economic development. An interpretive model*, Praeger, Westport and London.

Kwon, Ik-Whan, L Cordell and JH Kim 1985, 'Public policy and economic development, the case of the Republic of Korea', *Indian Journal of Economics* 65/3(258).

Kyujugonen SSM Chosa Kenkyukai 2000, *Nihon no Kaiso Shisutemu* [The social stratification system in Japan], 6 volumes, Tokyo Daigaku Shuppankai, Tokyo.

Lall, S 1991, 'Explaining industrial success in the developing world' in Balasubramanyam, V and S Lall (eds), *Current issues in development economics*, Macmillan, London.

Lam, WWL 1999, 'NPC deputies to push more amendments', *South China Morning Post*, 26 February.

Lau, LJ, Y Qian and G Roland 2000, 'Reform without losers: an interpretation of China's dual track approach to transition', *Journal of Political Economy* 108(1).

Lee, H 2000, '*Xiagang*, the Chinese style of laying off workers', *Asian Survey* 40(6).

Lee, KY (2000) *From Third World to First. The Singapore story: 1965–2000*, Asia Pacific Press, Singapore.

Lee, TY and l Low 1990, *Local entrepreneurship in Singapore, private and state*, Singapore Institute of Policy Studies, Singapore.

Lenin, VI 1922, notes for a report 'Five Years Of The Russian Revolution And The Prospects Of The World Revolution' at the Fourth Congress of the Comintern (2) 13 November 1922, 'Marxists internet archive', http://www.marxists.org/archive/lenin/works/1922/nov/13b.htm

Li, X 1998, 'Looking at China's potential financial risks from the East Asian financial crisis: analyses of the assets operation of the state-owned commercial banks', *Reform* 3.

Lim CY et al 1988, *Policy options for the Singapore economy*, McGraw-Hill, Singapore.

Lim KS 2002, media statement, 'Call for National Competitiveness Council to overcome major flaw of 2002 Budget and arrest the alarming deterioration of international competitiveness as reflected by Malaysia's 14-place plunge in three years in ranking in the Global Competitiveness Report 2001 and 12-place plunge in five years in the World Competitiveness Yearbook 2001', http://72.14.203.104/search?q=cache:CINQDi4KsgEJ:www.limkitsiang.com/archive/2001/oct01/lks1225.htm+malaysia%27s+global+competitiveness&hl=en&gl=au&ct=clnk&cd=9, viewed March 2006.

Lim, TC 1999, 'The origins of societal power in South Korea: understanding the physical and human legacies of Japanese colonialism', *Modern Asian Studies* 33(3).

Lo, D 1997, *Market and institutional regulation in Chinese industrialisation 1978–1994*, MacMillan, London.

—— 1999, 'Reappraising the Performance of China's state-owned industrial enterprises, 1980–96', *Cambridge Journal of Economics* 23(6).

Lo, D and R Smyth 2005, 'Industrial restructuring and corporate governance in China's large-scale state-owned enterprises' in Smyth, R, OK Tam, M Warner and C Zhu (eds), *China's business reforms: institutional challenges in a globalised economy*, Routledge London.

Low, L 1993, 'The Economic Development Board' in Low, L, MH Toh, TW Soon, KY Tan, H Hughes and KS Goh, *Challenge and response: 30 years of the Economic Development Board*, Times Academic Press, Singapore.

Lu, L 1997, 'Shunde: transformation of government function based on property rights reform' in *Realistic choice: preliminary summary of the practice of reforming small state-owned enterprises*, China Reform and Development Report, Far East Publishing House, Shanghai.

Ma, S-Y 1999 'The role of spontaneity and state initiative in China's shareholding system reform', *Communist and Post-Communist Studies* 32(3).

Macintyre, A 1994, 'Power, prosperity and patrimonialism: business and government in Indonesia' in Mcintyre, A (ed), *Business and government in industrialising Asia*, Allen & Unwin, St Leonards.

MacIntyre, A and Budy P Resosudarmo 2003, 'Survey of recent developments', *Bulletin of Indonesian Economic Studies* 39(2).

Malaysiatoday 2005, 'New Proton chief plans export drive', 11 December, www.malaysia-today.net/Blog-e/2005/12/new-proton-chief-plans-export-drive.htm, viewed March 2006.

—— 2006, 'Mitsubishi rules out JV with Proton', 15 January, www.malaysia-today.net/Blog-e/2006/01/mitsubishi-rules-out-jv-with-proton.htm, viewed February 2006.

Malhotra, J 2003, 'Pardesi in search of his roots', *Indian Express*, 26 August, www.indianexpress.com/res/web/pIe/archive_full_story.php?content_id=30276, viewed February 2005.

Mathur, S 1993, 'The trade performance of India and Australian since 1950—a comparison', in Vicziany, Marika (ed), *Australia India—economic links past, present and future*, Indian Ocean Centre for Peace Studies, University of Western Australia, Nedlands.

Maynard, M 2001, 'Private sector, to the rescue, quietly, at Hyundai', *New York Times*, 17 June.

McCormack, G 1995, *The emptiness of Japanese affluence*, ME Sharpe, New York.

McDonald, H 2002, 'Remembering the prince of polyester', *Time Asia*, 15 July, www.time.com/time/asia/magazine/article/0,13673,501020722-320795,00.html, viewed February 2005.

McKay, J and G Missen 1994, 'The problem of being big in Korea and small in Taiwan: restructuring firm and institutional networks', Centre of Southeast Asian Studies, Monash University, Clayton.

McNally, C and P Lee 1998, 'Is big beautiful? Restructuring China's state sector under the *zhuada* policy', *Issues and Studies* 34(9).

McNamara, DL 1988, 'Entrepreneurship in colonial Korea: Kim Yon-su', *Modern Asian Studies* 22(1).

—— 1996, *Trade and transformation in Korea 1876–1945*, Westview Press, Boulder.

Mendelsohn, O and M Vicziany 1998, *The Untouchables: subordination, poverty and the state in modern India*, Cambridge University Press, Cambridge.

Menon, R 2002, 'ONGC keen to ensure India's energy security',14 November, www.rediff.com/money/2002/nov/14bizsp.htm, viewed February 2005.

MiGHT 2004, *Annual report: upscaling innovation and skills for competitiveness*, Malaysian Industry-Government Group for High Technology, Kuala Lumpur, www.might.org.my, viewed March 2006.

Millett, M 1999, 'Korea faces its biggest hurdle yet—reform', *Age*, Business Section, 20 September.

Min, T 2004, 'Promoting private enterprise in China', *Korea Herald*, 12 March.

MIO (Media Indonesia Online) 2004, 29 June, www.mediaindo.co.id/berita.asp?id=43746, viewed 14 August 2004.

Mok, V 2000 'Post-Mao economic transition: the role of non-state enterprises', *Issues and Studies* 36(2).

Moon, Chung-In 1994, 'Changing the patterns of business–government relations in South Korea' in MacIntyre, A (ed), *Business and government in industrialising Asia*, Allen and Unwin, St Leonards.

Morgan, SL 2004, 'Professional associations and the diffusion of new management ideas in Shanghai 1920–1930s: a research agenda', *Business and Economic History Online*, volume 2, www.thebhc.org/publications/BEHonline/2004/Morgan.pdf.

Morris, J, J Sheehan and J Hassard 2001, 'From dependence to defiance? Work-unit relationships in China's state enterprise reforms', *Journal of Management Studies* 38(5).

Morris-Suzuki, T 2000, 'Anti-area studies', *Communal/Plural* 8(1).

Morse, EL and J Richard 2002, 'The Battle for Energy Dominance', Foreign Affairs, March–April, 81(2).

Mouer, R 1989, 'The Japanese model of industrial relations: warnings or opportunities?', *Hitotsubashi Journal of Social Studies* 21(1).

Mouer, R and H Kawanishi 2005, *A sociology of work in Japan*, Cambridge University Press, Cambridge.

Mouer, R and Y Sugimoto 1995a, *Nihonjinron no Hoteishiki* [The structure of Nihonjinron], Chikuma Shobo, Tokyo.

—— 1995b, *Nihonjinron at the end of the twentieth century: a multicultural perspective*, School of Asian Studies, La Trobe University, Bundoora.

MPI/PC (Ministry of Planning and Investment/Pricewaterhouse Coopers) 2003, *Viet Nam: a guide for business and investment*, Hanoi.

MT (Ministry of Textiles) 2006, 'Public sector undertakings—National Textile Corporation Ltd', http://texmin.nic.in/tex_08.htm#L01, viewed March 2006.

MTCP (Ministry of Transport, Communication and Post) 1994, *Vietnam railways network*, Hanoi.

Mukerhjee A and M Mukherjee 1983, 'Imperialism and growth of Indian capitalism in the twentieth century', *Economic and Political Weekly*, 5 March.

Muni, SD and G Pant 2005, *India's energy security: prospects for cooperation with extended neighbourbood*, Rupa Books, New Delhi.

Muscat, R 1994, *The fifth tiger: a study of Thai development policy*, United Nations University Press, Helsinki.

Mustapa, Mohammed YB Dato' 2004, Speech at the 'Car of the Year 2004 Award', Kuala Lumpur, December, www.epu.jpm.my/new%20folder/speech/dato%20pa/carcosa%20sri%20negara%20kl%201%20dec.pdf, viewed March 2005.

Nakamura, Tadafusa 1995, *The postwar Japanese economy: its development and structure*, second edition, Tokyo University Press, Tokyo.

Nakayama, I 1975, *Industrialization and labour management relations in Japan*, translated by Ross Mouer, Japan Institute of Labour, Tokyo.

Navaratnam, Tan Sri Ramon 2006a, *Quo vadis, Malaysia: where to, Malaysia?*, Malaysian Institute of Management, Kuala Lumpur.

—— 2006b, 'National unity, the NEP and beyond', paper delivered to the Malaysian Public Policy Forum, Monash Asia Institute, 2 June.

Ng SH, R Goh, B Lai and HL Lim 1998, 'Foreign direct investment and related issues' in Tan TM, AM Low, JJ Williams and TM Choo (eds), *Business opportunities in Indonesia*, Prentice Hall, Singapore.

Nguyen, T 1995, 'Interview—Citibank Thailand to boost 95 profit', *Reuters News*, 8 June, http://global.factiva.com, viewed 1 April 2006.

Nielsen, I, R Smyth and M Vicziany (eds) 2007, *Globalisation and labour mobility in China*, Monash University Press, Clayton.

Nolan, P 1996, 'Large firms and industrial reform in former planned economies: the case of China', *Cambridge Journal of Economics* 20(1).

—— 2002, 'China and the global business revolution', *Cambridge Journal of Economics* 26.

Nolan, P and G Yeung 2001a, 'Big business with Chinese characteristics: two paths to growth of the firm in China under reform', *Cambridge Journal of Economics* 25.

—— 2001b, 'Large firms and catch-up in a transitional economy: the case of Shougang Group in China', *Economics of Planning* 34(1–2).

Oh, Myeung-Ho 1993, 'Current reform politics in Korea', paper presented at the conference 'Korea under the Kim Young-Sam presidency: political, economic and security issues for the 1990s', National Korean Studies Centre, Melbourne.

Oishi, Toshikazu 1997, *Eigo teikoku shugi ron—Eigo shihai o do sura ka* [*Arguments about English language imperialism—what can be done about the way English controls the world?*], Kindai Bungei Sha, Tokyo.

Ong, Andrew (2006) 'Study: 30% bumi equity target exceeded', 23 September, http://www.malaysaikini.com/news/57219

ONGC 2005, 'History', www.ongcindia.com, viewed February 2005.

Ouchi, W 1981, *Theory Z: how American business can meet the Japanese challenge*, Addison-Wesley, Reading.

Ow CH 1986, 'The role of government in economic development: the Singapore experience', in Lim CY and PJ Lloyd (eds), *Singapore: resources and growth*, Oxford University Press, Singapore.

PBNRC (Production Bureau of National Reform Committee) 1999, *One hundred questions and answers on the modern enterprise system*, Reform Press, Beijing.

Pearson, B 2004, 'Seoul searching for a place in the sun', *Australian Financial Review*, 4 June.

Porter, ME 1990, *The competitive advantage of nations*, Macmillan, London.

—— 2003, 'Malaysia's competitiveness: moving to the next stage', presentation in Kuala Lumpur, 6 May, www.isc.hbs.edu/pdf/caon_malaysia_2003.05.06_v2.pdf viewed, March 2006

Pun, P 2003, 'D'Long at the helm of GZI Travel', *Standard*, 26 August.

Puteh, M 2006, *Electronic learning and the Malaysian universities: past, present and future*, PhD thesis, Monash University.

Pye, L 1990, 'China: erratic state, frustrated society', *Foreign Affairs* 69(4).

Rajah, R 2003, 'Investment policy and human development country study: Malaysia', Asia Pacific Regional Initiative on Trade, Economic Governance, and Human Development, UNDP, December 2003, www.asiatradeinitiative.org/docs/2004-Feb/31.%20Malaysia%20Investment%20(unedited).pdf, viewed February 2005.

Rajan, R 2001, '(Ir)Relevance of currency-crisis theory to the devaluation and collapse of the Thai baht', *Princeton Studies in International Economics* 88.

Ramesh, M 1992 'Social security in Singapore redrawing the public-private boundary', *Asian Survey* 32(12).

Ranjan, Amitav 2003, 'OVL pipeline to Sudan gets govt clearance', *Indian Express*, 26 August.

Rapaczynski, A 1996, 'The roles of the state and the market in establishing property rights', *Journal of Economic Perspectives* 10.

Rashid, A 2003, 'Business response to the regional demands and opportunities: a study of the Malaysian automobile industry', Seventh International Conference on Global Business and Economic Development, International Trade Counselling Centre, Bangkok, January, http://blake.montclair.edu/~cibconf/conference/DATA/Theme6/Japan.pdf, viewed January 2006.

Ray, D 2003a, 'Decentralization regulatory reform and the business climate', Partnership for Economic Growth Publication 126a, August, www.pegasus.or.id/publication.html, viewed 14 August 2004.

—— 2003b, 'Survey of recent developments', *Bulletin of Indonesian Economic Studies* 39(3).

Rediff.com 2002a, '5 Indians in Forbes billionaires list', 1 March http://update.im.rediff.com/money/2002/mar/01forbes.htm?h=splitinfinity&d=get&sony, viewed February 2005.

—— 2002b, 'Key statistics on Reliance Group', 7 July, www.rediff.com/money/2002/jul/07amb6.htm, viewed February 2005.

—— 2002c, 'Obituary—Dhirubhai Ambani rewrote India's corporate history', 7 July, www.rediff.com/money/2002/jul/06obit.htm, viewed February 2005.

RI (Republic of Indonesia) 2003, Articles 145 and 156, *Act Number 13 Year 2003 Concerning Manpower*, www.nakertrans.go.id/perundangan/UU-13_eng.pdf, viewed 23 August 2004.

Rice, RC 1983, 'The origins of basic economic ideas in New Order Indonesia', *Bulletin of Indonesian Economic Studies* 19(2).

—— 1998, 'The Habibie approach to science, technology and national development' in Hill, H and KW Thee (eds), *Indonesia's technological challenge*, Institute of Southeast Asian Studies, Singapore.

—— 2004, 'The contribution of household and small manufacturing establishments to the rural economy' in Leinbach, TR (ed), *The Indonesian rural economy: mobility, work and enterprise*, Institute of Southeast Asian Studies, Singapore.

Richardson, M 1997, 'Financial crisis leaves Asian leaders shaky', *International Herald Tribune*, 6 November.

Rodan, G 1985, *Singapore's second industrial revolution: state intervention and foreign investment*, ASEAN-Australia Economic Papers 18, ASEAN-Australia Joint Research Project, Kuala Lumpur and Canberra.

—— 2001, 'Singapore: globalisation and the politics of economic restructuring' in Rodan, G, K Hewison and R Robinson (eds), *The political economy of South-East Asia: conflicts, crises and change*, second edition, Oxford University Press, Melbourne.

Rodo Daijin Kanbo Tokei Joho Bu [Statistics and Information Department, Minister's Secretariat, Ministry of Labor, Japan] 1982, *Rodo Tokei Yoran 1982* [Handbook of Labour Statistics 1982], Okura Sho Insatsu Kyoku, Tokyo.

Samuels, RJ 1987, *The business of the Japanese state: energy markets in comparative and historical perspective*, Cornell University Press, Ithaca.

Sato, T 2000, *Fubyodo Sahaki Nihon: sayonara sochuryu* [Japan, the inegalitarian society: the end of Japan's middle class], Chuo Koron Sha, Tokyo.

—— 2003, *Nihon no 'Kozo Kaikaku'—Ima, Do Kangaeru Beki ka* [Structural reform: how should we evaluate the present situation?], Iwanami Shoten, Tokyo.

Saul, SB 1960, *Studies in British overseas trade 1870–1914*, Oxford University Press, Oxford.

SEEN (Sustainable Energy and Economy Network) 2002, 'Project profile: Bombay offshore oil and gas field developments', 24 July, www.seen.org/db/Dispatch?action-ProjectWidget:728-detail=1, viewed February 2005.

Serambi Indonesia 2005, 'Setahun SBY–JK: Premanisme Berkurang', 12 October.

SERI 2002, 'Economic briefing to the Penang State Government unemployment situation in Penang', Socio-Economic and Environmental Research Institute, Penang, April 2002, www.seri.com.my/oldsite/EconBrief/EconBrief2002-04.PDF, viewed February 2006.

Shamsul, AB 2006, 'Managing collateral damage: an anthropologist's viewpoint of the Abdullah–Mahathir controversy', seminar, Monash University, 13 July.

Shieh, S 1999, 'Is bigger better?', *China Business Review*, May–June.

SFD (Siam Future Development PLC) 2004, *Citibank Thailand*, Siam Future Development PLC, www.siamfuture.com/WorldInThai/citibank.asp, viewed 25 May 2005.

SinoCast 2003, 'D'Long Group approaches aircraft industry', Comtex News Network, 1 July.

—— 2004, 'Chinese appliance makers face difficulties in overseas expansion', SinoCast China IT Watch, Global News Wire, 18 February.

Sivasomboon, B 1995, 'Firms still rushing into Thai credit card market', *Bangkok Post*, 15 February, http://global.factiva.com, viewed 1 April 2006.

SMERU 2001, *Wage and employment effects of minimum wage policy in the Indonesian urban labour market*, October, SMERU Research Institute, Jakarta.

Smith, C 2000, 'Wars and rumors of wars: Sudan gets Chinese jets', *WorldNetDaily*, 13 July, http://www.wnd.com/news/articel.asp?ARTICLE_ID=20622, viewed February 2005.

—— 2000, 'China's tiny private sector faces giant obstacles', *International Herald Tribune*, 13 July.

Smyth, R 1997, 'The township and village enterprise sector as a specific example of regionalism: some general lessons for socialist transformation', *Economic Systems* 21(3).

—— 1998, 'Township and village enterprises in China: growth mechanism and future prospects', *Journal of International Economic Studies* 12.

—— 1999, 'Rural enterprises in Jiangsu Province, China', *Development Policy Review* 17(2).

—— 2000a, 'Asset stripping in Chinese state-owned enterprises', *Journal of Contemporary Asia* 30(1).

—— 2000b, 'Should China be promoting large-scale enterprises and enterprise groups?', *World Development* 28(4).

Smyth, R, Deng X and Wang J 2004a, 'Equity-for-debt swaps in Chinese big business: a case study of restructuring in one large state-owned enterprise', *Asia Pacific Business Review* 10(3&4).

—— 2004b, 'Restructuring state-owned big business in former planned economies: the case of China's shipbuilding industry', *New Zealand Journal of Asian Studies* 6(1).

Smyth, R and Zhai Q 2001, 'Reforming China's large-scale state-owned enterprises – the petrochemical sector', *Asia Pacific Journal of Economics and Business* 5(2).

Somu Sho [Ministry of Public Management, Home Affairs. Posts and Telecommunications] 2001, *Joho Tsushin Hakusho: Joho Tsushin ni Kansuru Genjo Hokoku* [The white paper on the communication of information: a report on the transmission of information], Somu Sho, Tokyo.

Song, Byung-Nak 1990, *The rise of the Korean economy*, Oxford University Press, Hong Kong.

Song, Jung-a 2006, 'Accused Hyundai chief faces arrest', *Australian* 28 April.

Sridhar, V 1998, 'ONGC: coping with competition', *Frontline* 15(8), www.flonnet.com/fl1508/15080890.htm, viewed February 2005.

Srinivasan, TN 2004, 'China and India: economic performance, competition and cooperation: an update', *Journal of Asian Economics* 15.

State Department 2006, 'Background note—Malaysia', Washington, www.state.gov/r/pa/ei/bgn/2777.htm, viewed August 2007.

Steinfeld, E 2001, 'China's program of debt–equity swaps: government failure or market failure?', paper presented at the conference 'Financial Sector Reform in China', 11–13 September, John F Kennedy School of Government, Harvard University.

Steinfeld, E and V Hulme 2002, 'Free lunch or last supper? China's debt–equity swaps in context', *China Business Review* 27(4).

Steinherr, A 2000, *Derivatives: the wild beast of finance, a path to effective globalisation*, John Wiley & Sons, Chichester.

Stewart, R and C Chan 2003, 'Beijing authorities may bail out lenders again', *International Herald Tribune*, Business Asia Section, 28 November.

Stewart, S 2004, 'Reliance Industries Ltd', *Economic Times*, 23 November, http://economictimes.indiatimes.com/corpambanishow/932760.cms, viewed February 2005.

Sugishita, T 2001, *NPO NGO Gaido* [Guide to NPOs and NGOs], Jiyu Kokuminsha, Tokyo.

Sui, C 2004, 'Protection of private property moves China closer to capitalism', *Agence France Presse*, 11 March.

Sun Q and WHS Tong 2003, 'China share issue privatization: the extent of its success', *Journal of Financial Economics* 70(2).

Sutherland, D 2001, 'Policies to build national champions: China's "national team" of enterprise groups' in Nolan, P (ed), *China and the global business revolution*, Palgrave, Basingstoke.

Tachibanaki, T 1998, *Nihon no Keizai Kakusa* [Economic inequality in Japan], Iwanami shoten, Tokyo.

Tam, J 2002, 'Region hit by 33 per cent surge in problem loans', *Standard*, 13 July.

Tan, AHH 2001, 'The Asian economic crisis: the way ahead for Singapore' in Low, L and DM Johnson (eds), *Singapore Inc. Public policy options in the third millennium*, Asia Pacific Press, Singapore.

Temasek Holdings 2004, www.temasekholdings.com.sg, viewed 7 December 2004.

Tian G 2000, 'Property rights and the nature of Chinese collective enterprises', *Journal of Comparative Economics* 28(2).

Trace, K 1996, 'Transport in Vietnam: creating a new market orientation', Economic Society of Australia (Qld), Third International Conference on Economics in Business and Government, Brisbane, July.

TI (Transparency International) 2003, wwwuser.gwdg.de/~uwvd/downloads/CPI_2003.xls, viewed 3 August, 2004.

—— 2005, www.transparency.org/policy_and_research/surveys_indices/cpi/2005, viewed 1 February, 2006.

Treerapongpichit, B and S Bunyamanese 1997, 'Corporate focus—Citibank sees retail success', *Bangkok Post*, 18 April, http://global.factiva.com, viewed 1 April 2006.

Treisman, D 2004 'Derivative markets in the South-East Asian political economy: the Thai case study (1997–2000), Masters Research Report, University of Witwatersrand, Johannesburg.

Tsuchiya, S 1995, *Ajia e no Kigyo Shinshutsu to Kaigai Fu-nin—Sono Keikakuk to Jikko* [The movement of Japanese firms into Asia and working overseas], Toyo Keizai Shimposha, Tokyo.

Undang-Undang Otonomi Daerah Tahun 2004 2004, Penerbit CV Tamita Utama Jakarta.

Unger, J and A Chan 1996, 'Corporatism in China: a developmental state in East Asian context' in McCormick BL and J Unger (eds), *China after Socialism: in the footsteps of Eastern Europe or East Asia?*, ME Sharpe, Armonk.

Van Wolferen, K 1989, *The enigma of Japanese power: people and politics in a stateless nation*, Vintage, New York.

Veale, J 1988, 'This time it's for real, Kim warns *chaebol*s', *Australian Financial Review*, 22 January.

Vicziany, M 1969, 'The Indian invasion of Portuguese Goa', Honours dissertation, University of Western Australia, Crawley.

—— 1998, 'Ecological Dimensions of the Development of the Piparwar Coal Mine, Bihar, Eastern India' in Grove, R (ed), *Nature and the Orient,* Oxford University Press, New Delhi.

—— 2001, 'Opportunities in the Indian IT industry', consultancy report for Department of Foreign Affairs and Trade, Canberra, www.monash.edu.au/casestudies/css/651_it.htm, viewed December 2005.

—— 2005a, 'The Indian economy in the twenty-first century: the tough questions that just won't go away', *South Asia* 27(2).

—— 2005b, 'Dalit responses to unemployment in contemporary India', *South Asia* 28(1).

—— 2006, 'Malaysian anti-imperialism and the role of US consultancy firms', forthcoming.

Vicziany, M (ed) 1993, Australia India– Economic Links Past, Present and Future, South Asian Issues Monograph no 1, Curtin University, Perth.

Vicziany, M, TSR Navaratnam, K-N Wong and T Thornton 2001, 'Australian business attitudes to Malaysia' in Nyland, C, W Smith, R Smyth and M Vicziany (eds), *Malaysian business in the new era*, Edward Elgar, Cheltenham and Lyme.

Vicziany, M and M Puteh 2004, 'Vision 2020, the MSC and the IT revolution in Malaysian universities' in Cribb, R (ed), Refereed Conference Proceedings, Asian Studies Association of Australia, Canberra., July 2004.

Vogel, E 1979, *Japan as number one: lessons for America*, Harvard University Press, Cambridge.

Wade, R 1990, *Governing the market: the role of government in East Asian industrialization*, Princeton University Press, Princeton.

WB (World Bank) 1987, *Korea: managing the industrial transition*, volume 2, World Bank, Washington.

—— 1993, *The East Asian miracle: economic growth and public policy*, Oxford University Press, Washington.

—— 1994, *Vietnam transport sector: serving an economy in transition*, August.

—— 2000, *Malaysia: Malaysia public expenditures – managing the crisis; challenging the future*, 22 May, Washington, www-wds.worldbank.org/servlet/ WDS_IBank_Servlet?pcont=details&eid=000094946_00061605362942, viewed March 2006.

—— 2001a, *From safety net to springboard: social protection sector strategy*, World Bank, Washington.

—— 2001b, *Vietnam: preparing for take-off?*, www.worldban.,org.vn/rep6/, viewed 6 September 2001.

—— 2002, *Vietnam: delivering on its promise*, Development Report 2003, Hanoi.

—— 2003a, *Indonesia development policy report: beyond macroeconomic stability*, 4 December, www-wds.worldbank.org/servlet/WDScontentserver/WDSP/IB/2003/1 2/11/000160016_20031211122325/Rendered/PDF/273740IND.pdf, downloaded 13 August 2004.

—— 2003b, 'Project appraisal document on a proposed loan in the amount of US$141 million to the Republic of Indonesia for a Java-Bali power sector restructuring and strengthening project, report No: 25414-IND', 4 June, www-wds.worldbank.org/ servlet/WDSContentServer/WDSP/IB/2003/06/16/000112742_2003061612011 5/Rendered/PDF/254140ID0Java1Bali0Power0revised.pdf, viewed 11 August 2004.

—— 2004a, '2003 country policy and institutional assessment (CPIA) overall rating', http://siteresources.worldbank.org/IDA/Resources/Quintiles2003CPIA.pdf, viewed 3 August, 2004.

—— 2004b, *Economic and social update*, Consultative Group on Indonesia mid-year review meeting, Jakarta, 2 June, http://siteresources.worldbank.org/ INTINDONESIA/Resources/CG103/midtermCGI-Jun2-04/cgi_main_report_ June2004.pdf, viewed August 3, 2004.

—— 2004c, 'World development indicators', www.worldbank.org/data/ onlinedatabases/onlinedatabases.html, viewed March 2006.

—— 2005, *East Asia update: countering global shocks*, Washington, http:// siteresources.worldbank.org/INTEAPHALFYEARLYUPDATE/Resources/EAP-Brief-final.pdf, viewed March 2006.

—— 2006, 'Malaysia country brief', March, Washington, http://siteresources. worldbank.org/INTEAPHALFYEARLYUPDATE/Resources/Malaysia.pdf, viewed March 2006.

WBG (World Bank Group) 2005, *Thailand economic monitor*, prepared by Bhaopichtir, K, W Atsavasirilert, R Thongampai, A Luangpenthong and K Matin, http://siteresources.worldbank.org/INTTHAILAND/Resources/Economic-Monitor/2005april.pdf, viewed 10 May 2005.

WEF (World Economic Forum) 2002, *The global competitiveness report 2001–2002*, Oxford University Press, New York and Oxford, www.weforum.org/site/homepublic.nsf/Content/Global+Competitiveness+Programme%5CGlobal+Competitiveness+Report, viewed March 2006.

—— 2006a, 'Growth competitiveness index rankings 2005 and 2004 comparisons', www.weforum.org/site/homepublic.nsf/Content/Growth+Competitiveness+Index+rankings+2005+and+2004+comparisons, viewed March 2006.

—— 2006b, *Global competitiveness report*, Oxford University Press, New York and Oxford, www.weforum.org/site/homepublic.nsf/Content/Global+Competitiveness+Programme%5CGlobal+Competitiveness+Report, viewed March 2006.

Wei Z, O Verela, and MK Hassan 2002, 'Ownership structure and performance in Chinese manufacturing industry', *Journal of Multinational Financial Management* 12(1).

Wei Z, O Verela, J D'Souza and MK Hassan 2003, 'The financial and operating performance of China's newly privatized firms', *Financial Management* 32(2).

Weiss, L 1994, 'Government–business relations in East Asia: the changing basis of state capacity', *Asian Perspectives* 18(2).

Weitzman, M and Xu C 1994, 'Chinese township and village enterprises as vaguely defined cooperatives', *Journal of Comparative Economics* 18(2).

Wen M 2003, 'Further reform of SOEs and state banks', in Smyth, R, OK Tam and C Zhu (eds) *Institutional challenges for the global China*, conference proceedings, Monash University.

White, G and R Wade 1988, 'Developmental states and markets in East Asia: an introduction' in White, G (ed), *Developmental states in East Asia*, MacMillan, London.

Wilson, D and R Purushothaman 2002, *Dreaming with BRICs: the path to 2050*, Goldman Sachs, Global Economics Paper 99, 1 October.

—— 2003, *Dreaming with BRICS: the path to 2050*, Goldman Sachs, Global Economics Paper 99, 1 October, www2.goldmansachs.com/insight/research/reports/99.pdf, viewed 20 August 2006.

Woo WT 1999, 'The real reasons for China's growth', *China Journal* 41.

Wu, B 1998, 'Comrade Wu Banguo stresses that if you want to "grab the big" then you have to grab the real "big"', *Gaige neican* 20.

XGTGZ (Xinbian Gongye Tongji Gongzuo Zhinan) 1999, *A guide to industrial statistics*, China Statistical Press, Beijing.

Xinhua News Agency 2002, 'Banks, auctioneers team up for non-performing assets', 23 August.

Yabuno, Y 1995, *Rookaru-Inishiateibu—Kokkyo o Koeru Kokoromi* [Local initiatives: efforts to go beyond national borders], Chuo Koron, Tokyo.

Young, MB 1991, *The Vietnam Wars 1945-1990*, HarperPerennial, New York.

Young, A 1994, 'Lessons from the East Asian NICS: a contrarian view, *European Economic Review* 38.

Young, MB 1991, *The Vietnam wars 1945–1990*, Harper Perennial, New York.

Yuan, G 1999, 'Bad debts of China's state-owned enterprises', paper presented at the Conference of the Association for Chinese Economic Studies, 15–16 July, Melbourne.

Zhang, G 2006, 'Informal financing and the rise of the private sector in Chengdu, China', PhD thesis, Monash University.

Zhang Houyi and Liu Pingqing 2003, 'Entrepreneurs energize economy', *China Daily*, 29–30 November.

Zhang, X 2002, 'Analysis of capital flight from China', *Journal of Beijing Polytechnic University* 2(3).

Zhou, F and Y Shen 1997, 'Letting go small SOEs is good for enhancing the quality of state assets' in *Realistic choice: preliminary summary of the practice of reforming small state-owned enterprises*, China Reform and Development Report, Far East Publishing House Shanghai.

Zweig, D 2001, 'China's stalled "fifth wave": Zhu Rongji's reform package of 1998–2000', *Asian Survey* 41(2).